Arthur T. Pierson

Arthur T. Pierson

A Spiritual Warrior, Mighty in the Scriptures;
A Leader in the Modern Missionary Crusade

A Biography by his Son
DELAVAN LEONARD PIERSON

ILLUSTRATED

WIPF & STOCK · Eugene, Oregon

Wipf and Stock Publishers
199 W 8th Ave, Suite 3
Eugene, OR 97401

Arthur T. Pierson
A Spiritual Warrior, Mighty in the Scriptures
By Pierson, Delavan Leonard
ISBN 13: 978-1-5326-7987-2
Publication date 1/25/2019
Previously published by Flemming H. Revell Co., 1912

To

MY MOTHER

whose fifty years of sympathetic comradeship and life of unselfish devotion made possible my father's world-wide ministry. Her children and grandchildren also rise up and call her blessed

Preface

A PORTRAIT

SINCE none can truly know a man but his Maker, none can paint a perfect portrait. Each artist will be influenced by his own mood and by sympathy with or antipathy to his subject. The peculiarities, the beauties, or the defects that loom large in the eyes of one painter will sink into insignificance in the view of another. Even a series of portraits drawn at different periods and under varying circumstances must fail to present a complete likeness.

Probably no two of those who study this portrait of Arthur T. Pierson will agree in their interpretation of the man. One will see in his face the beloved pastor, another the eloquent preacher and learned teacher, and still another the ardent advocate of world-wide missions. Some who look will be moved by the memory of a loving, faithful friend, others by thoughts of the man who led them to the Saviour, and still others by the recollections of the Ambassador of Christ who brought them into closer fellowship with the Master and who inspired them to render more devoted service to their King. A few may recall most vividly a rebuke or may be unable to overlook some real or fancied defect in character or conduct. None can see the whole man, but all can see one who fought well and nobly the battles within and without—battles for purity, truth and the supremacy of the will of God.

Preface

At one time my father planned to write his own biography—to paint his own portrait—for he longed to make known, as he alone could, God's gracious dealings with him and the marvellous way in which he had been led. But before he had even sketched the rough outlines he was called home to the land where he knows as he is known.

It has been a difficult and delicate task for a son to portray the character and life of his honoured and beloved father. And yet a son's picture may be the truest; certainly it is sketched from sympathetic knowledge, as every interpretive likeness should be.

In this life portrait I have sought to give a true picture of the man and of his ideals and to sketch some of the most important scenes from his world ministry. The glimpses of my father's inner soul may perhaps seem too intimate, for they are taken from his private prayer diary that was intended for God's eye alone, but these glimpses are necessary to unveil the man as he was when in the presence of his Maker. It was in these hours of devotion that he developed likeness to his Lord.

Although it was my privilege for the last twenty years to be my father's intimate companion and co-worker, this study of his life, his conflicts and ministries private and in public, has brought a fuller revelation of the man and his mission. Such an uplift has resulted that I hope and pray that even the partial view here given may bring a like blessing to others.

The joy of the work has been doubled and the difficulties vastly decreased by the constant and efficient help of my beloved wife. She has been at once my severest critic and my most appreciative and sympathetic co-worker. The mutual love that existed between her and my father also made her coöperation doubly appropriate and effective. To my friend, Rev. William J. Hutchins, for his most helpful literary criticism of the manuscript, and to others who have contributed bits of local colour to make this portrait and its background more perfect, I acknowledge my debt with heartfelt gratitude.

DELAVAN L. PIERSON.

Brooklyn, New York.

Contents
THE MARCH OF EVENTS

I. LOOKING BACKWARD—A RACE OF WARRIORS   17
Abraham Pierson, the First—Caleb Wheeler and Newark in 1666—Birth of Arthur T. Pierson in 1837—A Lost Boy—First Day in Sunday-school—Early Poems and Sermons—Wilson Phraner and Mount Washington Institute—Boyhood Temptations.

II. BOARDING-SCHOOL DAYS—ENLISTING FOR LIFE   30
1850–1853—Leaving Home at Thirteen—Conversion at Tarrytown—School Life at Ossining—The Young Editor and Publisher—Early Essays—Prize Temperance Oration—Business Experience in New York—A Charter Member of the Y. M. C. A.

III. AT HAMILTON COLLEGE—IN TRAINING FOR SERVICE   40
1853–1857—A First Stand—Humour of the Entrance Examinations—Necessity for Economy and Industry—Freshman Experiences—Personal Appearance—College Sports—Secret Societies—Hazing—Social and Religious Life—Literary Honours—Poetry—President North's Tribute.

IV. IN THE THEOLOGICAL SEMINARY—STUDYING TECHNIQUE   61
1857–1860—Union Theological Seminary—Famous Professors—The "Annus Mirabilis" in Missions—The Revival of 1857—A Lesson in Giving—Influence of Wendell Phillips—Beginning to Preach—Experience at West Winsted—Ordination.

V. FIRST CHARGE AT BINGHAMTON—TESTING HIS WEAPONS   74
1856–1863—Marriage to Miss Benedict—Installation at Binghamton—Key-note to Preaching—Rules for Reading—Ministerial Ideals—Infidel Attacks—Questions to Church-members—Shots that Struck Home—Spiritualism—Financial Straits—Lessons Learned—Resignation.

Contents

VI. THE WATERFORD PASTORATE—A BROADER
VISION 91

1863–1869—The Call to Waterford—Mr. Pierson's Peculiarities—Missionary Interest—A Revival in Church and Sunday-school—Rebuilding—First Visit to Europe—Charles H. Spurgeon—Fund of Humour—Call to Detroit.

VII. AT FORT STREET CHURCH, DETROIT—A
STRATEGIC CENTRE 106

1869–1876—Program for Work—A Visitor's Impression—Rules for Preaching—The Prayer-meeting—Missionary Interest—Bible Classes and Daily Study—Ministry in City and State—The Great Michigan Fires—Methods in Pastoral Work—A Stranger Converted—A Rich Man Offended—Family Life—An Escape from Drowning.

VIII. FROM CHURCH TO OPERA HOUSE—A
CHANGE OF TACTICS 127

1876–1882—Whittle and Bliss—Stirrings of the Spirit—The Burning of the Church—Opera House Services—Plans for a New Church—Reaching Out for the Masses—An Infidel Converted—George Müller's Influence—A Change of Field.

IX. A YEAR IN INDIANAPOLIS—VICTORY OR
DEFEAT? 148

1882–1883—The Pastoral Committee—Conditions of Acceptance—Leaving Detroit—Difficulties Encountered—Dr. Henry C. Mabie—Friction and Resignation—The Tabernacle Movement—A Critical Period—Healing a Breach—Lessons Learned—The Call to Philadelphia.

X. THE PHILADELPHIA PASTORATE—THE FIELD
AND THE FORCE 165

1883–1889—Bethany Church and Sunday-school—John Wanamaker—Problems to be Solved—Teachers' Meetings—The Lay College—The Evangelistic Band—An Ideal Installation Charge—Church Standards—Paying Off the Mortgage—Private Prayer Life.

Contents

XI. CONFERENCE AND MISSIONARY WORK—A WORLD-WIDE CAMPAIGN . . . 185

1884–1889—The Prophetical Bible Conference—The Second Coming—Influence on Men—D. L. Moody and Northfield—Mount Hermon and the Student Volunteers—Editor of the *Missionary Review*—The London Missionary Conference—Resignation from Bethany.

XII. SCOTLAND AND THE CONTINENT—MISSIONARY CRUSADES 210

1889–1891—Visitation of the Scotch Churches—Quotations from Missionary Addresses—Pilgrimages to Famous Homes—Meetings in London—Preaching for Charles H. Spurgeon—Visit to the McAll Mission—An Amusing Experience in Naples—Results of the Tour.

XIII. AT SPURGEON'S TABERNACLE—TWO YEARS AS A SUBSTITUTE 226

1891–1893—A Remarkable Chain of Circumstances—The Call to London—The First Service—A Visitor's Description—Methods of Sermon Preparation—Notes on Preaching—The Death of Spurgeon—Results of His Ministry—A Difficult Situation—Thomas Spurgeon—A Second Year at the Tabernacle—Newspaper Critics—An Officer's Tribute.

XIV. IMMERSION AND ITS CONSEQUENCES—A BATTLE OF CONSCIENCE 252

1893–1896—The Debated Question—Reasons Against Rebaptism—Letter to the Presbytery—Death of A. J. Gordon—Return to Great Britain—Immersion at Croydon—Attacks of the Press—Answer—Mission in Ireland—Dropped from the Presbyterian Church—Again at the Metropolitan Tabernacle.

XV. LATER BRITISH MINISTRIES—SPIRITUAL REINFORCEMENT 272

1897–1909—Views on Health and Divine Healing—The Life of George Müller—Experiences in Bristol—Answers to Prayer—Habits of Giving—Exeter Hall Lectures—Methods of Bible Study—Keswick Teaching—Experiences at Keswick—A Remarkable Meeting—Letters to His Children—Brighton Ministries.

Contents

XVI. LATER AMERICAN MINISTRIES—RECRUITING IN VARIOUS CAMPS **299**

1897–1909—An Unsettled Preacher—Providential Deliverences—In Conventions Oft—Preaching Engagements—The Parliament of Religions—Northfield Conferences—With Mount Hermon Students—Recreation Days—Among Neighbours—Influence on His Children.

XVII. THE JUBILEE YEAR—A VISIT TO THE FRONTIER **313**

1910–1911—Anniversary of Ordination—An Opportunity for Testimony—Golden Wedding Celebration—Reunions—A Visit to the Mission Fields—A Crowning Joy—Return to America—Final Home-Going—Unique Funeral Service—Resting Place in Greenwood—A Message in Stone.

Illustrations

Portrait of Dr. Pierson at Seventy
The Pierson Coat of Arms
Arthur T. Pierson's Motto and Emblem
Stephen H. Pierson and Wife
Arthur Pierson at Seventeen
Hamilton College in 1854
Union Seminary, New York, in 1857
Arthur T. Pierson in the Binghamton Pastorate
Sarah Frances Benedict at Time of Her Marriage
The Congregational Church at Binghamton
The Presbyterian Church at Waterford
Arthur T. Pierson at Forty (1878)
The Fort Street Presbyterian Church, Detroit
The Second Presbyterian Church, Indianapolis
Bethany Presbyterian Church, Philadelphia
Interior of the Famous Bethany Sunday-School
Spurgeon's Metropolitan Tabernacle, London
The Speaker's View of the Audience Room
Dr. and Mrs. Pierson at Bible Study
Bible Study Chart Used at Exeter Hall

Illustrations

Page from Dr. Pierson's Annotated Bible	*Facing page*	286
A View of Keswick and Derwentwater from Skiddaw	" "	292
Dr. Pierson Speaking in the Keswick Tent	" "	292
The Believer's Bank Note	*page*	298
View of the Northfield Home from the Study on the Hill	*Facing page*	310
Off Duty at Northfield—Dr. Pierson and His Grandson	" "	310
The Home in Brooklyn, New York	" "	328
A Message in Stone	" "	332

I

LOOKING BACKWARD—A RACE OF WARRIORS

ARTHUR T. PIERSON was a warrior, and came of a race of warriors. A few of his ancestors won renown upon fields of battle where the weapons were of steel, where the strength and skill required were those of nerve and muscle, where the foes were of flesh and blood and the rewards were temporal power and authority. But the majority of his forebears, and he, himself, were engaged in a different contest. They were trained, not in the military schools of the state, but of the Church. Their book of tactics was the Bible, their officers were men chosen and appointed by the almighty Commander-in-chief, their battles were for truth and true living, and their campaign was for the conquest of the world. Moral courage was counted of greater worth than physical bravery; the weapons of mind and spirit were more highly esteemed than those forged in earthly arsenals; the foes against which they contended were principalities and powers in spirit realms, their victories were over the enemies of character, of humanity and of God. These were battles worth waging. There have been tactical mistakes and temporary defeats; at times the forces have been divided; the great Commander's orders have been mistaken or disobeyed, but there have also been notable victories, the progress of the campaign has been steady and the final success is assured.

Arthur Tappan Pierson never prided himself on being a self-made man. He rather rejoiced in the conviction that every man's life is a plan of God. As he looked back in later years he saw in his ancestry and birth, in his early home and training, in his temptations and trials, in his opportunities and successes, the working out of the plans and purposes of his Creator. After his conversion, when he deliberately chose to follow Jesus Christ as his Lord and Saviour, the boy and then the man sought to discover and to obey the directions of his Sovereign.

It was not by accident that the man who was to enter upon a world-wide ministry traced his ancestry to a Church of England clergyman, that his conversion was in a Methodist revival and class-meeting, his theological training in a Presbyterian seminary, his first pastorate in a Congregational Church, and his largest field in a Baptist tabernacle; that he learned some of his deepest lessons among the Brethren in Bristol, England, and that he closed his career connected with no human organization,—a subject only of the universal Church and Kingdom of God.

In semi-humorous vein Dr. Pierson wrote a few years before his death: "It is amazing that Anglicans welcome me—a renegade Presbyterio-Baptist-Brethren compound, belonging to nobody but the Lord."

The Pierson ancestry was a godly one and gave promise of a goodly fruitage. The first of the American line was Abraham Pierson of sturdy Yorkshire stock who, although in the way of special preferment from the Crown, left his parish in Newark-on-the-Trent at the call of God. Like Father Abraham the first, he went forth not knowing whither he went, irresistibly driven by a desire to find a home where he could worship God according to his newly-acquired Puritan ideals. Although two centuries intervened between the life of this pioneer and that of his descendant, Arthur T. Pierson, the latter was in some ways a most striking replica of his forefather—the brilliant orator of Trinity College, Cambridge, the intrepid pioneer, the independent non-conformist preacher, the autocratic ruler of the infant settlement, and the zealous missionary to the savage Indians.

Abraham Pierson and his two brothers, Henry and Thomas, landed in Plymouth, Massachusetts, in 1639, and for forty years he was the spiritual as well as the civil leader of a consecrated band of colonists, who founded successively the towns of Southampton, Long Island; Branford, Connecticut; and Newark, New Jersey. Everywhere he went this Abraham followed the example of the Hebrew patriarch in first erecting an altar for the worship of God. He was a strong character, a leader with authority in Church and state, and united in himself the offices of pioneer and patriarch. He conscientiously held that no one who was not a church-member in good standing should vote or hold office in the body politic. This position was not popular with all, and twice for the sake of conscience and for the sake of peace, Abraham Pierson, with such of his following as were like minded, removed to new fields and reëstablished their homes and altars and church. All this meant much hardship and privation, but the beloved shepherd suffered with his flock, and while they recognized in him a man of unyielding principles and a strict disciplinarian, they loved and revered him for his sympathy, his uprightness and his genuine piety.

Abraham Pierson's eighteen years of pastorate in Branford, Connecticut, brought him into close contact with the Mohegan and Mohican Indians, and the missionary fire which two centuries later burned so brightly in the soul of his descendant was kindled in the old Puritan as he saw the ignorance and savagery of his Red neighbours. About this time occurred the awful massacre by the Indians of Anne Hutchinson and her thirteen defenseless children. The tragedy came very close to the Pierson home, as Anne was a relative of the wife of Abraham. He proceeded to "heap coals of fire on their heads" by setting himself to learn their language, as he said, "that he might inform the Indians concerning the things of their peace." He preached to them in their own tongue and acted as an interpreter and mediator between them and the civil authorities. Thus Pierson was the friend and spiritual adviser of the Indians of Connecticut as John Eliot and Mayhew were of the Indians of Massachusetts. A quaint catechism, which he wrote for their guidance, is still in existence.

The first church of Newark, New Jersey, founded in 1666 (now Presbyterian), had Abraham Pierson "to its father." He builded so wisely and so well that the organization is still standing, and among the present officers are some of the descendants of its first members. One of the few remaining documents of the old preacher is a sort of will wherein he asserts that he is "persuaded of the everlasting welfare of his soul's estate and his body's resurrection to eternal life by Jesus Christ, his dear and Precious Redeemer." He died in 1678 at the age of sixty-five, and was succeeded in his pastorate for a few years by his son, Abraham, the second.

The Founders of Yale and Princeton 21

In those primitive days a library of 440 volumes, such as Father Abraham Pierson possessed, was significant of a man's love of study and research. He placed great value on education and we find his son, Abraham, and grandson, John, taking prominent parts in founding two great American universities.

Twenty-three years after his father's death, Abraham Pierson second, with four other ministers of southern Connecticut, presented a petition to the General Assembly to draft a charter for a college and engaged to give books from their scanty libraries as a nucleus of the college property. Abraham Pierson was chosen president or "Rector," and he accepted in the following words: "I durst not refuse such a service for God and my generation, but submit myself to take the charge and work of Rector upon me." This "Collegiate School of Connecticut" is now Yale University, with thousands of graduates who have loyally responded to the calls of Church and state.

John Pierson, another descendant of Abraham the first, held a pastorate in Woodbridge, New Jersey, and when in 1746 the College of New Jersey (now Princeton University) received its first charter his name stood next to Dickinson in the list of trustees. Thus the Piersons had a hand in moulding the educational life of the American colony and gave evidence of the genius for study which, eight generations later, showed itself in Arthur T. Pierson, as a legacy transmitted from the long past.

By a singular coincidence we find among those who came with Abraham Pierson from Branford to Newark,—a Pilgrim son named Caleb Wheeler, a man of rugged piety, of splendid physique and of comparative wealth. Over one hundred and fifty years later two descendants of those two devout settlers, Sally Ann Wheeler and Stephen Haines Pierson, met and were married in the city of Newark. From this union of God-fearing parents came Arthur Tappan Pierson, spiritual warrior and a leader in the modern missionary crusade.

The time and place of Arthur Pierson's birth were themselves significant. The event occurred on March 6, 1837, in Chatham Street, New York (now Park Row), in apartments over an arched passage which led to the old Chatham Garden Theatre. Here many famous actors and actresses had entertained New York audiences, but the theatre had been renovated and leased for a chapel by the two well-known philanthropists and antislavery leaders,—Lewis and Arthur Tappan. The famous evangelist Charles G. Finney became the first pastor of this Presbyterian church and here he held the remarkable revival services which so mightily moved New York, and which also greatly influenced the minds and hearts of the young father and mother of the coming child. The chapel was a centre of antislavery agitation, and here were enacted real dramas more thrilling than any ever produced on the stage during its playhouse days.

These were stirring times in New York. The great eighteen million dollar fire of 1835 had been followed by the financial panic of 1837, when every bank in New York suspended and when business failures amounted to one hundred million dollars in that city alone. Among the hundreds of prosperous firms forced to make assignment was the well-known wholesale silk house of Arthur Tappan. Poverty stared in the face both the employer and his cashier and confidential clerk, Stephen Haines Pierson. Arthur Tappan himself was the soul of honour and though his income had been $100,000 a year, he sold all that he had, even to his watch, to satisfy his creditors and afterwards entered the employ of the firm of which for many years he had been the head. The price of food climbed abnormally high with coal $10.00 a ton and flour $20.00 a barrel. One month before the birth of Stephen Pierson's youngest son, Arthur, an angry and starving mob gathered in the City Hall Park within sight of the little home and there organized for plunder. Warerooms were entered and hundred of barrels of flour were thrown from the lofts by these desperate men.

The whole country was staggering under the financial policy of President Jackson which had awakened deep distrust, but the day of March 6th brought with it a gleam of hope when a new executive, Martin Van Buren, took the oath of office; it brought also a new influx of love and joy to the home of Stephen and Sally Pierson, as they held in their arms their little son—a gift of God to them and to the world. In this same year were born three others with whom in later life this newcomer was to be closely associated,— Dwight L. Moody of Northfield, John Wanamaker of Philadelphia, and James Archer Spurgeon of London.

This year ushered in an important period in the history of the world. The youthful Queen Victoria then ascended the British throne; the mission fields began to be explored as never before and several foreign missionary societies were founded. The *Great Western* crossed the Atlantic in 1838 and at about the same time Morse completed his telegraph. God was preparing the world and the Church, His physical forces and His messengers, for a great advance.

The ancestry, the time, and the contemporaries of young Arthur were in the plan of God. The same is true of his home and his parents. Stephen Haines Pierson, the father, is described by those who knew him as a highly respected godly man of staunch principles and quiet manner. Though he was without remarkable gifts, he moved for forty years among the business men of New York City and faithfully performed his duties as a Christian citizen. He was a careful and capable accountant, a strict and conscientious father and an elder in the Presbyterian church. His trust in God and his faith in the Bible was impressed upon his children. The great-hearted merchant, Arthur Tappan, exerted a marked influence on his life, and as he shared his employer's fortunes and misfortunes, so also he sympathized with his high standards of honour and his hatred of slavery. With loaded musket he stood guard when the Tappan store was attacked by opponents of the brave abolitionist, and when the financial crash came, Stephen Pierson, with his employer, was obliged to curtail his expenses to meet his depleted income.

The mother, Sally Ann Pierson, was an "elect lady," born in Newark, New Jersey, on February 2, 1802. She was one of a family of fourteen children of Joseph Lyon and Phœbe Jones Wheeler. Although her own family numbered twelve or more, she still found time to entertain many friends, to engage in church and other charitable work and to look after the affairs of her household. She was a woman of indomitable energy and a warm heart, an unusually bright conversationalist and of a hopeful, cheerful disposition—otherwise even her strong physique would never have stood the strain of hard work that fell to her lot. Many of her gifts and graces reappeared in her youngest son.

Arthur was the youngest of four boys and the ninth child in a family of ten. He experienced in early life some of the advantages and disadvantages in a home where the wolf was never far from the door, and where the demands of many brothers and sisters left little opportunity for selfish individualism. Activities in the home and church did not give the parents much time to cultivate the æsthetic in the manners of their children, but the weightier matters of their soul training were diligently looked after. The children were taught the catechism and Scripture verses, and the family altar, morning and evening, brought blessing to children's children unto the third generation.

While Arthur was still a babe his parents moved to 13 Renwick Street, the new "up-town" settlement near the Hudson River above Canal Street. Soon the boy was sent to a near-by private school, and is still remembered by some of his schoolmates as an active, talkative lad, always busy and full of life. In those days, as in these, the passing fire engine was an irresistible attraction and boys followed it through the crooked down-town streets with all the pleasure of a chase. Arthur even at the early age of four was interested in the passing engines and one day when he had followed the crowd he was lost in the maze of the city streets. His parents searched for him far and near, with aching hearts and visions of a little body floating somewhere in the river. But this was far from God's purpose for the lad. Towards sunset the father and mother of a little playmate found him near the City Hall Square with one shoe and one stocking gone, vainly trying to satisfy himself with some bread and molasses which the kindly matron of the almshouse had given him. The memory of this experience remained vividly with him to his dying day as a warning against allowing the allurements of this world to entice him away from his heavenly Father's sheltering arms.

The earliest religious impressions of the young boy, outside his home, were associated with the old Spring Street Church, where Dr. William M. Patton was pastor, and which was famous as an antislavery centre. On the first Sunday morning in May, 1843, when Arthur was six years old, he was taken by his sister Annie to Sunday-school. After church his mother met the superintendent, a young theological student, Wilson Phraner, and asked:

"Did my boy Arthur join your school to-day?"

"Yes," replied Mr. Phraner, "and I put him in the infant class in charge of Miss Connors."

With an intensely earnest expression on her face the mother said: "Be sure you make a Christian of him. I want all of my children to be Christians and to grow up to lead honourable, useful lives."

Those were the days when Christian parents gave first place to the religious training of their children; when nothing was permitted to interfere with church duties, and when non-churchgoing habits had not emptied the pews nor set evil examples to the youth. There were Sunday-school sessions both morning and afternoon, and it was never a debatable question whether Arthur should go. He attended both sessions and the church service as well. Nearly sixty years later

Early Religious Education 27

this boy, grown to be an honoured preacher, wrote to the pastor, Roswell Bates:

"I attribute to Dr. Patton and the few years I attended the Spring Street Church the convictions that have remained with me to the present hour as to the inspiration of the Scriptures, the deity of Christ and regeneration by the Spirit of God. We had occasional revival services and these were always fruitful in conversions. Here also I received my first interest in missions. In the Sunday-school I was taught by two young women—one of whom was a missionary volunteer about to sail for a distant field."

The boy made an impression on his teachers, his superintendent, and his pastor as a "youthful fact" that might later become a factor in shaping the world's history. When he was only seven years of age he joined the junior Mission Band and was always ready to say or do anything that might be required of him. He used to remark in later years that one of his great dangers was "an over-confidence in his own sagacity and capacity."

The boy's thoughts were early turned towards the ministry and one of his favourite pastimes was preaching to his sisters or to a row of empty chairs—the latter proving to be the more quiet audience. He also began to write essays and verses, many of which are still preserved. His first attempt at poetry was written in 1846 at the age of nine and shows even then the character of his early religious training which meant so much to him. The verse reads:

> "I don't care, I will bear—
> Ever in my heart will bear—
> Blessed Jesus, died to save us,
> On the cursed Cross He died."

He recollected that as a boy he had a fiery temper and was led to excuse outbursts of anger on the theory that it was ingrain, like the grain in wood. He says: "I was told that I might plane and polish it but the disposition would remain. All I could hope for was that it might be mollified. I bless God that I have learned that if we let God have the stronghold, the devil must give up control."

One of the factors that counted most in Arthur's education was the character of the teachers under whose instruction he was placed. From first to last they were Christians and emphasized the necessity for moral and spiritual as well as intellectual development. In 1848, at the age of eleven, he entered the Mount Washington Collegiate Institute, facing Washington Square, and there came under the influence of the principal, George W. Clarke, an earnest Christian man, later very active in state politics and charitable work.

Wilson Phraner was here the teacher of Greek and Latin and under his careful tutelage were laid the foundations of classical learning that proved so useful in later years. At twelve Arthur began to read the New Testament in Greek, and for the next sixty-two years he kept it up with increasing enjoyment and profit.

Dr. Phraner, his beloved teacher who still happily survives at the age of ninety, says that Arthur was "studious in his habits, quick to learn, and remarkably intelligent and ambitious to win the approbation of his teachers."

Among the prominent citizens who were educated in Dr. Clarke's school and who, like Arthur, there learned lessons in the things worth while, for time and eternity,

Boyhood Temptations

were the millionaire philanthropist, William Earle Dodge; the merchant prince, Morris K. Jesup, William Walter Phelps, George D. Baker, James Talcott, H. O. Havemeyer, the sugar king, and Roscoe Conklin, the United States senator. When, a few years ago, the students gathered to honour the old principal on his ninetieth birthday, they reminded him that he had never spared the rod, but he replied with deep feeling: "No horticulturist ever watched with more pleasure the budding and blooming of his flowers than did I the mental and the moral growth of my students."

Temptations were present in Arthur's young life as in the experience of other boys. He used to tell with a touch of humour how he was once induced to try smoking a pipe, but he added with a note of thanksgiving that the God-given warning of a gastric revolt took away all desire to make any second attempt. The city streets were full of vice and traps, and he was full of life and curiosity and self-confidence. Companions were ever ready to lead him into forbidden paths. Worse than this many summers were spent away from his family in the country where, all unknown to his parents, he found a veritable Sodom. It was, as he said, only the prayers of his father and mother, their example and early training and the overshadowing mercy of God that prevented his young life from being blighted. Such experiences led the man in later years to emphasize, with burning earnestness, the duty of parents to safeguard the early moral and religious surroundings and habits of their children.

II

BOARDING-SCHOOL DAYS—ENLISTING FOR LIFE

AT thirteen years of age Arthur left home, never again to return for any length of time. His parents noted their boy's talents and tendencies and took the advice of his instructors to give him every opportunity to stir up the gift that was in him. They determined to follow the Scriptural injunction to "train up a child in *his* way,"—according to his own God-given bent—and at no little sacrifice to themselves they sent their son to attend the Collegiate Institute at Tarrytown-on-the-Hudson.

Before his departure his father gave him as a life motto the injunction and promise from Proverbs iii. 6— "Trust in the Lord with all thine heart and lean not unto thine own understanding. In all thy ways acknowledge Him and He shall direct thy paths." Sixty years later the son said: "Since my father gave me that motto, no important step has been taken in my life without looking to God for His guidance and never have I looked in vain. I have learned that if His guidance does not come at once, it is safer to wait until He sees fit to show the way. After all it is His work, His time, His way that are of consequence. A step taken too soon will be pretty sure to be a misstep."

Stephen H. Pierson was not a man of many words and was not given to parental lectures, but his life was clean and upright and his words carried weight.

Another bit of advice he gave to his son as he sent him from home with his blessing and prayers: " My son, you are going among strangers and will find some who think it a clever thing to call in question your faith and your father's faith and teachings. Whatever else you think or do, stand true to God and always give Him the advantage of your doubt."

Thus fortified, with bright prospects before him, Arthur set out for school in the autumn of 1850. Homesickness and loneliness are evident in his letters as his thoughts turned lovingly to his parents with a new sense of his own shortcomings, and with a new tenderness. He wrote several little poems dedicated to his father, his mother and his sisters, in which he asked pardon for hasty words and recalled acts of loving thoughtfulness by members of the family.

Arthur's parents had not chosen the school hastily or with reference merely to intellectual and worldly advancement. The instructors were Christian and the principal made it his aim to help every boy to find in Jesus Christ his friend and Saviour and then to stand by him in every trial.

Although Arthur had attended church and Sunday-school since the age of six, and all his training and most of the influences that surrounded him had been Christian, he had never yet deliberately surrendered his heart to Christ. At Tarrytown there came the crisis that comes to so many boys when they first leave home, an experience which tested his earnestness and his courage. He came face to face with the question, " Shall I seek great things for myself in my own way, or shall I give my life to God and surrender to the claims of Jesus Christ ? "

During the one year of Arthur's stay in Tarrytown, a series of special revival meetings were held in the Methodist church, and the earnest but quiet message of the evangelist made a deep impression on him. What followed is given in his own words:

"One night I was much moved to seek my salvation. When the invitation was given I asked for the prayers of God's people and decided to make a start in serving God by accepting Jesus as my Saviour. On my way back to the school I was forced to ask myself: How am I to act as a Christian before the other boys? We all slept in large rooms with five or six beds and with two boys in each bed. As I went up to the ward where I slept I felt that now or never I must show my colours. If my life were to count, I must give some testimony before my schoolmates.

"The boys were not yet in bed and as some others had attended the meeting, the word had preceded me, 'Pierson is converted.' The boys were waiting to see what I would do. There was not one other Christian in the ward and my own bedfellow was perhaps the most careless, trifling and vicious boy in the school. My first hour of testing had come; much depended on how I would meet it.

"As I undressed for bed, I asked God for courage and then when ready to turn in, knelt down beside the bed and silently prayed. The boys were quiet for a moment, then a few began to chuckle, and presently a pillow came flying at my head. I paid no attention to it, though praying was not easy just then—if by prayer is meant consecutive, orderly speaking to God.

"My schoolmates were not malicious but only bent on 'fun,' and when they saw that I did not move, their

Conversion at Tarrytown

sense of fair play asserted itself. One of the older boys said: 'Let him alone,' and silently they all picked up their pillows and got into bed. I was never again disturbed when praying before my fellows."

The initial victory was won and it was the man's conviction in later years that this was a turning point in his boy life. He found that an apparently heavy cross when taken up with the help of God proves light and easily borne. From that time, whatever other faults he may have had, no one could justly accuse Arthur T. Pierson of a lack of moral courage.

His next step was to join the probationers' class-meeting at the Methodist church and when he left the school he took with him a certificate, dated March 20, 1850, and signed by Charles C. Kuntz, "Station Preacher."

"This is to certify that Master Arthur T. Pierson has been an acceptable probationer for about six weeks in the Methodist Episcopal Church of Tarrytown."

Two years later, on March 14, 1852, he joined the Thirteenth Street Presbyterian Church, New York, in which his father was an elder.

Immediately after his conversion, Arthur began to take his share in Christian work either by testimony in the boys' prayer-meetings or by leadership in the junior society. Several of his carefully prepared talks show thought and study quite beyond the ordinary boy of thirteen. One is on a subject that exerted such great influence on his after life—"*Faith in God.*" The text was taken from Psalm lxii. 8, " Trust in Him at all times." Several of his sermons or talks are preserved written in a neat boyish hand. The manuscripts are bound and have the titles elaborately penned in shaded letters on the cover.

The next autumn, Arthur was transferred to the Ossining School, at Sing Sing, New York, which was taught by his brother-in-law, Rev. J. P. Lundy. Here he could be under the care of his eldest sister, Annie, while he continued his classical and religious training. In the course of long walks in the country, the boy also acquired a taste for botany and mineralogy. Many times he was subjected to the bantering of his brothers and cousins on account of the pockets full of stones that he insisted on carrying around with him as specimens. This interest he never lost and in later years he wrote and lectured much on natural science. The subject also opened up a rich mine from which he took a wealth of illustrative material for future sermons.

The Ossining School aimed at the education of the whole boy. Especial attention was given to literary training and public speaking. By definite, practical oversight and criticism the teachers cultivated in the pupils a taste for good books and clear, forceful expression of ideas. The boys were obliged to memorize and recite difficult passages from famous orations so that they could enunciate clearly every consonant and vowel. In this way they learned to have full control over tongue and palate, lips and teeth, until nothing was too difficult for their vocal gymnastics. Particular stress was also laid on truth, morality and industry. These were deemed even more important than overcrowded memories and forced intellectual growth.

Only a limited number of boys were admitted to this school so that each might receive individual attention. The catalogue announced that the aim of the school was

Experiences at Ossining 35

to "imbue the pupils with an admiration for virtue, and a high purpose to live brave, noble, useful lives, to become worthy patriots, dear to God and famous to all ages. The Bible, as the best of all classics, is a prominent textbook and each boy is required to read it daily and to study some portion of it each Sabbath. They are also encouraged to pray habitually and to live in the consciousness that there is a world beyond this for which the present life is but a school."

At Ossining Arthur was a wide-awake lad and entered heartily into the school life. He made many friends and some of his early poems—falsely so called—were written at this time to boys and girls whom he loved. The poetry was not such as would make the boy famous, but the training in expression, in rhythm and in the use of synonyms was of real value. Some of the verses also show deep religious feeling and a desire to lead others to know his Lord.

The "literary remains" of this period include whole volumes of poems, plays written for the school, essays on many subjects, serious and humorous stories, and one novelette, entitled "The Baron's Will, or The Wonderful Inscription." Arthur was a frequent speaker on the school platform and graced many public occasions with prologues, monologues and epilogues. It became his ambition to excel in literary style and in public speaking and for a time this aim eclipsed all others. His first editorial experience was gained on the staff of the school paper, *The Ossining Gazette*, of which he was one of the editors. He was also publisher and printer, for he wrote out the four pages by hand for each subscriber! *The Gazette* was published every Wednesday and was declared on its title page to be "devoted to Literature, Science and the productions of Genius"—there is no doubt about the genius. When Arthur left the school in the winter of 1853 *The Gazette* died a natural death from insufficient nutrition and from lack of circulation.

The youthful author and student was in danger of being spoiled by overmuch praise and it is not surprising that he developed some conceit and a superabundance of self-confidence. Nothing was too difficult or too delicate for him to undertake, but he was in earnest and apparently wasted no time. That he was conscious of some of his faults is seen in the fact that in a farce which he wrote for a school entertainment he gave himself the character of "Samuel Valorous—A Great Bragg." But the faults were superficial, the real gold was underneath and often appeared on the surface. Many of the qualities which manifested themselves during those school days were such as marked his work in mature life—fine penmanship, originality, accuracy, painstaking research, earnestness of purpose and high moral tone.

Arthur's ambition received fresh impetus at about this time. In the spring of 1852 a prize was offered by Dr. P. A. Skinner, of Philadelphia, to the youth of what is now Greater New York, for the best essay on the subject: "How Shall the Rising Generation Protect Themselves Against the Daily Increasing and Destructive Influence of Alcoholic Drinks." Over five hundred and fifty boys and girls under eighteen years of age entered the contest and Arthur was awarded second prize. He was one of four appointed to read his essay twice before large audiences (that paid twenty-five cents admission) in the Broadway Taber-

Prize Temperance Oration 37

nacle, New York. The prize was advertised as a "splendid library" of fifteen volumes. They included such titles as "Pike's Persuasives to Early Piety, interspersed with suitable prayers," "Baxter's Saints' Rest" and others equally far removed from the daredevil literature usually supposed to be attractive to a boy of fifteen.

The period between school and college was an important one in young Pierson's experience. He completed his course in Ossining early in the winter of 1852-53 and matriculated for Columbia College, New York, but was still too young to be received. It was therefore decided that he should live at home and enter the employ of the mercantile house of Alfred Edwards and Company, Park Place. This enabled him to earn something towards his college expenses, gave him a new idea of the use of money and trained him in business principles and methods. He was always thankful for this brief experience and its influence was evident throughout his life. It taught him accuracy in keeping his records and accounts, inculcated reliability in handling other people's money, trained him to rightly estimate values, taught promptness in paying debts, and in other ways gave him the business sense that is too often lacking in clergymen. He learned the solemn obligation of a promise and was always known for his absolute honesty and truthfulness. He was greatly pleased by one experience at this time. The young man was never spoiled with an oversupply of spending money, for while his parents were thrifty they had a large family and his father was not in a position to supply all his boy's needs, much less his luxuries. He had, however, a wealthy uncle who one day asked

Arthur if he was in need of money. When the young man candidly admitted that he was, the uncle took out a blank card and wrote an order to his cashier:

"Give the bearer, Arthur T. Pierson, as much money as he wants and charge to my account. JOHN GRAY."

The boy took his uncle at his word, drew as much money as he needed and repaid it to the cashier as soon as he was able. The uncle never asked how much he drew nor when he returned it. In commenting on this incident in later years Dr. Pierson said:

"How like God's unbounded grace is the promise 'Ask what thou wilt.' How rich we are when God is our banker! It is not *our* name or account that makes our request honoured but the name of Him who endorses it—'Whatsoever ye shall ask in My Name.'"

The temptations of city life were not unknown to the young clerk. Many sought his companionship and tried to induce him to follow them into questionable amusements. It is estimated that there were, in 1850, 150,000 young men in New York. Many of them came from farms and were unable to stand their ground against the temptations that met them in city life. Away from the restraints of home, they gave up church-going habits and withdrew from other Christian influences. Pierson saw four or five of his fellow clerks who had come from the country, ignorant and innocent, wreck their manhood and constitutions through drink and debauchery. The evident results of gambling, strong drink and theatre-going led him to form the conviction that these should have no place in a young man's life.

It was the problem of caring for the thousands of youth in the city that led to the founding of the first Young Men's Christian Association in New York—the fifth to be established in the world (1852). With Morris K. Jesup, William E. Dodge, Howard Crosby and Samuel Colgate, Arthur T. Pierson became one of the first one hundred members. Forty years later he said: "Although no institution in the world is perfect, it seems to me that the Y. M. C. A., when its Christian character is maintained supreme, is as nearly complete as any human organization could be. I know no other institution that has, on the whole, so mighty a lever to uplift the young men of the community."

III

AT HAMILTON COLLEGE—IN TRAINING FOR SERVICE

IN harmony with the wishes of his parents and the advice of his teachers and friends young Pierson early decided to prepare for the Christian ministry. Although he was not yet conscious of any special "call," his talents, inclination and training all pointed in this direction. Without seeing the final goal, he took the next step in the divine program and every detail in this program is important.

He did not enter Columbia College as he expected, for his parents thought it best to send him away once more from the distractions of city life. Hamilton College was chosen as a Christian institution of high scholarship, large enough to offer the advantages of contact and competition with many classes of young men, yet small enough to allow for individual instruction and the impression of the personality of professors on students. Rev. Albert Barnes, the eminent divine, was one of the famous alumni and Dr. H. G. O. Dwight of Constantinople was pointed out, with pride, as a missionary product of the college. The early morning of September 19, 1853, saw Arthur cutting loose once more from his moorings and sailing out upon an unknown sea. It was of immense advantage that the decision as to his life-work had already been made, since it saved him from aimlessness and from a consequent waste of time and energy. He kept his port in mind, studied his chart, trimmed his sails, steered by his Polar Star and made a straight course for his desired haven. He says of himself, "I was precociously mature mentally—a thing I should not like to have true of my children,—but I was lacking in ripe judgment and maturity of character." He was ambitious and energetic and had confidence in his own ability to succeed. In the new world into which he was entering he was destined to receive some hard knocks that were calculated to give him a more modest estimate of himself. He took these experiences philosophically and acknowledged in after years that he greatly needed any discipline he received.

The entering class of which Arthur was a member numbered forty—which was, up to that time, the largest in the history of the college. God knows how much depends on a first stand in such a new world, and He gave young Arthur an opportunity to place himself at once definitely on His side. On the drive from Utica to Clinton, Arthur fell in with some students who took him to their boarding-house in town to spend the first night. After supper the landlady asked him, though an under classman and the youngest of the group, to lead family worship. It was a real ordeal, but he consented. This act marked him at once as an out and out Christian, and some of the companions of that first evening became his lifelong friends.

At the beginning of his college course he resolved to keep a journal—a resolve that many have made—and he kept it up for sixty years—a feat which few can equal. This unique record reveals the systematic perseverance so characteristic of the man. From these records and from contributions to the local press we glean many of the facts that follow. In the opening sentences of his description of his first day at college, we recognize the earmarks of a youthful grandiloquence.

"The richness of youth's golden twilight had not yet deepened into the sober light of manhood, when I entered college. The irresistible fascination of boyish romance yet held sway over my soul, clothing whatever was dark and cheerless in the prospect, in the attractive habiliments of hope. . . .

". . . The day following my arrival, I went to the house of the president, called, in the sacrilegious language of the students, the 'Prex.' I was met at the door by a tall, cadaverous, skeleton-like gentleman in black, on whose long nose rested that scholastic badge, a pair of spectacles, and from whose black silk gown I shrank in indefinable horror. It was the 'Prex' himself. His long, straight hair, combed back, gave to his already rigid features an air of peculiar sternness. I know nothing of his origin further than the report which the students circulate as authentic, that an Egyptian mummy, conveyed to this country, on being opened, revived and became the president of this college."

Before his freshman year was passed young Pierson had acquired a high respect and affection for this "mummy" who went in public by the name of President Simeon North. He was a good friend to the students, honest-hearted, level-headed, strong-handed, a man who taught the youth under him how to think for themselves and to do the work of men in the world.

Pierson's story continues: "While I was waiting my trial, in a roomful of professors and candidates, I noticed on my right one of the greenest looking speci-

A Trying Ordeal 43

mens I ever saw. He was facing a large pompous professor who was questioning him in mathematics. The eyes of the youth stared vacantly around. . . . If he ever *had* any ideas they had entirely evaporated. Circles, parallelograms, diameters and tangents, cubes and spheres were all one to him. His mind was evidently chaotic. . . . At the other extremity of the room, facing a thin, pale-looking LL. D., sat a richly dressed New Yorker whose expression reminded me strongly of a 'Baboon,' and who acted as though it were his firm conviction that what he did not know was not worth knowing. But he was more ready than correct in his answers. It was amusing to look first at the fellow on my right, fairly expecting to be devoured and then at the ignoramus on my left whose awkwardness was only equalled by his self-satisfaction. . . .

"But *my* time had arrived. . . . First came mathematics. It seemed to me that my examiner applied figures to everything, for every movement and question seemed measured by compass and square. My recollection is indistinct but my impression is that I gave the 'rule of three' for the process of algebraic multiplication. . . . Then came Greek. The professor handed me a Greek Reader. For some reason I became dizzy; the Greek text became a black mark and I suffered martyrdom. The professor, seeing my difficulty, read the text for me while I translated slowly and not very surely. As to the rest I willingly let fall the curtain. I left the house like Ulysses when

"'He fled with joy pernicious Cyclop's den
Not wishing ever to return again. . . .'"

In justice to the young freshman, however, it should

be said that he was ill that day and returned later to request the professor to give him a second trial. He was told that, contrary to his expectation, he had passed successfully. In his diary he remarks, with his usual fondness for a play on words: "The fire of questions had been so slight that I was not scorched." The early years of faithful study had enabled him to stand the severe test.

The next day he set out to secure a room on the campus and to furnish it according to his means. This was not a simple task for a young man almost without funds, for Stephen Pierson's recent business ventures had not proved successful and he could supply his son with very little money. Everything beyond tuition and the bare necessaries of life must be provided by Arthur's own industry and ingenuity. He faced the situation manfully, secured a room in Kirkland Hall, and furnished it "luxuriously" with a chair, a table, a cot, and a straw mattress. He paid for his rent, light and heat by acting as caretaker of the sophomore recitation room.

The necessity of adding to his small store of funds led him to constant economy and industry. Though he was only a self-taught musician he had some real talent, and secured a position as organist in the village church. His carefully balanced account books show a total income of only $150 a year, and frequent items marked "benevolence."

A vein of humour runs through much of his college diaries, side by side with signs of what would seem to many an overabundance of pious expressions. He thus describes his first attendance at chapel:

"All the students assembled at 9 A. M. according

The Chapel Service

to custom. . . . The chapel is a curious building designed by an old-fashioned deacon who evidently regarded any ornament or comfort as an invention of the devil. The backs of the benches are at right angles to the seats and the pews are very narrow as if the designer meant to

> ' 'Brace our backs against a board
> To make us tall and straight.'

"The chapel formerly had an organ, but one day some hilarious students took out the pipes and used them to serenade the faculty and ladies of the town. Since then the instrument has been silent. . . .

"By the kindness of a friend I was shown to the freshman seats but some were not so fortunate. One wag, seeing a freshman enter and look around in a perplexed way, directed him to the faculty seats. The poor fellow did not discover the joke until the president and professors entered. . . .

"After prayers it is customary for the classes to leave chapel in order of their seniority but some of the freshmen started to go out first. They were promptly hissed and one poor fellow, who heard shouts of 'Fresh' coming from every side, stood transfixed like a statue, almost frightened to death at the enormity of his offense."

College students in those days enjoyed less freedom than now. None could leave town without special permission; study hours were rigidly enforced and no student was permitted to be out of his room after 10 P. M. Bonfires and fireworks on the campus were prohibited and the use of intoxicants spelled expulsion.

Chapel services were held both morning and evening and there was no provision for "voluntary" attendance. A strict system of demerits was applied to all breaches of discipline such as reading during public worship, which cost five demerits. Twenty such marks called forth a warning to the student, a letter to parents, and might result in suspension.

Pierson was, at this time, a slender, nervous youth with dark waving locks that he used to shake gallantly. He wore a small silken skullcap on the campus and was "always going somewhere"—never idling. He was ever ready to assume the responsibilities of leadership which at times brought embarrassing publicity. In after years he was fond of telling how at one of the first student prayer-meetings he attended, there was one of those long pauses, so uncomfortable to an active youth unaccustomed to "Quaker meetings." After enduring the silence as long as possible, the young freshman, ignoring the leader, called out: "Brother ——— (naming an upper classman), will you pray?" It was many weeks before Pierson could meet any of his college mates on the campus without being bantered by a clearing of the throat and the salutation, "Brother ———, will you pray?" Such good-humoured chaffing was not resented and the experience helped to teach a needed lesson.

Prof. Anson J. Upson took a kindly interest in the lad of sixteen, and many years later Dr. Pierson spoke his gratitude. "It pleased God," he said, "that there should be one of the instructors in college sufficiently friendly to come to me and tell me where I was making a fool of myself. I had been trotted out so frequently at home to speak in public that I did not

Student Fraternities 47

know that silence was especially golden in a freshman. Professor Upson rendered me a great service by his friendly warning as to the rocks ahead."

College sports in those days were not the highly developed, semi-professional games of modern times, and did not supplant the studies entered in the curriculum. Pierson entered heartily into college life but he was not strong physically and did not take any large part in athletics. He took long walks and maintained his health by care in eating, sleeping and fresh air. While always slender (he weighed only 124 pounds) he was of that nervous, wiry build that could endure great strain. In fifty years of strenuous public life after graduation, with duties that compelled him to travel many thousands of miles and to speak often two or three times a day, he was seldom obliged to break an engagement because of illness.

Hamilton College, in the fifties, was a hotbed of secret societies. Fierce rivalry existed between the "Alpha Delts," the "Sigma Phis" and other Greek letter fraternities, but fiercer still was the contest for supremacy between the secret and non-secret organizations. There was a great rivalry for college honours and any suspicion of favouritism was a signal for energetic remonstrance. At one time there were serious riots, college windows were smashed and other property was damaged. The pulpit ("bear-box" as it was called) as well as the stoves and benches were carried away from the chapel. In sophomore year the non-secret fraternity seriously debated the question, "Is it expedient for the whole fraternity to leave college and publish its protest to the world?" Several students actually did withdraw.

The question as to which society a student should join was an important one, since this determined a man's associates and his social position. "Secret" men looked down upon the "Antis" as low caste and considered them only a step above the "neutrals" or outcastes.

Pierson's evident talents caused it to be reported that he would lead his class and he was urged by both the secret men and the "Antis" to join their fraternities. He may have been misinformed on some points, but it is interesting to see that even at this early age he determined to make his decision not because of social or intellectual advantages but from moral motives. We find his arguments and convictions rehearsed in his journal and letters:

"Politics on a small scale," he writes, "have entered college life. Since coming here I have been surrounded by men electioneering for the different societies. There are four secret fraternities and one non-secret, but I will not pledge myself to any until I know more about them. . . . The Anti-Secret Society (which later changed its name to the Delta Upsilon to escape from the consequences of the initial letters) is composed of some of the best men in college. The majority of them are pious and industrious, are opposed to secrecy and are of the best moral character. That is far more important than talent."

The reasons he gives for joining the "Antis" reveal characteristics which marked his choices through life. (1) While the secret fraternities seemed to have the advantage in numbers, talent, and influence among students and faculty, the "Antis" were, he thought, standing on higher moral ground. (2) The men in the

Social Life and Friendships 49

latter seemed to have a more general reputation for piety, while many in the secret societies were said to have loose habits. (3) He approved of the standard set up in the motto οὐδεν ἠδήλον ("Nothing Concealed") as better calculated to produce harmony in the college. In answer to the suggestion that he ought to join the less moral society in order to reform its members, he remarked: "My Bible is my only guide. While it encourages me to endeavour to make the wicked better, it in no case tells me to join hand in hand with them (Psalm i.)."

Pierson was always opposed to any hazing that seemed like a cowardly attack by superior numbers, but there were some pranks which he could contemplate with relish. He tells of one unsuspecting freshman whom the sophomores volunteered to drill in declamation. At one point in the selection where an excited Hungarian exile addresses the hated Emperor Nicolas of Russia, the sophomores suggested that the freshman turn about towards his right hand, and with a very expressive and emphatic gesture address himself to the Russian autocrat as though he were beside him. The result exceeded their wildest expectations, for the gullible freshman, waxing warm, turned about, and shaking his fist in the face of the dignified professor of rhetoric thundered out, "And you—you old northern bear, sit there quietly on your imperial throne warming yourself in furs," etc., etc.! This climax brought a tumult of applause which the freshman appropriated as his due for his dramatic eloquence!

There were not many social advantages in Clinton, but Pierson was not a recluse. As a member of the Glee Club and of the chapel quartette he spent many pleasant evenings in the homes of his professors or with the young people of the town.

Friendships always filled a large place in his life and thought, and in nothing did he show more wisdom than in his choice of intimate associates. Even at this early age he was a careful student of human nature and sought his comrades not for their wealth or brilliancy but for their real worth. His whole life was enriched by the friendships he formed in college. Among those whom he admired and loved were William J. Erdman, who later became a well-known preacher and Bible teacher; Herrick Johnson, later professor of homiletics in McCormick Seminary, Charles E. Robinson, a well-known Doctor of Divinity in New York, and Delavan Leonard, who was afterwards an editorial co-worker for over twenty years. From these friends we gather the following picture of Pierson during his undergraduate days. Johnson, who was class president when Pierson was secretary, writes:

"From the first day I met Pierson on College Hill I had confidence in him, and we became friends. He was fresh, eager, impulsive, warm hearted, enthusiastic. He was the best linguist in the class and among the first in intellectual clearness and scholarly culture. As a writer and speaker he commanded attention and kept a high place of honour and influence throughout his college life. He was fervid, imaginative, genial, a good story-teller, nimble in speech, swift in perception, large in mental poise and full of cheer. His face was a sunbeam, and there were prophecies that found fulfillment in his large and useful life. He was pelted with jokes but without sting. His very foibles were winsome.

His enthusiasm was boundless and found its chief joy in usefulness."

"His quick repartee, brilliant smile and love of fun," writes Dr. Charles E. Robinson, "his open-heartedness, confiding disposition, general benevolence towards all and decided ability were marked even in freshman year. He took high rank in speaking and scholarship, in debating and literature."

Dr. Leonard thus describes his first meeting with Pierson in October, 1855:

"He had then just entered his junior year, and a few hours before I had arrived on the campus a freshman and an utter stranger. After supper I was standing on the steps of South College taking in my new surroundings and oppressed by more than a touch of loneliness and homesickness. Just then Pierson came up with extended hand, inquired my name and gave his, and with the utmost cordiality invited me to his room. I went, without fear of hazing, and almost at once we fell into a friendship and intimacy unmatched by any other in my life. I had come from a farm in western New York and was clad in plainest attire. My face was sunburned and my hands were hardened with toil; while Pierson was city born and bred, and arrayed in garments which seemed to me to surpass anything I had ever seen! Though a member of the junior class, he treated me as an equal, and appeared to desire my friendship. That first evening in particular I was fairly stunned by my new friend's musical ability, both vocal and instrumental, as with voice and nimble fingers upon his melodeon he rendered not only hymn-tunes and anthems but also passages from this and that oratorio and opera. The fellowship thus begun continued until his graduation two years later, and again for a year in Union Theological Seminary.

"On the platform before an audience, he was at his best. Scarcely ever did he fail to please and edify. He always had something to say which was worth hearing, and he was also certain to say it in such a way as to hold the attention of his hearers. Though at graduation he was as yet scarcely out of boyhood, being only just twenty, the evidence was conclusive that, should he live, his achievements were destined to be far more than ordinary."

Most of the professors at Hamilton were not only men of high intellectual attainments and moral standing but of deep religious conviction and experience. Under these influences young Pierson developed greatly in spiritual ideals and strength of character. He was known among his fellows as pure minded and earnest, and many were the times when a ribald jest was cut short at his appearance on the scene. He refused to furnish the gallery of his imagination with evil pictures or the storehouse of his memory with vile stories such as are often passed around among college men. On one occasion when the students were observing the old custom of "Burning of Demosthenes" to celebrate the close of the year, Pierson joined in the fun until it came to the oration. "That," he says, "was a complete embodiment of filth and filthy language; insomuch that I was obliged to leave the room."

One day he saw a circular of fifty books distributed by a Utica firm and wrote in his journal: "All were of licentious character. It is terrible to assume the responsibility of issuing and advertising fifty books to pollute the hearts of youth! Abominable, to think how

A Religious Revival

much evil is thus done. I would avoid them as I would a coal of fire."

The spiritual life in college was at a low ebb in freshman year but during his junior year there was considerable religious interest, largely due to the neighbouring revivals under Charles G. Finney. This interest was increased by an accident to one of the students which resulted in death. On November 26, 1855, Pierson wrote:

"The spirit of God is here and F——'s death has produced a deep impression. On Saturday evening at prayer-meeting four spoke, all professing to be Christians, and referred to this providence as having forcibly impressed them. . . . To-day at 9 A. M. a prayer-meeting was held."

This student had been deeply concerned in the spiritual condition of the college and now his prayers for a revival of religion were answered through the interest awakened by his death. Pierson's diary records many conversations with college mates, professors and others on religious subjects, for here he began to do personal religious work. He records with thankfulness many promising conversions—among them that of one of his professors. The death of his sister Annie at this time also made him more sensible of the importance of working while it is day.

During a part of his college course, Pierson acted as secretary of the village missionary society and taught a Bible class in the village church. In senior year, during the revival period of 1857, there was special religious interest in Clinton as in other parts of the country, and he was instrumental in leading many of his Bible class to confess Christ. This work also led him to adopt a plan of systematic Bible reading. By taking one chapter a day and three on Sundays, he read the New Testament through twice and the Old Testament once in a year and a half. True to his early training, he had strict views of Sabbath observance and made it his rule on that day "not to think his own thoughts nor speak his own words" even in the writing of ordinary letters.

Birthdays and other anniversaries were always important mile-stones to him. At seventeen (1854) he wrote: "May there be fewer unimproved blessings to be mourned over at the close of another year;" at eighteen: "I would that I could feel that in all respects my time has been well spent. I fear it has not been, but with St. Paul I can say, I will 'press forward to the things that are before';" at nineteen: "May God so aid me to improve my time that it may not be reviewed with regret when passed." A year later his prayer was still more serious: "Oh, that the next year of my life may be a holier one."

This same youthful earnestness enabled Pierson to take a high stand in his classes, and in literary society work. "I came to college," he says, " with the resolve that if by assiduous application, punctuality and attention to duties I could lead my class, without injuring my health, I would do so." In view of his chosen calling he devoted much attention to training in writing and speaking and his compositions always had the salt of sincerity and the spice of novelty. They were written with a definite purpose to gain attention and also to convince.

Public speaking was not as easy for the young man as it seemed to his audience. When he first appeared on the college chapel stage he says that he experienced "a tremulousness of the limbs"—which he overcame by stamping forcibly. By steady perseverance he gained the mastery over his nerves, so that before he left college he was acknowledged to be one of the best orators in his class. He won honours in classics, poetry, English composition, debating, rhetoric and oratory and was elected a member of the Phi Beta Kappa when that society entered Hamilton. After one unsuccessful competition he wrote: "I care not for these things. My ambition is to excel, not as an end but as a means to an end, in hope of doing good. I seek humbly to win for the glory of God. All the honour that the world can confer is not so precious as my own honour. Nothing must be allowed to throw a shadow over my Christian character."

Hamilton College excelled in the cultivation of able writers and speakers. The students were assembled every Saturday to hear essays from the lower classmen and orations from the juniors and seniors. These performances were judiciously criticized by the professors and plagiarism was severely rebuked as stealing. The training in the fraternities and literary societies was also excellent, for here the students criticized each other—sometimes with relentless candour. Some of the characteristics of Arthur Pierson at this age are noted by those who passed on his work. One critic said, in reviewing an essay on "The Embodiment of Thought":

"Man is a progressive animal. Mr. Pierson has been harping on the strings of architecture, painting, sculpture and music long enough. He would better lay aside this class of subjects for at least six months."

Another criticism related to his overabundance of illustration; of imagery and of underscoring. In general, however, he was highly commended for neatness, logic, thoughtfulness and style.

During his college course he began his career as an author and wrote frequently for New York and local papers. His printed poems and essays of this period would fill volumes and yet he wrote solely for practice or to give vent to his overflowing exuberance of thought—never for money. Before he was twenty-one he had seen over one hundred of his productions in print and yet had never received a cent in return. This characterized his work throughout life. At one time he entered in his diary: " Mr. ——— is anxiously inquiring how much I expect for the article I wrote for him. I told him not to be disturbed—that I did nothing for hire." He counted himself as God's steward and placed his talents freely at the disposal of others. The number of noms-de-plume which he used to hide his identity is astonishing—among others we find " Amicus, Felix, Pierre Fils, U. Donough Outis, A. Nonymous, Esq., Skezix, Hujus, Am. Phibius," etc.

Many poems of this period were highly praised and widely published. Some appeared in the New York *Evening Mirror* with which Thomas Bailey Aldrich was associated. This author took a great fancy to the young student and encouraged him to write. One poem, in imitation of " The Bells " by Edgar Allen Poe, was publicly attributed to Mr. Aldrich, and in reply the well-known poet wrote: " I did not write it— but I am pleased to have been thought its author. As a general thing I rank imitations below parodies. A parody is an understood burlesque, but an imitation is too often a mild name for an unpardonable plagiarism. Not so in this case, however. It is true that the author owes the shape of his verse to E. A. Poe, but the thought, now as delicate as the summer zephyr, now solemn like the sepulchral moan of an autumn midnight, lifts the poem even above 'the tintinabulation of The Bells.'"

The poem referred to was entitled "The Winds," and was written when Arthur Pierson was seventeen:

> "Hear the gentle summer winds,
> Zephyr winds.
> Of what sweet Æolian music their melody
> reminds;
> How they whisper—whisper—whisper
> Through the balmy air of night,
> While their strains so sweet and floating,
> All their joyfulness denoting,
> Fill the spirit with delight.
> How they glide—glide—glide
> By the window at your side.
> Ah, what charming undulation every lis'ning
> person finds
> In the winds—winds—winds—winds—
> Winds—winds—winds—
> In the breathing and the playing of the
> winds.
>
> "Hear the cold winter winds,
> Icy winds.
> Of what joyous fireside home-scenes their chill-
> ing blast reminds;
> Hear them whistle—whistle—whistle
> In the freezing air of night,
> And the constant clamour blowing,
> Ever loud and louder growing,
> How they chill and blast and blight!
> Hear them roar—roar—roar,
> Now more fiercely than before.
> 'Tis a banging, slamming uproar that everybody
> finds
> In the winds—winds—winds—winds—
> Winds—winds—winds—
> In the rushing and the brushing of the winds.

"Hear the solemn churchyard winds,
　　　Mournful winds ;
Of what agony and sorrow their direful chant
　　　reminds.
　　How they mutter—mutter—mutter
　Round those graves and vaults at night.
　　Their unceasing moan and sighing
　　Makes you think of dead and dying,
And of ghostly shrouds of white.
　　Hear them blow—blow—blow,
　　As if saying only ' woe ! '
Ah ! what sorrowful vibration the weeping
　　　mourner finds
　　In the winds—winds—winds—winds—
　　　　　Winds—winds—winds—
In the moaning and the groaning of the winds.

"Hear the awful tempest winds,
　　　Stormy winds ;
Of what wrecks and sad destruction their angry
　　　roar reminds.
　　How they grumble—grumble—grumble
　Through the wood and vales at night,
　　While their mad terrific lashing,
　　Through the trees and buildings crashing,
Really chills you with affright.
　　Hear them howl—howl—howl,
　　With a fierce and angry growl.
Sad and cheerless desolation every human being
　　　finds
　　In the winds—winds—winds—winds—
　　　　　Winds—winds—winds—
In the grumbling and the rumbling of the
　　　winds."

During summer vacations Pierson set himself to follow systematic courses of reading in literature, biography, history and poetry and made it a rule to read at least one hundred pages a day. Much of his time also was spent in writing, that he might gain facility of expression, beauty of diction and definiteness of ideas.

Betrothal

He was still in training for service and did not believe that vacations should be periods in which a man loses the impetus gained in the period of study.

But vacations were not all work days. The summer months and winter holidays were used for delightful outings and to cement many friendships. During the Christmas holidays of his junior year—when he was eighteen years of age—he met Miss Frances Benedict who was keeping house for her father Seth Williston Benedict in the Pierson home. Arthur's parents were at that time living in Chicago and the two young people thus brought together were immediately attracted to each other. Other young women friends had previously impressed the young man and he might have allowed himself to succumb to their charms—but God graciously prevented him from making any such serious mistake and providentially brought together the two eminently fitted for each other. Both were Christians so that there was little danger of disagreement on the most important questions of life.

Arthur Pierson was graduated from Hamilton with high honours, but the best part of his college course was perhaps that outside the curriculum, including the personal influence of some of his professors. Concerning two of these men he wrote:

"Prof. Edward North—'Old Greek,' as we called him—had the culture of an Athenian scholar and the consecration of a Christian teacher. He was a magnificent man mentally and morally, though not impressive physically. He took a personal interest in his pupils and I spent many an evening in his home. He could read Greek as we would read English. His contagious enthusiasm and childlike reverence for the

Scriptures inspired me to read the Word of God in the original. Then there was Professor Root—'Square Root' as we nicknamed him. He was a noble man of highest integrity, and not to be trifled with in his classes. The students did not dare to play tricks with him and could not recite successfully with only 'intuitive knowledge.' This thoroughness made him universally respected and his moral influence was most impressive."

Even more than the literary honours Arthur Pierson valued the manifest confidence and esteem of these professors. He was greatly pleased when at the end of junior year the president, Simeon North, called him to his office, and after commending him for the way in which he had taken care of the sophomore class room, offered to give the college bell into his charge for the next year. The diary thus closes the account:

"Prex said to me most solemnly, 'Mr. Pierson, this is the post of greatest responsibility. The bell is the regulator of the college and therefore must be put in charge of the man who can most be depended on for punctuality and responsibility.' The course of integrity is its own reward."

IV

IN THE THEOLOGICAL SEMINARY—STUDYING TECHNIQUE

COLLEGE did not turn Arthur Pierson aside from the ministry, although in the course of his scientific studies his inquiring mind became a little skeptical on some points which he had been taught to believe. There were not lacking companions and even professors who suggested more doubts than the twenty-year-old student could answer. Of this period he says:

"Just as I was leaving college, I felt myself in danger of sinking into the horrible pit and miry clay of doubt. I had been much interested in the study of the natural sciences and read many books on the subject, written by unbelievers. A shallow knowledge of science was leading me into skepticism, but I found that the deeper I went into the study, the more surely I came upon the reality of God. I found ' a little learning to be a dangerous thing,' but that all true science leads to the divine Creator and ruler of the universe."

He determined to prepare for the ministry at Union Theological Seminary which had been established in New York City in 1836. It was then located on University Place, near Washington Park, and when Mr. Pierson entered in the autumn of 1857, there were one hundred and twenty students and five professors. The seminary was not housed in the palatial quarters of to-day, and there was nothing in the surroundings that were calculated to unfit young men for the strenuous life of simplicity and self-denial that awaited them in their chosen calling. Union Seminary was founded as a conservative seminary reporting to the " New School Assembly" of the Presbyterian Church. The prospectus stated that it was intended to be "a training school, not to foster religious controversy but to unite a divided church, . . . a place where all men of moderate views who desired to stand free from the extremes of doctrinal speculation, practical radicalism and ecclesiastical domination, might cordially and affectionately rally."

Here Pierson spent three years of special study and practical training. His debt to the professors who guided his thought and inspired his life could never be adequately acknowledged. There was Dr. Thomas H. Skinner, professor of Sacred Rhetoric and Pastoral Theology, whom he mentioned as the holiest man he had ever met up to that time. "The atmosphere of heaven seemed about him. Piety beamed from his eye, gleamed in his smile and almost made his footsteps radiant. He may not have been an intellectual giant but his spiritual insight and influence were remarkable and in a great measure Union Seminary of those days was poised upon him as a spiritual centre. Though the students were wont to imitate his lisping speech and his habit of gazing steadfastly into the corner of the room while he lectured, they nevertheless loved and honoured him. He had a marvellous power in reading the Scriptures and many times, after reading a chapter like Ezekiel xxxiv. or Daniel ix., I have gone to my room to verify the passage and make sure that what seemed

The "Annus Mirabilis" in Missions 63

so new was really old. His reading and his prayers made me a better man."

Prof. Henry Boynton Smith, who taught Systematic Theology, was characterized by Pierson as a man of great learning and the clearest thinker he ever knew. "He taught us to know God, for his system of theology was nearly perfect." He was genial in manner, full of humour and a great favourite with the young men.

For one year Dr. Elias Riggs, the famous missionary to Turkey, taught Hebrew in the seminary and stamped the impress of his character and missionary enthusiasm on the students. Under his influence and through lectures by Dr. Schauffler of Constantinople Arthur Pierson's missionary interest was greatly stimulated.

The year 1858 was in fact an "Annus Mirabilis" in modern missions. During that one year doors in heathen lands were opened, giving access to one thousand millions of the human race. Japan was opened to the Gospel, China by the treaty of Tientsin gave access to her interior provinces and provided that any Chinese might accept Christianity without fear of persecution. The control of India was also taken from the sordid East India Company and Christian England came into control of the Indies. In the same year the first woman missionary penetrated the Zenanas of Hindustan; in Italy the foundations of religious freedom were laid; David Livingstone entered Africa the second time to prepare the way for the missionary; in Mexico, Benito Juares overthrew the Papal power. These events stirred the Church from sleep and called forth volunteers. George E. Post, a classmate and personal friend of Pierson, decided for foreign service, and the question came home to his own conscience with an insistence which the plea of poor health would not silence. He says:

"I heard the question answered by the argument from conceit, that we students had forsooth too great capacity for acquisition and culture to go into foreign lands, and that we should remain where our gifts would be appreciated. These arguments may have tended to shape my course, but I had before me the example of the wonderful linguist and scholar, Dr. Elias Riggs, the cultured gentleman who was giving his life to the Turks. The vision of the marvellous events in heathen lands also stirred my apathetic soul to a further study of missions; but I said to myself 'home ties bind me to America.' In reality it was my ambition that prevented me from truly and conscientiously considering at that time my duty in regard to the foreign field."

Among friends and classmates in the seminary were William J. Erdman, Arthur Mitchell, afterwards secretary of the Presbyterian Board of Foreign Missions, and D. Stuart Dodge, a philanthropist and the son of a philanthropist. He met these men and others not only in the class room but in debating societies and in social circles that developed character and cemented friendship.

It was according to the plan of God that Arthur Pierson was brought back to New York at the beginning of the great revival of 1857. What he saw and heard during those days of spiritual quickening helped to mould his ideals and convictions as to evangelism. The period between 1843 and 1857 had been marked by stagnation

The Revival of 1857

in New York churches so that the accessions to membership scarcely equalled the losses by death and discipline, and attendance upon church services had fallen off to an alarming extent. Then a small cloud arose on the horizon and with it came hope of a downpour. Mr. Jeremiah C. Lamphier, a merchant, decided to give up his business and devote himself to the work of a lay evangelist. Commerce was crowding out religion in the mercantile district and Mr. Lamphier planned to set up a counter current by establishing a noonday prayer-meeting for business men in Fulton Street. There were six present on the first day (September 23, 1857), twenty on the second and before long four rooms were filled with an attendance of hundreds. The interest spread throughout the city until there were twenty places in New York and Brooklyn open for daily services. Henry Ward Beecher, Theodore L. Cuyler and others began to preach with new power and religion became the chief topic of conversation. The daily papers aided by printing sermons and reports of the revival. Men and women of all classes were aroused, and early morning and evening meetings were conducted daily in many of the churches. Large union services were also held in the afternoons and many were converted and organized for Christian work. At about this time came also a financial crisis in which banks suspended payment and men were brought to a fresh realization of the uncertainty of earthly things.

The Thirteenth Street Church, of which Arthur Pierson was a member, shared with others in the renewed activity and received 245 at two communions. The young theologue was pressed into service and took charge of a Bible class in the Sunday-school. This class grew in membership from sixteen to eighty-four and through God's blessing on the teacher's faithful efforts every member was led to Christ. The last to surrender himself to God joined the church on his young teacher's twenty-second birthday. Mr. Pierson himself was greatly blessed and records in his diary thanksgiving for a special baptism with the Holy Spirit. He wrote (April 1, 1858):

"I am every night in the meeting for inquiry and feel that the experience is of incalculable value to me. I have just begun to realize the true worth of souls and the true secret of living near to Christ. Now I am constantly and perfectly happy. Christ manifests Himself to me very clearly and closely and I feel that 'for me to live is Christ and to die is gain.' How sweet it is to do anything for Christ! How strange it is to be permitted to do anything for Him at all. I feel that I have been baptized with the Holy Spirit and am fully resolved never again to pass a day when I cannot feel at its close that I have done something for my Saviour."

He was much exercised over the unconverted members of his own family and among his friends, and expresses words of praise as one after another they surrendered to God.

This was the West Point period of the young cadet's training for service in the army of the King of kings. In the distractions of the city and the opportunities for social engagements, there were many temptations to divert his attention from hard work, but Arthur Pierson did not allow even the absorbing interest of his love for his affianced wife to interfere with what he considered his duty as a soldier of the Cross. While social calls and pleasures were not entirely neglected they were not permitted to interfere with his theological studies nor with his devotion to Bible class teaching and personal work. He often visited city prisons on Sunday evenings, helped in city missions, made personal calls and aided his pastor in church work. More and more he came to appreciate the goodness and wisdom of God in leading him to a life-partner who not only put no serious stumbling-block in his way but who sympathized with him in his ideals and supported him in his efforts to win spiritual victories.

These years of training in theology and Christian service brought also new lessons in the value and use of money. The necessity for self-support added to the perplexities and problems of the young student not yet of age. The firm by which Stephen Pierson was employed had failed and he had been obliged to move to Chicago in search of other employment. Relatives and friends were ever ready to help, but Arthur Pierson preferred to be independent. There were hardships to be endured and temptations to distrust God. In September, 1857, after two weeks' illness with chills and fever, and in the absence of his family, he had not even money enough to pay his car fare to ride to the doctor's. But he was not deserted and a few days later he recorded with gratitude: "During the whole of my illness I have been most kindly provided for and have wanted scarcely anything. So can Providence take care of us. Why did I even for a moment fear?"

When he had recovered sufficiently, he turned his spare time and his talents to account, and secured the position of organist in Dr. Burchard's church, tutored his young cousins, and at the age of twenty-one lectured in various churches on Palestine and other subjects.

Financial straits involved important discipline and taught Pierson to value money as one of the requisites for effective service. At this time also came his first lessons in giving out of all proportion to his income. He caught a glimpse of the unlimited resources of his Great Captain which enabled Him to supply every need of His followers. When Mr. Pierson had secured the position of organist, which brought him in $150 a year, he wrote that all his worldly wishes were fulfilled since he could now be somewhat independent. "The situation I consider a gift from God and as such I shall appropriate at least one-fifteenth of the salary to His work."

The summer vacations were spent in preaching and in evangelistic work and as a result Pierson returned to the seminary in his senior year with $100 to his credit. It was the largest amount he had ever possessed at one time and the questions arose: Should he use it all for his own necessities and long desired comforts; should he save a part of it for future needs; should he enjoy the luxury of giving to those he loved or should he "lend to the Lord" and trust Him for the future? How he answered these questions is best described in his own words:

"I found myself in possession of my first one hundred dollars as the result of my summer work. My board and lodging were otherwise provided for, so that I felt free to 'salt down' the precious gold against a day of future need or indulgence. Greed had unconsciously begun to tighten its grip upon me. For the

A Lesson in Giving 69

first time in my life I tasted the luxury of hoarding money and the taste was sweet.

"Just then another young man—a dear personal friend—came to the seminary to begin his theological studies. A few days later I learned accidentally (or providentially) that he had only fifty cents left. He had come from a home of poverty, without funds, in the hope that the city would afford an opportunity for outside employment, but he had been disappointed. His money was exhausted but he made no complaint and his face was unclouded by doubt or anxiety. That hoarded one hundred dollars began to trouble me and the battle between greed and grace began. The thought kept persistently recurring: I have money and no immediate need and this other child of God has dire need and no money. I consulted my Bible—that ever faithful guide-book—until I was convinced that God taught His children not to hoard earthly treasure, but to use what they have for the relief of the destitute and to trust Him for the supply of future needs. This teaching is unpopular but it is Scriptural and I could not gainsay it. After much thought and prayer I decided to give my friend one-half the money as a loan. I told him that I had no present use for it, and added that if, as my own funds became exhausted, God Himself should supply my need, the loan would become a gift; if not, he could repay it as he was able.

"This was not a very bold venture perhaps, but it was a beginning in the primary school of faith. Now mark the result. After spending what I had held in reserve, there were four separate occasions on which I needed a part of the loan to buy clothes or other actual necessities. *In each case on the very day and in the exact amount required* my wants were supplied. Thus God repaid the entire loan through friends who knew nothing of the circumstances, and I was able to tell my friend that the debt was cancelled."

This first lesson was never unlearned. It relaxed the giver's love for gold and taught him how to transmute material things into spiritual power. About this time he wrote in his diary: "This morning I feel like tracing a memorial of God's goodness. Uncle John has invited me to make my home with him without expense. All my wants are thus supplied for some time to come. In my religious life too I seem blessed of God and enjoy one continuous smile. If I were only a holier man I would ask nothing more, and with God's help that shall be my constant aim. So happy am I that I often think it may not be the design of God to spare me long."

But a mercurial temperament did not permit him to remain long in such a state of exaltation. Ill health, the criticisms of friends, failure to secure what he felt to be his due, or the yielding to some temptation of pride or ambition often cast him down again into the depths for a period. But on the whole there was progress, and each experience taught him some new lesson of his own weakness or of God's strength.

Among the extra-curriculum courses during these days of preparation were the opportunities to attend musicals and lectures, and these he turned to good account. Classical music was his delight, and lectures such as those by Wm. Lloyd Garrison, Edward Everett, and others gave him many practical points on the use and abuse of the powers of thought and speech. On several

The Influence of Wendell Phillips 71

occasions he heard Wendell Phillips speak in Cooper Institute on the subject of human slavery and on other topics and thus describes the result :

" The man that moulded my ideas of oratory and taught me the necessity of having something to say and of knowing how to say it, simply and effectively, was Wendell Phillips. He had great oratorical powers and great charm. When I first heard him he talked so quietly that I thought he was giving us only the introduction and that the lecture proper would soon begin. When he sat down I found to my surprise that he had been speaking for an hour and a quarter. To me it seemed fifteen minutes. It was marvellous how he held the people. I heard him many times and studied his wonderful simplicity and directness. I came to the conviction that he had a deep moral basis for his oratory and never said anything for artistic or dramatic effect. He had been converted under Lyman Beecher's preaching and made up his mind that as God had created him, He had a right to all his faculties and talents and he determined to use them for God."

The first attempts at preaching by the young theologue were in 1858 in a little church at Fiftieth Street and Broadway, New York. He also preached frequently at Green Village, near Chatham, New Jersey, where as a boy he had been accustomed to spend his summers. Quite appropriately for a young man of his energy his first sermon was on " Christian Activity " (Titus iii. 8). His second sermon was on " Rest " (Matthew xi. 28). His own pastor, Dr. Burchard, took a great interest in the young man and pointed out many opportunities for service. He was a ready speaker and had no hesitation in making impromptu addresses if necessary. One good elder in the Thirteenth Street Church remarked to him one day:

"You will do well, young man; all you need is the bit and bridle on you."

One of his seminary classmates, Rev. A. L. Clark, says that he was a faithful student of the Bible, and was regarded as the ablest sermonizer in his class. Pierson himself says: "In the seminary we were drilled in the analysis and illustration of texts, but preaching in the power of the Holy Spirit is one of the things that God alone can teach."

Considerable success had attended Mr. Pierson's preaching in neighbouring towns and there had been several professed conversions. Dr. Hitchcock proposed to take him as an assistant pastor, but he preferred to be independent and accepted another call as temporary supply for the Congregational church in West Winsted, Connecticut, at $15.00 a week. Here he preached until after the close of his seminary course, and in this field he learned something of his own strength and weakness. The trustees, naturally perhaps, distrusted some of the views of the young theologue and they had been in power too long to change their course at his dictation. The result was considerable friction and little progress. The Winsted church did not at this time ask Mr. Pierson to remain as pastor, but at the farewell meeting they showed keen regret at his departure.

"Everybody cried and heads were bowed," says the journal. "Mr. B—— thanked me for preaching so plainly. Had a long talk with C—— as to things that had hindered my usefulness, among which he mentioned—too familiar with clerks, too frank to speak of myself, too incautious. I have given the impression of egotism by saying some things that other men are shrewd enough to keep to themselves."

This congregation gave him a call a little later but it was not unanimous and he refused. After an examination in Hebrew which Dr. Riggs pronounced the best that he had ever heard, Pierson was licensed to preach on April 3, 1860. The following month he was graduated from the seminary and was ordained as an evangelist, although this was against the general practice of the presbytery. The ordination charge by Dr. Walter Clarke made a deep impression on his mind.

"Dr. Clarke bade me remember," he says, "that I was from that hour a minister first of the Word of God; second, of the Lord Jesus Christ; third, of the Holy Spirit; fourth, of the Church of God, and fifth, to the souls of men. That half hour speech affected my whole life. I have always taken especial joy in the fact that I was set apart to the work of an evangelist and I have never forgotten that fact in my ministry. Every pastor should be an edifier of saints and a saver of souls."

V

FIRST CHARGE AT BINGHAMTON—TESTING HIS WEAPONS

MARRIAGE is a divine institution and in one man and one woman truly united in heart and soul, in love and in loyal service to God, we see the ideal unit of the human race, for "in the image of God created He them male and female." Together, these two made one, can do a work for their Creator which would be impossible for either to accomplish alone. But without agreement in " the things of the Lord " there can be no true unity in the home and no lasting happiness.

In his choice of Sarah Frances Benedict as his future wife, Arthur Pierson was unconsciously guided by an all-wise Father. His betrothed was as quiet and retiring as her fiancé was active and aggressive. By education and home training she was well fitted to be a minister's wife, and love prepared her to share his lot in poverty or in wealth. Positive ideals and quiet persuasion enabled her to influence her husband by loving words and ways rather than by willful self-assertion. After four years of close acquaintance these two heart mates were married, July 12, 1860, by Rev. Joseph W. Pierson, a brother of the groom.

Thus began a happy half century of true union. The husband found in his wife one who did not allow personal preference to hinder service. Her economy and industry relieved him of many cares and her tact

Marriage to Miss Benedict

saved him from many an awkward predicament in his pastoral work. His marriage gave the young clergyman freer access to homes in his parishes and made his home a haven of hospitality. In her husband, the wife found a faithful protector and companion, one who, while in every sense head of the house, made it his aim to cherish his wife and to assist in the training of his children. Together they learned the truth of God's marital mathematics that when two are one, joys are multiplied and sorrows are divided, and that in Christian work, if one alone can chase a thousand cares and troubles, two-made-one can put ten thousand to flight.

While on their wedding trip Mr. Pierson received calls both to West Winsted, Connecticut, and to the First Congregational Church at Binghamton, New York. The latter invitation was unanimous and urgent and seemed to offer the better opportunity for service; he therefore wrote his acceptance.

Binghamton was an attractive town of some ten thousand inhabitants, prettily situated on the banks of the Chenango River. It was well supplied with churches but laxity in life and the lack of harmony among professing Christians made it a difficult and needy field. Hither came the young ambassador and soldier to test his ammunition and try the spiritual weapons that he had been gathering and learning to use. He was only twenty-three years of age, but his experience in preaching and the commendation of his friends led him to expect a successful ministry.

On Wednesday evening, September 5, 1860, Mr. Pierson was installed in a crowded church which held perhaps three hundred people. Prof. Benjamin F. Martin of the University of New York, who preached the sermon from Ezekiel iii. 17-19, urged the young pastor, as the herald of the Almighty, to faithfulness and fearlessness in warning his people. Rev. Thomas K. Beecher, of Elmira, a brother of Henry Ward Beecher, gave some wholesome advice to the people—advice which is not yet out of date. He reminded them that they should trust their pastor and give him freedom of conscience as one responsible to God and not to them; (2) that his family life was to be sacred and not subject to gossip or intrusion; that the wife was not to be expected to lead in everything—since she had married her husband, not the parish; (3) that it was as incumbent on the people to live the Gospel as it was the duty of the pastor to preach it. "Living epistles have even more influence in a community than spoken sermons. The world has a right to ask the Church not only for a display of its machinery and a statement of what it can do, but for samples of its products."

The pastor began his ministry full of hope and enthusiasm. His ideals were high and his energy was unfailing. He desired conversions and expected them. His first sermon showed the goal that he had set before him. It was on 1 Corinthians ii. 2: "I determined not to know anything among you save Jesus Christ and Him crucified." In this sermon, he set forth the sublimity of Christ as the incarnate Son of God, as the revealer of the divine Father, as the perfect pattern for man, as the ideal friend and brother and the all-powerful Redeemer. Christ was lifted up as the Crucified One who meets the deepest needs of the human soul.

The resolve to put Christ first in everything was adhered to throughout his ministerial life. "Too many modern preachers," he says in one of these early sermons, "are not content with using the plain Sword of the Spirit, which in its naked simplicity thrusts deep and cuts quickly. Scholars, instead, forge for themselves swords of gold, diamond-hilted, that are brilliant but have neither point nor edge." So while this young swordsman sought beauty of style (in late years he thought he had done so too much) it was to bring out more clearly the keenness and power of the Word. He studied history, science, biography, poetry, philosophy, literature, that he might mould these into ammunition with which to fight battles for truth and against error.

Some practical rules for reading, which he tested and found useful, are the following:

1. First, never lose a valuable fact or a good thought. Make a note of it, preserve it, and put it into shape for future use.
2. Never read a vile, coarse, or worthless book. Time is too short, character is too priceless.
3. Never pass by a word, a reference to an historical or scientific fact, or anything else worth knowing, until it is understood.
4. Mark in the books you read the matter contained in them. It has been my habit to indicate with a pencil on the margin of a book by single, double, or triple lines, and again by a line underscoring words and sentences, whatever I desire to have for ready reference and future use. Then, on the fly-leaves, I make a brief index, under subjects, of such portions of the contents as are specially valuable.
5. Read some books at least that *tax all your powers*. It may be well to read now and then books that do not by their contents particularly attract, and are what we call "dry reading," for the sake of learning concentration of mental powers, of acquiring the voluntary exercise of attention aside from attractive features that draw out our mental powers by fascination.

6. Let reading be varied. After a philosophical work, the mind will, without fatigue, turn to romance, poetry, history, or biography. We rest in such a variety of mental occupation, and not in absolute repose of mind.

7. Ordinarily, do not buy a book which you do not need as a permanent possession. There is vanity in accumulating a large library. There are comparatively few books that you will ever examine after you have once read them. Those few you want to keep, and keep at hand.

At Binghamton Mr. Pierson looked older than his twenty-four years would lead one to expect and his high broad forehead, clear blue eyes and waving brown hair gave him an impressive appearance. His intellectual ability, his growing faith in the Scriptures and his sense of responsibility as an ambassador of God added dignity to his manner and authority to his message.

In the pulpit the pastor spoke plain words to his people, for in all his ministry he believed that straight shots are the only ones that can be counted on to hit the mark. He was not given to shooting at random nor with bullets made of putty. In the evening of his first Sunday after the installation he preached on "The Pastor's Reception," and took his text from John xiii. 20, "Verily, verily, I say unto you, he that receiveth whomsoever I send, receiveth Me." This struck another key-note in his conception of the minister as an ambassador of Christ entitled to attention and respect (2 Cor. v. 18). He said:

"A minister is not to lord it over his flock. An unsanctified pride of office is nowhere more repulsive than in a Christian minister. . . . Yet by virtue of his post and profession, a measure of dignity invests his advice in spiritual matters. . . . He is a man like men fallible. . . . But he is professionally a student of spiritual things and on these subjects it ought to be presumed that he is right until it can be shown that he is wrong. . . . Otherwise measures over which a pastor has studied long and earnestly may be defeated by the crude and ignorant opposition of some layman."

He asked his people, if they took exception to his public utterances, to use the right of private remonstrance, and when possible to speak words of encouragement. "It is a sin to flatter a preacher with compliments," he said, "but to tell him that his sermon led you to the Cross or saved you from danger or brought comfort to your soul, helps to make life sweeter."

Few people realize how they tempt a minister to glorify self by pleasant but unwise compliments on the sermon he has just delivered. All through his early life, Mr. Pierson fought the temptation to accept for himself the praise due to God alone, and many an abrupt or cold reply to an enthusiastic admirer was the honest effort of a beset soul to avoid what seemed an ambuscade of the enemy. The nervous exhaustion and physical drain of preaching were often so great that he felt it necessary to slip quietly away and be alone after he had delivered his message.

In later years he expressed the same conviction that influenced him in youth:

"So long as an ambassador of Jesus Christ confines himself within the limits of his instructions the whole authority of the Godhead is behind him. I am grieved when I see ministers descending from the lofty pedestal of an ambassador for Christ, to talk about what other men can deal with just as well, and sacrificing their dignity thereby."

In the beginning of his ministry, the pastor thus realized some of his responsibility and the dignity of his office. Like David, he also determined not to go to war with weapons that he had not tested. "I resolved," he said, "that I would not preach on any subject that had not been opened up to me by some personal experience. A man may exhort others to believe and obey the Word of God that is as yet beyond his own full experience, but he cannot preach with power that which he does not believe and endeavour to practice."

Not long after he had raised the standard in this field the fight began to wax hot. As the uncompromising character of the pastor became known, enemies began to test the strength of his armour. He found himself the target for a fusillade from infidels who sent him pamphlets and books by the score in their efforts to find a joint in his harness. Under the guise of a desire to ask him to solve perplexities, these unbelievers sought to lodge doubts in his mind as to the truth of Christianity. Mr. Pierson was unable to meet these attacks at first, for he had learned to use the weapons forged by others. From his parents and teachers he had come to believe the doctrines of the Church, but now he saw that the basis for his faith must be investigated. For a time his confidence in the inspiration of the Bible, the Deity of Christ and even in his own salvation was severely shaken. He became alarmed but refused to beat a retreat. Instead he determined to take refuge under the banner of his Master while he built anew his fortifications, refitted his armour and looked well to his ammunition. He began to study systematically the "reason for the faith" that was in him and tested the foundations and the superstructure. It was not long before earnest, prayerful study of the evidences had established him so firmly that his faith in the eternal verities was never again shaken. Attacks which were meant to weaken were used by God to strengthen him. After one of the periods of doubt he wrote: "My gloom lasted for days, but was then dispersed by a most marked communication of the Holy Spirit, conducting me to a full assurance of faith. It was an uncommon experience of the grace of God."

This study of Christian evidences led him to say: "My reason was convinced at that time largely by the argument from prophecy. I came to the conclusion that the Bible is indeed the Word of God and I was prepared to receive it, with all its apparent errors and contradictions, and to wait calmly for their explanation either here or hereafter. It was a great day for me when I learned to stand on the immutable Word of the immutable God, on the inspired Word of the inspiring God. This Word has brought to millions salvation and sanctification and no weapon that has been formed against it shall prosper. . . . I was now prepared to expect some mystery in God's Word, as I saw that otherwise I would be claiming equality with Him. I found that to understand the Bible rightly I must be taught by the Spirit of God and not lean to my own understanding."

This battle won and his armour tested the soldier was ready to lead a charge. He began to seek out the unconverted men and women of his congregation and to point them to Christ. On various occasions we find in his diary the record of those who rose for prayer, or of "blessed prayer-meetings when all kneeled at the close" and when the Spirit seemed present in power. A class of young people from the Sunday-school was formed to meet on Saturday afternoons that they might be instructed for church-membership. Then interest and attendance increased, and the congregation voted to observe a day of fasting and prayer. This plan was carried out with unmistakable evidences of God's presence. Husbands, sons, and daughters for whom special prayer had been offered were converted and united with the church. Candidates for membership were asked the following questions:

1. What reason have you for believing that you are a child of God?

2. Why do you desire to unite with the church?

3. What assurance have you that you will be faithful?

4. What do you propose to do for God in your Christian life?

Each candidate was also asked to assent to a carefully written "Confession of Faith," which covered statements about the Trinity, the Bible, the Sabbath, the Resurrection and Judgment, man's sinful state and his only hope of redemption in Jesus Christ. All new members covenanted to study the Word, to forsake the world, to attend the church and to live a truly Christian life.

In his enthusiasm the young minister was confident that in a short time his whole church would be converted, that Binghamton would be transformed and that the world would be brought to Christ in his lifetime. He preached with enthusiasm and faith but he found that only here and there were men and women gathered into the church. The great mass of people appeared to be untouched, for when he preached on the dishonesty and iniquities practiced in public and private life, while some were moved to confession, others were offended. On one occasion he preached from Isaiah i. 13 on the subject of "Iniquitous Solemnities." In this sermon he examined unrighteous motives which led people to the Lord's house, and experienced some unpleasant results from speaking the truth.

Evidently some of the shots struck home, for he wrote in his diary: "To-day I endured a personal excoriation for preaching what I believed to be the truth. I knew that it would strike right and left and it did. Afterwards I felt sad and gloomy—doubtful whether it were best to preach so plainly."

The objection to the sermon was, in fact, so strong on the part of some of the congregation that Rev. George Overhiser, a friendly clergyman who attended his church, took an opportunity to speak to the people in public and to commend the pastor for his courageous utterance. It "requires more nerve and grace," he reminded them, "to face men and to lay bare their faults than it does to face the cannon's mouth."

The inexperienced young preacher was learning how subtle are some of the attacks made on the church and on the individual Christian. Unfortunately all the enemies did not fight in the open and too many of them were in the camp itself. In the Binghamton Church there were two hostile parties who would not even sit on the same side of the church. The distressed young pastor laboured with each prayerfully in his endeavour to affect a reconciliation, but it was in vain. He says: "I was at last impelled to ask the Lord either to heal this hindering breach or to take me away. It was not long before one of the leaders in the strife was taken ill and died; the landlord of another raised his rent and the man moved away; the third lost his standing through scandal and so all the contestants were put out of commission." By this signal and literal answer to prayer Mr. Pierson learned that he could trust the Great Commander Himself to solve many difficulties that baffle human skill.

Early in the fifties, modern spiritualism had its birth in Rochester, a city about one hundred and fifty miles from Binghamton. The cult was spreading and Binghamton boasted the possession of a spirit medium. Here was a new enemy to be reckoned with, and one likely to do damage among the more ignorant members of the church. There was in Mr. Pierson's congregation a devout woman who for many years had been a leader in good works. After her husband died some one told her that he was appearing at a neighbouring séance night after night and was calling her. At first she refused to listen to these stories but at last she determined to go and see. "I do not really believe in these things," she said, "but what harm can come from looking into it? I will ask him to tell what happened on the 19th of March, 1860." She attended the séance and the reply came from the medium: "That was our wedding day and we went to C—— to celebrate it." The answer staggered the wife, for no one in the audience but herself knew the fact. The result was that before many weeks had passed she had become entangled in spiritualism, had lost her interest in the church, and deserted the prayer-meeting for the séance. The young pastor reasoned with her from the Scriptures and he himself invaded the enemies' camp, attending a course of spiritualist lectures and debates that he might study and counteract its influence. His people profited by his investigation and the straying member was finally won back by the clear teaching of God's Word. She, herself, gave this striking testimony:

"I found that their teachings and practices were contrary to the Word of God and I said to myself: I cannot explain these mysteries but I can test them by the Scripture principle—if a prophet shall perform a sign or wonder in your eyes either by predicting future events or by performing some inexplicable wonder, if he teach anything contrary to the Word of God, then he is a false prophet and not to be followed."

Mr. Pierson himself learned, by this experience, to "try the spirits whether they be of God," and was saved from following many false trails and false teachers. He steadfastly refused to consider any philosophy or practice, however plausible, that was contrary to the teachings of the Bible or that led to less devotion to Jesus Christ.

During these first years in the pastorate at Binghamton various forms of organizations were attempted, some of which are of interest. "A Maternal Association" was founded for the purpose of training children in the "nurture and admonition of the Lord." It was the forerunner of the present day "Mothers' Circles," and "Mothers of the Temple." The members met once a month to read books, pray and converse on child conversion and child training. Each mother pledged "to pray for her children daily and with them frequently, to set them a right example, and in every way to perform faithfully the arduous duties of a Christian mother."

No doubt the pastor felt special interest in this organization since in his own house there had been two additions to the family circle. The arrival of these little daughters added to the joy but also to the problems of the household. The Civil War had just broken out and the cost of living was extremely high. Mr. Pierson's aged parents had come to make their home with their son and the father was an almost helpless paralytic. During these hard times the promised salary of one thousand dollars was seldom paid promptly and as a result the pastor's family knew economy and even hunger. When house rent, doctor's bills, food and other necessaries had been paid for, it was difficult to keep the balance from being on the wrong side of the ledger. But Arthur Pierson hated debt as he hated sin and many days the family lived on oatmeal and potatoes or had nothing but pea soup to set before a dinner guest. They could not even afford ten cents for fruit. Apparently the trustees expected their pastor to "work on earth and board in heaven."

Finally he was forced to write to the trustees a letter calling attention to the long overdue salary. "I have lived this year," he said, "under great pecuniary embarrassment. For my own suffering I care nothing, though I have gone for a month without ten cents in my pocket. I was forced to go to housekeeping because of the increase in my family, but even with my household of six I might have met my debts if the money

Reasons for Resignation 87

due me had been paid on time. The church has owed me two hundred and fifty dollars for over two months and my creditors are suffering as well as I. . . . Privations I am willing to endure, but I feel that to be everywhere in debt damages my influence and my work suffers. If the church cannot pay one thousand dollars let them say what sum they can give and I will reply whether I can accept it, but what is promised must be punctually paid."

Before long other questions arose involving strategy and coöperation in the local campaign. The First Congregational Church, to which he ministered, had been established, on a mistaken policy of rivalry, near to the larger Presbyterian house of worship. There was no need for both churches in that neighbourhood, but there was an opportunity for a church across the river. The young pastor did everything in his power to strengthen his church but he was enough of a general to see the mistake that had been made, and to advise his people to move. This they hesitated to do because of their money invested and the expense involved in a change of centre. Some wished to remain where they were, others favoured dissolution, but Mr. Pierson determined that the only right course was to move and so save the church. His stand showed Christian faith, courage and common sense. He had a growing family dependent on him and was without other means of support or any other field in view, but in order to relieve his people from the necessity of paying his salary, he resigned his charge on January 4, 1863, with the understanding that they should sell the church property, pay their debts and move across the river.

The ecclesiastical council convened and advised that

the pastoral relations be continued on the ground that one Congregational church should be maintained in Binghamton, and also because the "present pastoral relations had been marked by an unusual degree of mutual attachment and good will and promised most desirable fruitfulness." They, however, advised the church's removal to the west side of the Chenango River. After some further consideration the pastor's resignation was accepted on account of "pecuniary necessity," and the relationship was dissolved with mutual regret. The advice of Mr. Pierson was followed, the church was transplanted, revived and became one of the strongest Congregational organizations in New York State—outside of the metropolis.

A comparison between Mr. Pierson's sermons at Binghamton and those of later years shows wonderful growth. He was not then the profound expository preacher and ardent evangelist that he afterwards became, but he showed some of the characteristics that were strengthened and developed in later years. His habits of Bible study had not matured, but his sermons were Biblical and practical. He depended for impression on facts as revealed in the Bible and in daily life rather than on emotional stories or elaborate ornamentation. The sermons were informing, inspiring and fearless, and often dealt with sins and with truth that made some of his congregation wince.

The two years and a half spent in Binghamton proved that the young minister could preach without fear or favour, but he learned that the truth must be spoken in love. Perhaps he had not yet accustomed himself to give due regard to the right of private judgment on the part of others, and needed to learn by experience that even a pastor with a divine commission will succeed better if he seeks to lead rather than to drive his flock. His sermons on slavery and the Civil War made some enemies, but when he preached to a company of soldiers en route to the field of battle the church was crowded to the doors morning and evening.

In Binghamton Mr. Pierson also learned the value of organization and coöperation and laid emphasis on personal work and on the religious training of the young. He was perhaps somewhat less self-confident when he left Binghamton, but his confidence in God had increased and he adopted as his life motto the words of the Apostle Paul in the Epistle to the Galatians (ii. 20): *Non ego sed Christus* ("Not I but Christ").

"In preaching the Gospel," he said, "I desire to preach not myself but Christ Jesus, the Lord, and myself your servant for Jesus' sake. I desire never to preach a sermon of which Christ shall not be the beginning, the centre and the end. . . . I pray that all my powers and energies may be simply and earnestly directed towards Him and His glory."

The lessons taught by poverty had been valuable but unpleasant and there had been temptations to increase his slender income by engaging in secular pursuits. He determined however to permit nothing to interfere with his main business and would not even allow opportunities to lecture or requests for articles from his ready pen to turn his attention from his ministry to men's spiritual needs. He wrote and spoke frequently on many themes, but these were only the overflowing of the cup.

In the summer following his removal from Binghamton Mr. Pierson's brother Joseph and his father both died and thereafter his mother made her home with her son Arthur, who for thirty-two years continued lovingly to minister to her comfort.

When he resigned his Binghamton pastorate, Mr. Pierson rather expected that, when the church had become established in its new location, they would recall him, but God had other plans. On the same Sunday when he resigned in Binghamton a much loved pastor in a distant town in the same state preached his last sermon and was soon after suddenly called Home. Later the eyes and hearts of the afflicted people were providentially turned towards Mr. Pierson, God thus releasing one servant to fill the place made vacant by the departure of another called to his reward. After a summer spent in supplying the Congregational Church at Norwalk, Connecticut, he received a unanimous call to Waterford, New York.

VI

THE WATERFORD PASTORATE—A BROADER VISION

THE change from Binghamton to Waterford was an important event in Mr. Pierson's life, for it meant a change from the Congregational to the Presbyterian ranks. But it was a return to his mother church and therein he spent the next thirty-three years of his ministry.

Waterford, whither he was called in August, 1863, was an attractive town on the banks of the Hudson River, a few miles from Troy. He saw in this invitation a greater opportunity for service, for the church was larger, the work was better established, and the general spirit more aggressive. To the salary of $1,000, paid quarterly, was added a parsonage with grounds running down to the river and an abundance of fruit trees. On October 6th he was duly installed, and on this occasion Prof. M. R. Vincent preached a sermon which sounded yet another key-note in the pastor's ministry. The theme was "Christian Action"—a true soldier's ideal—and Professor Vincent emphasized the folly of a church allowing their attention to be diverted by disputes and trivial technicalities while a perishing world is waiting for help and salvation. The one great question is, "How can we best save souls?"

Mr. Pierson brought to his work all the enthusiasm of a young man of twenty-six—and a minister's second charge usually benefits much by his first experience.

The field had been especially prepared also by the faithful work accomplished by the previous pastor, the Rev. Mr. Lee, a rare spirit greatly beloved by his people.

Into this field, to take up the work laid down by such a predecessor, Mr. Pierson entered with all his heart and soul. He is described by his contemporaries at this time as "a wide-awake speaker who did not believe in following the old beaten track made by our fathers to the neglect of more modern methods and advanced ideas." He was of nervous temperament, extremely intense in whatever he did. When he entered upon a course he did not allow himself to be diverted until he reached his goal. He seemed always in haste, and neighbours who heard his front door close would often look up just in time to see him disappear around the corner. He was known as "a man of one idea at a time"—the work he was doing absorbed all his attention. One evening he accompanied an elder of the church to his home, discussing a topic of deep interest to them both, and in order to come to some clear understanding in the matter went into the elder's house. After a lengthy conversation, Mr. Pierson suddenly became conscious that he was sitting on something unusual; he arose and thrusting his hand in his coat tail pocket, exclaimed with astonishment: "There is a steak for my dear wife," and taking his hat immediately, he made a hurried departure.

When his thoughts were on a sermon theme or pastoral problem, passing events made little impression on him, so that he often met members of his church in the street and passed them without a sign of recognition. This was a source of annoyance to them and caused him deep regret. When, however, his parishioners came to understand the reason they readily forgave the seeming slights. Others were not always so forgiving and he suffered all his life from the results of such misunderstandings. This same power of concentration, however, enabled him to accomplish much that would have been difficult otherwise. His family increased in Waterford by the addition of a girl and a boy, and as the nursery was never far from the study in his home, for years few sermons were written without the accompaniment of childish prattle. The only time when the doors were locked against intrusion was when "father was at prayer."

While he was sustained by a sense of his own right purpose, he was keenly conscious of personal failings and constant temptation so that prayer was indeed his "vital breath." On his birthday in 1867 he wrote: "I am thirty years old to-day—just the age when the Saviour began His public ministry. I solemnly covenant to overcome, by God's help, two especially besetting sins which interfere with my spirituality and usefulness. Every day must see new victories over self and for Christ."

As a preacher, even at this early period, he was versatile and forceful. His aggressive thought-compelling sermons aroused to action, and he became widely known as an unusually clear and inspiring teacher of the Bible. At his Sunday afternoon class there was an attendance of from 160 to 200 people and his novel and informal method of free discussion drew many from all parts of the town. He came into sympathetic touch with all classes in his parish, wrote rhymes and made out humorous programs for his young people and composed long poems for the postmen and messenger boys to present as New Year greetings to their patrons.

Many members of the congregation were devout and intelligent Christian men and women and contact with them meant much to the growing man. At the time of the centennial celebration of the church in 1904 Dr. Pierson wrote: "I owe much of my own enthusiasm for missions to my six years in this church. It was most active and aggressive in this department of service. It had its own missionary in the field and kept in living contact with him by correspondence, gifts and prayer. This missionary atmosphere I breathed with immense profit and I was compelled either to lead my people in missionary work or to resign my pastorate. My real missionary education began here in a church far ahead of me in intelligence and enthusiasm for God's work.

"I found myself to be lacking in my knowledge of missionary history and biography and set myself to gather new facts through the study of missions, the trials and the triumphs. Thus I began to see more clearly, on the one hand, the awful spiritual destitution of the world and on the other hand the perfect adaptation of the Gospel to human need. I began to feel more and more my previous ignorance and lamentable indifference, while the conviction took deep root that the interest and zeal of a congregation cannot ordinarily be expected to rise above the pastor's level. . . .

"Perhaps it may be well to indicate the steps by which success was attained in awakening interest, arousing activity and stimulating larger gifts. First I gave a series of lectures on prominent fields where missionary work has proven the power of the Gospel

Growing Missionary Interest 95

to cope with the lowest forms of heathenism and the worst phases of vice and superstition. The Hawaiian Islands, the Karens of Burma, Fiji, Tahiti and Madagascar were successively treated. Then, one by one the various forms of false faiths were presented—Mohammedanism, paganism, Brahmanism, Confucianism, etc.—and were compared with Christianity. Glimpses of the past and present condition of each of the heathen nations enabled me to marshall into array that grand host of facts which students of missionary history have found to constitute the resistless logic of missions and the overwhelming argument for a deeper devotion to the world's enlightenment. No man can study these subjects without his own missionary spirit burning with a fervour before unknown."

The missionary fire kindled in Mr. Pierson's heart was at the same time a "refiner's fire," for he passed through one of the most intense struggles of his life as a logical result of his missionary studies. He was too sympathetic and too loyal to Christ to see a need without wishing to supply it and too sincere to advise others to respond to a call to a mission which he himself was unwilling to undertake. Of this experience he says:

"As I studied the needs of the world and our Lord's commission I became conscious that I had never been true with God on the subject of consecration to missionary work. I wanted power in my ministry to convert souls at home, but I could get no peace with God until I reconsidered the entire question. I fell on my knees before God and asked Him to forgive me for the superficial manner in which I had considered the claims of the world upon me when I was in the theological seminary. I told Him that if He called me now to the foreign field I would leave my pastorate and, with my family, consecrate myself to this work."

Thus the needed surrender was made but God did not require more at this time. The way was not opened to Mr. Pierson for service abroad, but wider doors of usefulness were thrown open at home, and because he had honestly faced the question, he was, in after years, the means of turning hundreds of young men and young women and thousands of dollars into the mission fields.

But the far-sighted vision which came to be so characteristic did not by any means shut out the needs and responsibilities near at home. The work in Waterford suffered no neglect. Preaching and pastoral duties, the Sunday-school and the prayer-meeting received his closest attention, for he could not understand how any pastor who claimed to be evangelical could be anything else than evangelistic. In the Waterford church he found a prepared soil, ready for the sowing of the Word. Mr. Lee's sudden death had left his people very tender and the new pastor on the first Saturday evening with his flock appointed a special meeting for prayer for the outpouring of the Holy Spirit. For six months they patiently waited on God until a few encouraging signs of blessing appeared. The meetings that had been more or less of a formality became a delight. One Sunday evening in March the congregation were so moved that they remained for an hour beyond the closing time, to confess their sins and to pray for power. Three weeks of preaching and prayer service followed and the church was filled every night. Thirty-two rose for prayer and most of them subsequently united with the church. In his diary the pastor says:

"God is doing it all. We can see that the work seems to override ordinary agencies."

Just two years later, after another season of prayer, a deep interest in their own and the world's need of Christ was awakened in the young people of the Sabbath-school, of which the pastor was also superintendent. A special prayer-meeting was held after the school session, and all were invited to stay who wished to pray for God's blessing. Scarcely one left. Dr. Samuel R. House of Siam, who was at home on furlough, said a few quiet words and prayer was offered. There was nothing done to excite a child's mind, but the Holy Spirit's presence was evident. Of that Sunday afternoon Mr. Pierson says:

"Each teacher was asked to speak to each scholar on the subject of personal salvation. I never saw a more beautiful sight than the whole school melted to tears, talking quietly together about the soul and the Saviour. I moved from class to class with words of instruction and encouragement. Then one teacher arose and suggested that all stand who had resolved to make the decision of Joshua (about which they had been studying), 'We will serve the Lord.' The entire congregation responded and sang solemnly:

"'Here, Lord, I give myself away,
'Tis all that I can do.'

"During the following week most of the pupils came by classes to talk with me in my study and at the next communion thirty-eight united with the church on confession of faith."

The new communion table around which they gathered was the gift of the Sabbath-school. The spirit of earnestness spread to the church and resulted in the conversion of parents and friends. The distinguishing features of this revival are pointed out by the pastor in his diary as follows:

"1. A large increase in lay activity. Almost every silent member has received the gift of a tongue to testify for Christ or to lead in prayer. . . .

"2. The prayer of faith receives immediate answer. Even friends at a distance are converted.

"3. The means used by the Holy Spirit are simple and direct. A few practical words of exposition, followed by prayer and exhortation. The general gatherings are followed by separate meetings for men and women. I have called in no outside evangelist. My only colleagues are my own church-members.

"4. God is wonderfully blessing those who put themselves at His disposal."

This revival was followed by an increased spirit of giving and as fast as tithes came in the blessing increased. The foreign missionary offering that year was the largest in the history of the church and at the same time the contributions for congregational expenses were greatly increased. The church was remodelled and enlarged to double its former capacity at the cost of $17,000, and every department of benevolence and activity was strengthened.

The dedication of the renovated church was made memorable by the reception of forty-one members—the largest accession at any one communion in over twenty years. Husbands and wives met together at the Lord's table for the first time, and parents came led by their

First Visit to Europe

believing children, so that families were made complete in Christ.

The summer following the dedication of the remodelled church Mr. Pierson made his first visit to Europe at the invitation of a friend, Mr. David Blake. He saw in this invitation a God-given opportunity for rest and education.

They sailed from Boston on the steamship *Cuba* on July 18, 1866—just at the time when all the civilized world was aflutter with the expectation of the completion of the first transatlantic cable. As the *Cuba* neared the Irish shore a packet boat came out and Mr. Pierson asked for the news. He was told that the cable was completed and within a few hours the first message was flashed under the deep: " Glory to God in the highest and on earth peace, good will towards men."

Judging from letters and diary, Mr. Pierson must have been a most enthusiastic visitor to all the new scenes so full of interest to him. Nothing escaped that eager eye and receptive mind. After a visit to the Crystal Palace, where there were elaborate reproductions of ancient civilizations, he wrote:

"I tried to keep calm but it wrought a fever in my blood, for I had no one with me into whose ears I could pour the overflow of my soul. It will take the rest of my life to tell all that is laid up in my mind and heart."

He attended many churches and heard such famous preachers as Alexander McLaren of Manchester, Newman Hall and Charles H. Spurgeon of London.

The visit to the great Metropolitan Tabernacle and his first sight of Spurgeon is worth recording, not only on account of his later associations with the work there, but because of the influence it exerted on his whole life and ministerial ideals. Of that visit he says:

"On Sabbath morning, August 19, 1866, I crossed Blackfriars Bridge and leaving the Thames behind me, stood shortly as one of a large multitude before the door of a somewhat imposing building, not unlike an opera house. The building is so constructed that visitors, entering from the main vestibule, naturally turn to the gallery and are not ushered into the floor of an audience room already full. The impression is therefore that of a free church.

"We had been seated but a few moments when the preacher walked forward and raised his hand to invoke divine blessing. A more unclerical looking man you could scarcely imagine as occupying a metropolitan pulpit. But when he began to speak the physical was forgotten in the intellectual and spiritual. I have known many people who were good-looking until they opened their mouths; Mr. Spurgeon becomes good looking when he opens his.

"The service was lengthy but not long; plain but interesting, and Mr. Spurgeon's method of lining out the psalms and hymns is primitive but effective. The music is led by a precentor, without choir or instruments. One part of the audience follows another, out of time, like a duck dragging a lame leg. Nevertheless I never heard such singing. It was like a great wave of praise surging up against the pillars of the throne of God. No matter how refined your ear, all offenses against the laws of art were forgotten in the impression of music in which there was such devotion. In comparison with it, all the splendid swell of the grandest organ, all the finished culture of the costliest quartette are a parody on worship.

"Mr. Spurgeon's praying was marvellous. I have heard from others more pathetic confession of sin, more fervent supplication, more importunate intercession, but never before such adoration. We seemed to stand before God's throne and see His glory, to feel His power, wisdom and goodness smiting us with insufferable blinding splendour.

"The reading of the Scripture occupied half an hour and was interspersed with short, pithy, helpful comments which served to make the meaning plain and practical. Before he came to the sermon we had received a blessing. Everything had been conducted as though it was intended to bring God near. There was no hurrying over preliminaries, as though to sing, to read the Word, to pray were mere forms by which the sermon is approached. Each part of the service was itself a sermon and produced definite spiritual impressions and results.

"The sermon was preaching indeed,—it was the text expanded. One could not have said in this case that while 'the text was the gate to the Lord's garden the preacher, instead of going in, only got on it and swung to and fro.'

"Whatever may be the secret, Mr. Spurgeon has practically solved the problem: how to bring the multitude to the house of God. He is a prince among preachers. He is not a mere machine for talking or marrying, baptizing and burying people. He evidently aims to bring God's thoughts down to the minds and hearts and consciences of men. Nothing impressed me more than his simplicity and his entire freedom from all artificiality or affectation. He bends every power and purpose to reach and mould men for newness of life. How puerile some of the criticisms of this great man seem. He is the most effective preacher of the century and I rejoice to see a man who dares to know only the grand theme of ' Jesus Christ and Him crucified' have such a place filled with thousands of hearers."

The letters written home during this trip to Europe reveal the man's wide interest in the things he saw and his deep love for home and family. He wrote hundreds of pages to wife and children to help them to enter with him into the pleasure and profit of sightseeing. He told them of the wiles of cab-drivers and of the mischievous retailers of misinformation. He had a rare vein of humour and while too serious to be a joker he greatly enjoyed and contributed to innocent fun. His own witticisms usually took the form of plays on words, as a certain family in his congregation discovered, when they good-naturedly took him to task for his propensity for puns. Their comments were rewarded a little later by a carefully collected book of samples of puns picked up from each member of this family—prepared with infinite care and illustrated with marginal drawings. The whole was entitled, "The Aversions and Diversions of the C—— family, with the compliments of A. T. P."

Wood, tin and silver wedding celebrations in his own family or in those of his friends were occasions for many original programs, menus, puns and poems from his pen. These productions show much bright humour and ingenuity, and as master of ceremonies in such festivities he was in his element.

The work at Waterford had prospered under his

Some Tasks Completed 103

ministry, during which one hundred and eleven members had been added to the church. All departments were in a healthy condition, but the field was limited in its opportunities and the pastor saw providential signs that the pillar of cloud and of fire was about to move. The climate had not been conducive to health and he felt that the work for which he had been specially sent to the church had been largely accomplished. He enumerates some of the tasks completed:

"The church has been remodelled and nearly paid for. The church services have been built up. The Sabbath-school has been reorganized. Missionary work has been strengthened with the monthly concert of prayer and the organization of field reports. There have been two pervasive revivals of religion. Pastoral work has been thoroughly systematized. The people have been incited to greater generosity in giving. The church manual has been completed."

At this time invitations to other fields began to come from many directions, and he wrote for advice to Dr. Shaw of Rochester, his old time friend and counsellor of student days. Just before his letter reached Rochester another communication had come from the committee of the Fort Street Presbyterian Church of Detroit, Michigan, asking Dr. Shaw if he could recommend as pastor some man of growing spiritual power. He immediately answered: "Pierson of Waterford is your man." The committee made inquiries and sent a delegation not so much to hear the preacher as to learn what his townspeople and neighbours thought of him. The report was so favourable that the committee asked him to come to Detroit to preach, but Mr. Pierson was averse to candidating and refused. The Detroit committee then arranged for a stated supply who could not be considered a candidate and thus precluded the possibility of a divided church, while they patiently waited until Mr. Pierson could visit the field, on his way to meet an engagement in Chicago. When he did so he preached so acceptably that the committee immediately moved to extend him a call.

Still the question was not settled, for the chosen pastor had received overtures from many fields—Boston, Norwalk, Orange, Brooklyn, New York, Chicago and elsewhere. He examined the open door in Detroit carefully and was much attracted by the beautiful "City of the Straits." It was the metropolis of Michigan and its population of 80,000 was growing in wealth and influence. The broad streets lined with trees, the attractive homes, the parks and noble river that separates it from the Canadian shore, all made it a most desirable place in which to live and bring up a growing family. The salary of $3,000 was also a substantial increase in the income that had thus far supplied the minister's needs. The membership of the Fort Street Church was known as the most influential, wealthy and aristocratic in the city, if not in the West, and there were many men of influence and fame among the members. R. A. Alger, afterwards Governor of Michigan and Secretary of War; Senator Zachariah Chandler, James F. Joy, President of the Michigan Central Railroad, J. D. Hayes of the Royal Blue Line, Allan Sheldon and Ex-mayor Frederick Buhl, were all members and generous supporters of the church.

But none of these things furnished a determining motive for removal from Waterford. The supreme

The Call to Detroit

questions in Mr. Pierson's mind were: "Whither is God leading? Where can I best serve my Lord?" It was difficult to leave the village home where children had been born and to break ties which had grown stronger during seven years of labour, suffering and rejoicing together.

He watched for providential leadings in even seemingly insignificant details and wrote them down carefully that he might weigh them and pray over them. In this way he made a list of seventy-five reasons which led him to see in the Detroit call an expression of the will of God. His views of the situation are given in a letter to his wife written on the first visit to Detroit, January 19, 1869:

"If I have any confidence in the leadings of the most marked providence of my life, I must give an unequivocal acceptance. I passed an almost sleepless night, my heart palpitating with solicitude, lest I should decide wrongly, but now I have no doubt as to my duty, for I believe that here I can accomplish twice as much for my Saviour. . . . Pray that I may not think of mere prominence of position but may really be so absorbed in His work that I shall be content with the lowliest sphere that I may serve Him more truly and efficiently. I am conscious that I need to sanctfiy ambition rather than to crucify it."

As a result of this deliberation, Mr. Pierson resigned his charge in Waterford on February 14, 1869, to accept the call to the Fort Street Presbyterian Church, Detroit, Michigan.

VII

AT FORT STREET CHURCH, DETROIT—A STRATEGIC CENTRE

IN Binghamton, Mr. Pierson learned from practical experience the value of the Word of God as a shield against doubt and as an arsenal from which to draw his spiritual weapons. In Waterford his horizon was broadened to include the world in his vision and his field of service. In Detroit he was to discover more effective methods of reaching men as individuals and in the mass.

The Fort Street Church to which he was called worshipped in a beautiful stone Gothic structure considered one of the "sights" of Detroit. It had been organized in 1849, and the building was completed in 1855. Here Mr. Pierson found a congregation that had recently passed through some trying experiences and needed to be built up in numbers and in spiritual life. Of the two hundred and thirty-eight members on the roll many had drifted away and there were only eighty-two pewholders in a church accommodating eight hundred people.

The field presented some difficulties, but there was an inspiring opportunity for hard, faithful work, and the cordial, united welcome of the people gave promise of abiding and far-reaching results. The new pastor's first Sunday in the pulpit put his self-possession to a severe test and might have awakened forebodings in any one of a superstitious temperament. Just as the choir were singing the first anthem there was an alarm of fire that nearly emptied the church. The minister kept his seat calmly and as the alarm proved false most of the people returned. The experience was not conducive, however, to self-poise, nor was the fluttering of a bird that flew around the auditorium at the evening service and threatened to divert attention from the worship. But these were in no sense evil omens—they might rather have foreshadowed a coming baptism of fire and a descent of the Holy Spirit to purify and stir that people into newness of life.

Mr. Pierson was installed on May 5, 1869, and from the first proved to be the right man in the right place. Large opportunities for generalship in the church work called forth all his energy and latent ability, as we see from the list that he made of "Things to be accomplished by divine help." Later with characteristic system he entered in his journal the dates on which these desires were realized. Among the thirty objects mentioned are the following:

1. Increase congregation and church-membership.
2. Reorganize the Sunday-school.
3. Build up the evening service.
4. Make a thorough pastoral visitation.
5. Organize the young people.
6. Introduce systematic benevolence.
7. Start a mission school and church.
8. Increase sociability among the members.
9. Build up the prayer-meeting.
10. Revive the monthly concert of prayer for missions.
11. Induce people to take missionary papers.
12. Remodel the session and appoint stated meetings.

13. Establish a Bible class and teachers' meeting.
14. Improve public worship and congregational singing.
15. Induce all parents of the church to present children for baptism.
16. Pray for a revival of religion.
17. Start a young people's prayer-meeting.
18. Organize a women's prayer-meeting.
19. Publish a new church manual.
20. Promote Christian union among Detroit churches.

This list indicated a large program but it was only the beginning. Mr. Pierson built up the church attendance by giving the people his *best* at both morning and evening services and by organizing the men and women and the young people into bands to distribute invitations in the neighbourhood and to welcome strangers. He advertised very little, for he believed that his people were an even better medium than printer's ink, but he endeavoured to make certain that his congregation should never be disappointed by a half-thought-out sermon. No matter how stormy the night or how few were present he never preached an old sermon to save the new one. People came from miles around to hear his sermons, which, according to one parishioner, were "full of weighty and solemn truth: His addresses afforded entertainment while they were at the same time impressive and instructive. . . . The intensity of his convictions, the lucidity of his ideas, and his supreme loyalty to Christ were marked. His thought often flashed out like chained lightning and we sat fascinated by his earnest eloquence."

A newspaper writer of the day describes the pastor of the Fort Street Church as "one of Julius Cæsar's lean men, tall, sharp of visage, with dark hair and beard. His face is pale but eager and his eye penetrating. He has not a powerful voice but uses it admirably. He is slow and emphatic in speech, enunciating clearly so as to be easily heard. He dresses simply and his behaviour before a congregation is absolutely unaffected. There is no bravado about his sermons but much bravery, for he often teaches unpalatable truths. The thought of delivering some of his discourses would be enough to throw not a few prophets of the Lord into a cold perspiration. John Knox—of the grim visage and lion heart—would find a fellow in this mighty man of valour."

Mr. Pierson's ideals of a preacher's equipment are partially expressed in a reply to the offer of a chair of systematic theology in McCormick Theological Seminary. He wrote in his declination: "I confess that I do not feel in sympathy with the method of teaching theology from its polemic or controversial side rather than from its Biblical and practical side. In my opinion, students should be taught not so much how to throw up defenses as how to win souls and build up believers."

He was called "a prince among preachers," and his success was due in part to his painstaking preparation and to the mastery of his subject matter. The sympathy and enthusiasm with which he took up a subject proved his own strong conviction as to its truth and importance; his ability to understand his hearers also enabled him to speak with persuasive power.

Less than two years after the new pastor was installed, it became necessary to enlarge the auditorium and to remodel the basement of the church building to provide for the growing work. The interior was made in keeping with the exterior at a cost of nearly $40,000.

The prayer life of the church received particular attention. A young people's society was organized and held a prayer-meeting just before the evening service. A woman's weekly prayer circle was also formed and the midweek service grew in interest and power. Some of the methods that he used to improve this "gauge of church life" were:

First: Do away with all stiffness and formality. The leader should avoid lecturing and sermonizing. Let him open the meeting with a brief Bible study and cultivate a conversational style of speaking. His preparation must be thorough.

Second: The leader should come direct from his knees and carry the atmosphere of heaven with him. If the people also come from their closet-devotion there will be no spirit of criticism.

Third: Let there be good, lively, appropriate singing of familiar songs and hymns.

Fourth: Let there be time for testimony of young Christians, for special prayer and for reports on any work in which the people are or should be interested. This will give an object and subject for prayer.

Fifth: Let prayer be brief and to the point, not stereotyped and formal. Leave off the "preamble and resolutions" and begin in the middle. Prayer should unburden the heart.

The missionary interest and work of the church had apparently fallen to a low ebb and were next taken in hand. The monthly concert of prayer for missions was revived, a Mission Band of young people was organized and the Woman's Society was strengthened.

Church Organization

There was also formed what was perhaps the first *Men's* Foreign Missionary Society to support a missionary. The membership was intended to embrace all the men of the congregation and meetings were held quarterly. The pastor delivered carefully prepared missionary lectures and sermons and made judicious suggestions as to missionary books and periodicals; he developed other definite plans for practical work, so that his people soon came to be known far and wide as a missionary spirited church. This of course took time, study, tact and perseverance. According to Mr. Pierson's own statement, when he first assumed the pastorate of the church there was not one missionary organization or any regular missionary meeting in the congregation. "It took nearly ten years of patient sowing before the harvest was reaped, but there were then five missionary bands, one of which supported its own foreign missionary, and the monthly concert offerings alone outweighed the entire annual contributions to missions in previous years."

Systematic beneficence both for current expenses and benevolence was also made a subject of prayer and study, and a system of individual pledges was instituted. Members of the church were urged to "preach by proxy" in home and foreign fields while they enjoyed the privileges of the Gospel in their own luxurious building. As a result the gifts to both the local church and missionary work were doubled in the first five years and later were still more largely increased. Giving was made a part of worship.

The work of organization was important but by no means easy. Mr. Pierson believed that however destitute a pastor may be of efficient workers there are always in a congregation a few at least who may be called in to help conduct the temporal and spiritual affairs of the church. In Detroit he discovered a number of business and professional men, capable of leadership, and he set them to work. The elders, deacons and trustees were formed into a *Church Council*, which met once in two months or at the pastor's call. Every important matter that pertained to the church was brought before this council for discussion and decision. Objections and arguments were carefully and prayerfully weighed and only when there was substantial agreement were the plans brought before the congregation or put into effect. Thus the program was agreed upon in advance and no "half-baked" plans were put into operation.

Other members of the church he set to work in various ways, so that talents and tastes were utilized to good advantage, and individuals felt that they had definite responsibilities and interests in the organization. One man's artistic ability was employed to make signs and posters, another edited a church bulletin, women consecrated their voices in the worship of song; some called on new members and strangers; and others who could only use hands and feet distributed invitations.

The pastor's Bible Class and Teachers' Institute which met for some years every Monday evening soon became popular and this feeding of the people on the Word of God and teaching them how to feed themselves proved a valuable means of building them up in faith and conduct. This class later developed into a Saturday evening study for all the Sunday-school teachers of the city, and enabled the teacher to mould the Biblical beliefs and Christian life of a large part of the Protestant population.

Systematic Bible study had a great effect, not only on Mr. Pierson's preaching and teaching, but on his own spiritual life. He came more and more to regard the Bible, not only as a book of doctrine but as a living Counsellor and a Book of Life. He formed the habit of rising one or two hours before breakfast that he might have uninterrupted time for study and might begin the day with a personal fellowship with God. He found that the hour thus spent when his mind was fresh and when he was not distracted was worth more than three hours after other duties had begun to fill his thoughts. He would far rather go to his day's work without breakfast than without his hour of Bible study and prayer. He went to the Bible as to a personal friend, for in it he saw the Divine Author. When he wanted guidance, help, comfort, he found it in these pages and received not only spiritual light and strength for general problems but often found wonderful answers to specific inquiries.

The study of the Bible also led him to reconsider and ultimately to reconstruct his style of sermonizing. He found that when he preached the Word, God honoured it, but when he preached on popular themes, no matter how powerfully, the harvest was bare. He testified that when he ceased to care first for his own reputation and gave his people the results of Bible study, rather than the conclusions of his own philosophy, he never more experienced the sensation of ministers' "Blue Monday." His sermons became distinctly Scriptural, "thinking God's thoughts after Him," and he learned to expect God to fulfill His own promise, "My Word shall not return unto Me void."

"For myself," he said, "I feel constrained to bear

witness that no amount of study of commentaries or any other human product has been of such help as the spiritual, devotional study of the Scriptures (if possible in the original tongues). The case and number of a noun, the mood and tense of a verb, the relation of clauses and words to each other may throw new light on a passage. Above all prayer and the supreme regard for the mind of the Spirit will lead to a receptive attitude of mind and comparative indifference to mere literary standards."

This daily Bible study also led him to adopt Scriptural models and ideals for his church work. Not what *man* said but what *God* said was of chief importance to him. The supreme question on any subject was "What does the Bible teach?" The "pattern shown in the Mount," if it could be found, must be followed at all costs.

Daily Bible study brought such familiarity with the Word and such a love for it that it became a part of him; unconsciously his style and language were moulded and governed by its thoughts and words. Even when he wished to send a postal card to his mother announcing the birth of his second son he most naturally expressed the message in a Scriptural enigma as follows:

> " From sweet Isaiah's sacred song, ninth chapter and verse six,
> First thirteen words please take and then the following affix;
> From Genesis, the thirty-fifth, verse seventeen, no more,
> Then add verse twenty-six of Kings, book second, chapter four;
> Then last two verses, chapter first, first book of Samuel,
> And you will learn what on this day your loving son befell."

No doubt this was a means of leading some inquisitive postal employees to search their Bibles. In later years when he travelled much across the sea, though he had copies of a cable code with which to communicate with his family, he invariably used a Scripture quotation in preference.

As Mr. Pierson's fame grew he was beset with outside calls which offered wider spheres of service. He was a regular attendant at Presbytery and active in that organization. In Synod he was generally present and was a power. His addresses on systematic beneficence, Bible study and home, foreign and city missions became famous. He was also one of the moving spirits in the formation of the "Presbyterian Alliance," organized in 1872, to assist weak churches and to found new ones. This alliance was composed of all the pastors and elders of the city and was one of the early interchurch organizations formed to promote unity and coöperation in church work and city evangelization. The aim was to introduce into church affairs the ability and generalship more often seen in politics and business than in the affairs of the kingdom.

He was active in enlarging and equipping the Young Men's Christian Association in the city and was the leading factor in the purchase of a site and a building before the days of "Whirlwind campaigns." Nothing troubled him so much as to be idle or to have his money or other possessions in "Cold Storage." Gradually he had accumulated a carefully selected library of some two thousand volumes and rather than have their usefulness limited he allowed them to be circulated all over the city.

Throughout the state he was also known as the friend

of worthy but struggling institutions and many thousands of dollars were, through his persistent efforts, added to equipment and endowment of Kalamazoo Seminary and Olivet College.

On one occasion when attending Synod in Ann Arbor Mr. Pierson was stirred through and through by the reported irreligious condition of the university there. He announced that if such were the facts, there was need of immediate missionary work in that field, as many promising youth of the state and country were being saved or lost to God in that university. Whenever he felt or spoke like that, some practical plan took shape. The ultimate result in this case was the formation of the Tappan Presbyterian Association, which now owns property valued at fifty thousand dollars and has its own student pastor to look after the religious welfare of the eight hundred or more Presbyterian students at the university.

When the Chicago fire destroyed the office of *The Advance* he wrote suggesting that each of the subscribers help pay the loss by sending anew their year's subscription, and he himself offered to use his pen freely to supply poems and articles without charge.

In 1881, when great forest fires devastated large districts in Northern Michigan and made thousands of sufferers homeless, Mr. Pierson went to their help. He made a tour of that portion of the state and his subsequent appeal to the Christian public brought thousands of dollars for relief.

Outside calls increased, as is always the case with effective workers, but Mr. Pierson did not allow them to interfere seriously with the duties to his own congregation. Some of his most valued experiences came in

Methods of Work 117

connection with pastoral visitation. He formed the habit of carrying about with him a record book in which he entered in cipher the facts about each family —the names and birthdays, the character and peculiarities, the tastes, the physical infirmities, temptations and besetting sins of the children, the talents and capabilities of each for church work, the residence of absentees, and the characteristics of the spiritual life of each. These facts gave him an intimate acquaintance with the households in his parish and enabled him to enter into the family life and to pray intelligently and sympathetically for them individually and collectively.

Such systematic and faithful work produced results. Revivals in church and Sabbath-school rewarded the Scriptural teaching and prayerful spirit and at one time nearly the whole Sabbath-school remained week after week at the close of the session for religious conversation, and large numbers united with the church. The next step was to set these young recruits to work and in this Mr. Pierson had five rules:

1. Have definite work on hand in the local church or mission.
2. Endeavour to enlist every one in some unselfish service.
3. Emphasize this as among the normal duties of every one received into the church.
4. Keep an exact list of church-members with the work each is doing or able to do.
5. Carefully adapt the forms of work to individual temperament and fitness.

There were many individual instances which encouraged the pastor in his work. He aimed to save men, not to make them comfortable, and he believed that faithful preaching would attract those who were earnest seekers after God. One incident he relates as follows:

"One Monday morning a young man—a stranger—was ushered into my study. He sat down and said: 'Sir, I was led yesterday into your church and heard you preach on "The wages of sin is death, but the gift of God is eternal life through Jesus Christ our Lord." It made me feel that I am a sinner and have fairly earned those wages. But I want the gift of God. Can you tell me how to get it?' He was not ashamed to weep and I wept with him. Then I explained to him, with a satisfaction that can never be known by those who have never felt it, the simple way of believing on the Lord Jesus, taking Him at His Word and so receiving cleansing and redemption. As he listened I asked: 'Are you willing to accept this Saviour as your only hope of eternal life?'

"'I am.'

"'Now and forever?'

"'Yes, now and forever.'

"'Are you willing to give yourself unreservedly to Him?'

"'I am.'

"We knelt down and both prayed. He spoke in a trembling, stammering tongue that I am sure sounded as smooth and sweet in the ear of God as the most fluent dialect of heaven.

"As we rose to our feet I said: 'Now will you tell others of the Saviour you have found?' He promised and went from my house to a noonday prayer-meeting where he testified to his new joy in finding the Saviour. He followed this by confession in his home and the church and brought his wife also to the table

A Rich Man Offended

of the Lord. He took a class in the mission school and became a humble, active Christian. He will ever be in my mind an example of a man who seeks for God with all his heart."

In a church which included so many wealthy and influential men there must have been not a little temptation for the minister to preach generalities and to avoid direct and definite denunciation of sins which are often countenanced even by church-members. But moral cowardice could never be charged against Arthur T. Pierson. He had an overwhelming sense of his responsibility to preach the Gospel as an ambassador of Christ and could not take the responsibility of toning it down to please "itching ears." He believed that if he spoke his own words he might be held accountable for the result, but if he spoke the Word of God in truth and love he could leave the outcome in the hands of the Almighty. One experience in Detroit confirmed him in the determination to be faithful even in most trying circumstances, and the outcome taught him that such fidelity is respected even by those who may be offended. We give the incident in his own words:

"At a funeral of a rich, generous and popular but dissipated man who died of delirium tremens, I felt it my duty to be very plain in addressing straight words of warning to the large number of men who attended the funeral. I made a pointed appeal to the hundreds of his unconverted business associates who came to the last rites and asked them that old question of profit and loss, 'What shall it profit a man if he gain the whole world and lose his own soul?' With intense earnestness that question was pressed home to many who never showed themselves within church doors.

"Of course some took offense. Many came that day, expecting that the 'officiating clergyman' would pay homage to a rich and popular man, and gloss over with polite varnish his life of profligacy and inebriety. They hoped to have some salve applied to their own consciences from the ointment of praise with which such a man would be anointed for burial. The disappointment of a few was outspoken and violent. One man, who was a paying but not a praying member of my congregation, went away angrily cursing me and declaring that he would make a provision in his will that I should not have any part in his funeral ceremonies!

"Any minister of the Gospel who seeks first of all to be true to himself and to God as well as to man, knows at what sacrifice of feeling truth must sometimes be told. But sooner or later the compensation comes. In this case it came very unexpectedly and markedly. Within a few months that man was smitten with an incurable disease; and as he belonged to my congregation, I ventured to call upon him to offer him such help as I could. To my surprise he was not only glad to see me but he begged me to come often. He clung to me like a little child—opened his whole heart to me, confessed his lifelong sins, besought me to pray with him, and before he died wrote me a letter, with a trembling hand, in which, after lovingly acknowledging the attentions I had paid him during his illness, he said: '*Always tell men the truth;* be honest with them under all circumstances. They may be offended at the time, but they will believe in you and trust you in the end. As a man of the world let me say, my dear pastor, that when you or any minister of the Gospel can present the subject of religion to a sinner so that you make him feel that you have a *personal interest in him,* outside—if I may so say—of your clerical duty to present these great truths to all men, then you have made rapid strides into his heart and confidence.'

"That letter is a revelation of what passes in the breast of many a hearer who seems to give no heed. When they come to look at the great Hereafter they want no quicksand on which to stand."

One secret of Mr. Pierson's success with men was this personal interest in the individual members of his congregation. He often secured the coöperation that he needed by some unique method of approach. This is illustrated by a note written to a member of his church when he was in need of a pulpit clock. The trustees had purchased one, but it was lost in some way and they neglected to replace it. The pastor therefore wrote the following to one of his parishioners:

"Your pastor very meekly suggests,
 Not venturing any more earnest requests;
 A clock to the pulpit might be annexed
 To keep the people from being vexed
 By sermons that run to excessive length,
 And tax the popular patience and strength.
 Perhaps an hour-glass might do as well
 By which the swift passing of time he could tell;
 Or a beadle to tap with his gentle rod,
 Not only the hearer who ventures to nod,
 But the preacher whose words continue to run
 When the sand in the hour-glass ought to be done."

The pastor received his timepiece without delay.

It may be well to pause here to note the family life of this busy pastor. Before he was forty years old he had a family of seven children ranging in age from one to sixteen years. With his aged mother there was a family of ten and a busy, often noisy household it was. The children had inherited good physiques and the simple food and regular habits of life gave them health that was overflowing in animal spirits.

The father believed in ruling his household with a firm but loving hand, for he regarded the family as a miniature state and church. God's plan, he believed, was that the father should be priest and ruler leading in worship and, under God, shaping the policies of the household. The "first commandment with promise," "honour thy father and thy mother" was not an empty and antiquated regulation in the Pierson family but the father and mother saw to it that they themselves should be worthy of honour. Before their children knew that there was a Father in heaven they became acquainted with their father on earth and from him received their ideas of God. It was a basic principle in the Pierson household that while the children were under the parental roof and supported by father and mother, the parents were to be obeyed as God was to be obeyed. Nor were children allowed to wait for a reason else it would not be true obedience. "Spare the rod and spoil the child" was not an obsolete maxim. Anarchy in the household was looked upon as the precursor of anarchy in state and Church.

The rules established were few but reasonable and were strictly enforced by father and mother in harmony. Some of these rules were: No argument in matters of obedience; early bedtime regulated according to age; early rising and prompt dressing or little breakfast; no absence from school except for illness and then strict diet, and no playtime due to sudden recovery; no Saturday holiday until the Sunday-school lesson had been prepared and the memory verses had been recited to mother; church and Sabbath-school attendance not a debatable question; no books read that had not first passed parental censorship; no "parties" to interfere with school or on Saturday nights; a portion of all money received as an allowance, however small, to be set aside for benevolence.

But the regulations were not by any means chiefly negative or legalistic. The parents believed in sympathy as well as in strictness and they themselves set the example in Christian life and regular habits. The morning worship was as regular as clockwork and the singing, Scripture reading and prayer were generally adapted to young minds. The "blessing" at table also kept God in mind as the bountiful Provider to whom the heart's gratitude is due. Not only in summer but in the busy winter, father and mother took an active interest in their children's outings, friends were ever welcomed at the home and ten was not so large a number at table as to exclude additions. The long winter evenings, after lessons were finished, often saw a happy family circle gathered in the library, employed with sewing, drawing, or whittling, or making scrap-books, while the father read aloud from some interesting work of history, biography, travel, popular science or high-class fiction. This was a valuable means of cultivating the taste of the growing minds and the interests and sympathies of parents and children were firmly cemented together. In this way also they became familiar with most of the important books of the day, adapted to youth, and were saved from the temptation to indulge in pernicious or senseless literature.

One picture of the father in these Detroit days is indelibly impressed on the memories of his children. It was in the autumn of 1876 and the mother was confined to her bed with her youngest child a few days old when three of the children suddenly came down with scarlet fever. There were no surplus funds for special nurses, and if there had been the father would have preferred, if possible, to care for the sick ones himself. His church was being rebuilt and there were countless meetings of session and trustees as well as many outside calls, but Mr. Pierson for six or eight weeks daily visited with his wife, prepared his sermons, kept up his pastoral work and would then come in to spend an hour or two with his three young children all ill in one room. He himself would rub their hot little bodies with cocoa-butter and in the days of their convalescence he would read aloud from their favourite books. His great delight was to prepare with his own hand some delicacies that were permitted by the physician. His eyes would dance and twinkle like a child's when he came into the sick-room with some fine oranges, toys or other delightful surprise. After the time for his brief visit had flown—all too quickly—he would carefully bathe with carbolic soap and dress with entirely fresh clothing that he might without danger to others again visit his beloved wife and go about his usual duties.

The summers spent in Brooklyn, Michigan, were great seasons for strengthening the family ties. There work and regular duties were not lacking for each one in house, garden or stable, but recreation was provided for with equal care. It was a happy family that went off on long weekly drives and picnics to some of the neighbouring lakes. The children learned from joyful experience that the parents understood them and were as solicitous for their happiness as for their training in thrift, obedience and truthfulness.

Sorrows were not numerous in the household, for death did not enter and serious illness was infrequent, but some experiences made a profound impression on all and added to the seriousness of life. One of these, which brought home to all a deeper sense of God's loving care, occurred in the summer of 1877, when Mr. Pierson and three children, Laura, Louise and Delavan, narrowly escaped drowning in Vineyard Lake near their summer home. They had been out fishing in a leaky boat, as they had often done before, but this time the boat became unusually full of water. One child started to change her seat and more water entered over the sides. Suddenly the boat began to sink. The father leaped forward with one child clinging to his back and grasped a slender fishing stake with one hand while with the other he drew two children from under the water. There for half an hour they clung unable to summon assistance from the deserted shore. The father could swim, but was unwilling to leave his children. Between the calls for help to unseen men, they prayed to the unseen God and committed themselves to His keeping. They promised that if their lives were spared they would devote them loyally to His service. Finally a woman heard their calls for help and came to the rescue in another boat. She had never handled oars and Mr. Pierson, with his head just above water, had to direct her how to use them. Finally they climbed into the boat and reached the shore in safety. The joy and excitement of reunion with loved ones might have effaced from the young minds the covenant made with God and the deeper lesson of gratitude to Him, but the father wrote his children a loving letter which he asked each to sign:

"MY DEAR LAURA, LOUISE, AND DELAVAN:

"I cannot keep from thinking about you. . . . I cannot thank God enough for such a wonderful deliverance as that on last Tuesday when we were all saved from drowning.

"Now, dear children, do you not think that we ought to remember how we told God, when we were in the water, that if He would save us we would live for His service? We were in the very jaws of death and He put his arms under us and kept us alive. . . . What can we do to show our love to our dear Saviour? I thought I would like to write out my promise to God and sign my name. I think you will each be glad to sign your name also. . . . Let us ask God to make us such a blessing as that we shall see more and more reason to be grateful to Him. . . .

A Promise to God

"We owe our lives to God. He heard our cry and sent us aid when we were in danger of drowning in Vineyard Lake on July 27, 1877. Now we put our names to this promise to give ourselves to Him, praying Him to help us by His Spirit to live all the rest of our days unto Him."

[Signed]

Arthur T. Pierson
Laura W. Pierson.
Louise B. Pierson.
Delavan Pierson.

VIII

FROM CHURCH TO OPERA HOUSE—A CHANGE OF TACTICS

SUCCESS had thus far crowned Dr. Pierson's efforts. As the popular pastor of one of the leading churches in the Middle West he occupied an enviable position. His congregation was large, cultured, influential and wealthy; his people were harmonious, devoted and enthusiastic; his work was well organized and aggressive and the various departments of church activity seemed to be in a healthy condition. He had received the degree of Doctor of Divinity, his salary had been increased, and there were other tokens of appreciation and esteem. His fame had spread abroad, in city, state and nation so that he had many remunerative opportunities to lecture, and he was recognized as a power in civic and ecclesiastical affairs, especially as a leader in religious and missionary enterprises. God's blessing seemed to rest upon him so that he had very nearly reached the summit of his ambition, but still he was far from being satisfied. What lacked he yet? Some pastors might have been content to settle down with a consciousness of achievement. They would have cared for no greater sign of success than a well-filled and well-organized church. But this did not satisfy the soul of Dr. Pierson. Most of the additions to the church were by letter or were children from the Sunday-school, and while he rejoiced over these, he longed to see men and women born anew and manifesting their new birth by a new nature and a new life. His dissatisfaction grew as he saw and heard of multitudes converted under the simple preaching of comparatively unlettered evangelists. He realized that there was a power of God of which he knew nothing. There were promises of blessing which were not being fulfilled. He believed in God's Word and in His power, but something must be standing in the way.

While this burden was lying heavily upon him, God sent to Detroit two of His servants, Major D. W. Whittle and his associate, P. P. Bliss, the singing evangelist. They began to hold gospel meetings on Tuesday, October 6, 1874, and continued their Detroit campaign for six weeks. Dr. Pierson gladly sat at their feet, as a learner. He attended the services, studied their methods and observed the results. He learned three things: (1) The power of simple gospel preaching in contrast to that which emphasized literary style; (2) the power of God's Word when used to unfold the great Christian doctrines in contrast to non-Biblical preaching; and (3) the power of gospel song in contrast to elaborate music rendered chiefly for artistic effect.

Mr. Bliss wrote his music, as Major Whittle prepared his sermons, solely for spiritual impression, and when Dr. Pierson wrote for them a song, "With Harps and with Viols," he was impressed to see Mr. Bliss withdraw for a season of prayer before composing the music. All they did was "sanctified by the Word of God and by prayer."

The evangelists were entertained for a month in the Pierson home and their very presence was a benediction. The calm peace and joy in the Holy Spirit that pervaded their lives spoke even more loudly than their sermons and songs. Their host longed to experience more of the fullness of God's abiding presence and power in his own personal life and ministry.

One night after a meeting of unusual power, the pastor of the Methodist church, in which it was held, entered his lecture room and found Dr. Pierson alone with his head bowed on his hands, deeply moved. On being asked the cause of his distress he replied:

"I feel that I have never been truly converted nor have I preached the Gospel as I ought."

By many external leadings and by the inward "Still small voice" God was calling him to larger, more fruitful service. Just before the evangelists left the city, Major Whittle said to his host, with great earnestness: "Brother Pierson, Bliss and I are firmly convinced that God would mightily use you if you were wholly consecrated to Him. We have agreed to pray for you daily that you may be fully surrendered."

These words were not easy to forget, but for over a year they apparently bore no fruit. He became restless amid his worldly success until he finally felt that he must face the issue or give up his commission. The conviction had been growing upon him that before he could be used as he wished for the conversion of men he must be more fully consecrated to God. At his suggestion a room was fitted up in the church tower and thither he went for uninterrupted Bible study, meditation, self-examination and communion with God. On November 12, 1875, a day appointed by the Synod of Michigan for fasting and prayer, he was convinced that the great obstacle to his spiritual growth and power was his ambition for literary glory. This conviction had been slowly growing, but he had almost unconsciously fought against it. Now he asked God to deal with this ambition in His own way. He was brought to the depths of humiliation and almost despair. The steps by which he began to come out of the slough of despond, he describes as follows:

"I began to pray aloud in private and found this a great help to my realization of the presence of God, and I learned what real prayer meant. Then I was impressed with the necessity for honesty, absolute candour with God in asking what I really wanted, and what I was willing to give up everything else to obtain. I saw that my life had been full of self-seeking and idolatry, such as I had never realized. Next I felt the need of present faith in the sure Word of God which promises answer to such prayer. God gave me this assurance in the preparation of a special sermon to my people. Finally I saw that I must give up every ambition and every idol, and must place myself unreservedly in the hands of God. It was a terrible battle, but at last I said, with all my heart, 'Lord, let me be nothing, but use me if Thou wilt to save souls and to glorify Thee.'

"From that day I was conscious of the presence of the Holy Spirit in my life and work in a way that I had before never known. The text, 1 John v. 4, 'I have overcome the world,' was revealed to me in a new light and instead of depending upon my energy and ability to overcome the world, I saw that God must do it and all the glory was to be His, not mine.

"Just at this time the remarkable biography of Charles G. Finney was put into my hands and from it I saw how God's spirit could use a man wholly absorbed in the work of saving souls. From the hour

at I nailed my ambition for literary honours and
plause to the Cross of Christ, I began to feel a deep
d solemn conviction that God, in answer to prayer,
as about to commission me to a new work for Christ.
ithin one year this expectation was marvellously ful-
led."

One Sabbath morning, March 19, 1876, he preached on
The New Birth " with a keen sense of the help of the
oly Spirit. The impression made on the hearers was
ep and solemn. The pastor felt that many would
ve arisen for prayer but for the atmosphere and tra-
tions of the congregation, which restrained him from
aking any such innovation. Inquirers were asked to
me to the lecture room and two men responded and
ve themselves to God. At the evening service the
stor began a series of sermons suggested by facts in
inney's life, and there was evidence of still deeper
terest.

The next Friday evening, March 24th, was unusually
ormy, but seventy-five gathered for prayer and the
stor took his people into his confidence. He spoke
lainly and tenderly of the barriers that he felt stood
etween the church and larger ingatherings. He told
em of his own surrender and asked the church to
in him in a determination to remove any obstacles
at might be due to tradition, prejudice, fashion, over-
ttention to the æsthetic or to lack of sympathy with
e masses. The very character of the church building,
ith its imposing architecture, beautiful furnishings,
nd rented pews, was suggested as a possible hindrance
 drawing the poorer classes. God's promises to an-
wer prayer and to give power for service were quoted
om His Word. Then pastor and people knelt down

(this act itself was an innovation) and prayed that at all costs their church might be used to give the Bread of Life to the unsaved multitudes of the city.

While that prayer was being breathed out to God the church building was burning. As they rose from their knees smoke was noticeable in the room and some of the officers sought the cause but without success. They concluded that contrary winds were blowing the smoke down the chimney, and after a careful investigation they went home. The next morning the beautiful temple was in ashes. The fire had started in a defective flue and had crept along between the walls, so that in the early dawn the whole building burst into flame. When the fire engines arrived the interior was a roaring furnace.

In spite of the financial loss and the grief due to the devastation of a place so full of hallowed associations, Dr. Pierson saw in this seeming calamity the hand of God. The tower study, in which were a thousand books, and two thousand sermons—the work of twenty years,—was destroyed, but even then he felt that the spiritual lessons and experiences were beyond the reach of the flames. He wrote to D. L. Moody: "I felt as if God had laid His hand on my shoulder and said, 'I am thy God; henceforth be a man of prayer and faith and give thyself to the work of saving souls.' I replied, 'Lord, by Thy grace, I will.'"

Immediately the church officers were called together and at their pastor's earnest request decided to hire the large "Whitney's Opera House," and to open it freely for evangelistic services, with gospel hymns and a volunteer choir.

This was a great step for the aristocratic, exclusive

After the Burning of the Church 133

church to take. At the same time their pastor discarded forever the use of written sermons, for he saw in the loss of his manuscripts [1] a call to abandon what he believed to be a hindrance to direct preaching of God's message to the people. His first sermon in the Opera House was sought on his knees and he was led to preach on the words: "The fire shall try every man's work of what sort it is."

A newspaper writer of the day thus describes the first service in the Opera House:

"The audience began to assemble long before the doors were open and stood patiently reading the billboards, which announced the play 'The Black Crook.' As the people began to fill the house from pit to top gallery, two theatre men who dropped in out of curiosity remarked that such an audience would bring a good sum at fifty cents a head. When the audience joined in singing 'Praise God from whom all blessings flow,' it made the house ring as it never had rung before even for the grandest opera chorus. Some of the people, who were more accustomed to the opera than to church, were so impressed by the singing that they began to applaud. A hushed stillness pervaded the vast audience during the prayer and they listened sympathetically to the sermon on 'The Ordeal of Fire.' Two actors who came in at the stage door to look for their baggage stood behind the flies, with hats in hand, listening with rapt attention to the man who stood where they had performed the evening before."

The preacher seemed inspired as he gave what was reported to be "one of the most startling, plain spoken

[1] These manuscripts and his annotated Bible were afterwards recovered and were found to be in only a slightly damaged condition.

liscourses a nineteenth century audience ever listened to."

The power of God was immediately manifest in the Opera House not only at the preaching services but in the two Bible readings and two prayer-meetings held each week. God touched His servant's lips with a live coal from off the altar and his words burned their way into men's hearts. Hundreds rose for prayer and remained for personal conversation. Men and women, who had not been in church for years, began to attend; even standing room was taken, and often on pleasant evenings from 800 to 1,000 were turned away. In the next sixteen months Dr. Pierson saw more souls converted than in all the previous sixteen years of his ministry.

In a letter to Mr. Moody he expressed his own convictions: "I pray especially that neither I nor any one else may attribute these results to any human instrument. It is so plainly the work of God that I am comparatively lost sight of, as I desire to be, but I have a deep conviction that God is anointing me for some new service, new at least in some respects. . . . Pray that I may be wholly emptied of self and filled with Him."

On the second Sabbath the pastor preached another stirring discourse on "The Church and the Masses" (Luke xiv. 23), in the course of which he said:

"Men give three kinds of excuses to avoid coming into the kingdom of God: First there is the excuse of property, second of preoccupation, and third of domestic ties. Similar hindrances stand in the way of the churches that would minister to the unsaved. When churches are ornate and have rented pews, poor men will not come to be guests of the rich. . . . When Christian people are not willing to sacrifice their tastes for art, architecture, music and oratory in the house of God they do not reach the masses. A kid glove is often a non-conductor between man and man. . . . But the Church *must* have the people or it will die. The Church needs them as much as they need the Church."

Thus from the beginning of the new era Dr. Pierson spoke plainly to his people and urged them to prepare to follow God's leading and to build a simple tabernacle in which all classes would feel at home in the worship of God. He asked for a church building adapted to this purpose and for an unworldly administration.

One of his sermons presents some of his convictions on the church and free pews.

"1. We must magnify the idea of the *Lord's* House by some system that discourages all exclusive human rights of property in the sanctuary and discountenances all invidious social distinctions.

"2. The support of the ministry should be on the basis of voluntary contributions so as to promote true independence on the part of the Lord's ambassador.

"3. We must study economy according to the principles and practice of the Apostolic Church and be an example to other churches.

"4. We must so plan as to bring the Gospel into contact with the unsaved multitudes about us. Attendance at the house of worship should be as free as is consistent with the necessary cost of maintaining the work."

The pastor himself felt, with Paul, "Woe is me if I preach not the Gospel." He proclaimed with earnestness and power not only the attractive aspects of the Gospel but the sterner doctrines as well. He was never a prophet of smooth things. Sin was denounced and mercy was offered. The result was one of the greatest religious revivals the city ever experienced. Scores of converts were added to many churches and some of the most prominent men of the city date their conversion from the Opera House services.

These converts were not like paper, caught up and carried along only for a brief moment by the whirl of a passing enthusiasm. Twenty-one years later an investigation was made and it was found that of 294 members received into Fort Street Church on confession of faith as a result of these meetings 229 were satisfactorily accounted for as faithful to their Christian vows.

When the question arose as to the rebuilding of the church, Dr. Pierson urged his officers to aim to make it not so much "a model of art as a model of a church" —a building not for display but for work and worship, without unnecessary extravagance but adequately equipped for service. He asked not for a colossal tabernacle but for an auditorium adapted to work for the masses, planned for comfort but not for luxury.

He was also opposed to a church debt and exclaimed, "Better a frame chapel free from debt with Christian ideals, upheld with Christian manhood, than a stately temple built and controlled by the money of ungodly men, or obtained by bowing to those who do not bow the knee to Christ as Saviour and Lord."

The officers of the church listened patiently and courteously to their pastor's arguments and appeals, but while they loved and respected him they were not convinced. The church was rebuilt more beautiful than ever, but by way of compromise the pews were made free for the evening services. The pastor was disappointed and felt that they were not *wholly* following the Lord's leading. He however threw himself into the effort to win men to Christ by the use of such equipment as he had. Both pastor and people had been radically changed by their experience in the Opera House, and when they returned to their renovated temple after sixteen months' absence, a different spirit and atmosphere prevailed. Instead of formality and comparative coldness to strangers there was warmth and a cordial welcome for all.

The congregational singing took on new life and the mottoes " Preach the Gospel" and " Pray without ceasing" on either side of the pulpit were put into practice with new fervour. Many members had acquired a taste for soul winning, and every week young men visited hotels, saloons, and street corners to distribute invitations. "After meetings" were held each Sunday night and missionary work was carried on in neglected quarters of the city. Earnest men and women went out to hold cottage prayer-meetings, Sunday-schools and preaching services, and more than one new church grew up as a result. Dr. Pierson's motto for his people was " Let every hearer become a herald."

But with the return to the new and stately building it was found impossible to preserve the hold upon non-churchgoers, though the pewholders sought to make strangers welcome and the sermons continued to be simple, practical, and extemporaneous. The preacher did not disregard his talents and literary style, but he made them subservient to the one great end of reaching men.

During this period Dr. Pierson learned many lessons in dealing with inquirers. He himself testified that he had up to that time depended on argument in place of on the Holy Spirit. He thought he could interpret anything or solve any difficulty. He used to lay his plans to capture men as he would to capture a fortress, but he too often found that when he had taken one stronghold the garrison had fled to another. Now he learned that when he kept Christ in the foreground and depended on the Sword of the Spirit, God gave the victory. The heart cannot be captured by attacking the head, and spiritual difficulties must be overcome by spiritual weapons. The one dependence in this warfare is on the guidance and power of the Holy Spirit.

Some of the experiences of the inquiry room were of unique interest and permanent value as examples of effective methods in leading men to Christ. One of these Dr. Pierson described as follows:

"At the close of a sermon on 'Abiding in Christ,' according to my custom, I invited any person present who was impressed with his need of Christ to meet me in the inquirer's room.

"One young man of about thirty responded. He was tall, stalwart of frame, intelligent, and would have been fine looking but for a cloud that seemed to abide upon his countenance. In fact, his face seemed scarred and furrowed, as though his life had been a battle with sin and care, and he had been terribly worsted in the contest. I said to him:

"'I take it, sir, that you are here to talk with me

Dealing With Inquirers

about your spiritual interests. Will you let me into the very heart of your trouble or difficulty?'

"'Well, sir,' said he, 'I suppose you would consider my case a desperate one. I am a follower of Robert Ingersoll. I am an unbeliever, a disbeliever, an infidel.'

"'But I suppose there are some things you believe. You believe the Bible to be the Book of God?'

"'No, sir.'

"'You believe Jesus Christ to be the Son of God?'

"'No, sir.'

"'Well, at least you believe in a God?'

"'There may be a God; I cannot say that I believe there is, but there may be; I do not know.'

"'Then why are you here? I do not see what you want of me, if you do not believe in the Bible nor in Christ, and are not even sure there is any God.'

"'I heard you preach to-night, and it seems to me that you must believe something and that it gives you peace and comfort.'

"'You are quite right.'

"'Well, I don't believe anything, and am perfectly wretched; if you can show me the way to believe anything and to get happiness in believing, I wish you would. If you can help me, do it quickly, for I have been carrying this burden as long as I can. I am a law student, but I am so wretched I cannot study nor sit still. I wandered over here to-night, and heard the organ playing in your church, and went in expecting to hear some fine music. I heard nothing but simple congregational singing, but curiosity led me to remain and hear what you had to say, and one thing impressed me, —that you have faith in somebody or something, and you are happy in believing. My envy of you brings me in here.'

"I lifted my heart to God for special guidance, and drew my chair up close to this unhappy man and involuntarily put my arm around him.

"'Tell me something to read,' he said.

"'I would have you read nothing but the Bible. You have been reading too much; that is partly what is the matter with you. You are full of the misleading, plausible sophistries of the skeptics. Read the Word of God.'

"'But what is the use when I do not believe it to be the Word of God?'

"Opening my Bible, I turned to John v. 39, and with my finger on the verse slowly read: 'Search the Scriptures; for in them ye think ye have eternal life and they are they which testify of Me and ye will not come unto Me that ye may have life.' 'Now,' said I, 'it is God's testimony and my experience that he who diligently searches the Scriptures will find that they contain the witness to their own divine origin and inspiration, and to the divinity of the Lord Jesus Christ.'

"'Well,' said he, 'I'll read the Bible, but what beside?'

"Turning to Matthew vi. 6, I pointed to the words: 'Enter into thy closet, and when thou hast shut thy door, pray to thy Father which is in secret, and thy Father which seeth in secret Himself shall reward thee.' 'If that means anything, it means that if you sincerely pray to God He will reveal Himself to you.'

"'But of what use to pray to God if you don't believe there is a God?'

"For an instant I was perplexed. But a thought

An Infidel Converted

flashed across me, and although I never had given such counsel to any man before, I gave utterance to it, for I felt guided.

"'It makes no difference,' I replied, 'provided you are sincere. God will not disregard any genuine effort to draw near to Him. Go and pray, if only like the famous Thistlewood conspirator: "Oh, God, if there be a God, save my soul, if I have a soul."'

"'Anything more?' said he.

"'Yes,' and I opened to John vii. 17, and read: '"If any man will do His will, he shall know of the doctrine." That means that if you act up to whatever light you have, you shall have more light. In God's school, we never are taught a second lesson till we practice the first. "Then shall we know if we follow on to know the Lord."

"'I have given you three texts already to ponder and study. I wish to add one more: Matt. xi. 28, 29, 30, "Come unto Me, all ye that labour and are heavy laden, and I will give you rest." That means that if you come directly to Jesus Christ, He will give you rest. Now notice these four texts. One bids you to search the Scriptures; one, to pray in secret; one, to put in practice whatever you know; and the last, to come to Jesus Christ as your personal Saviour.'

"'Is that all?' he inquired.

"'That is all. Will you promise me to go and follow this simple prescription?'

"'I will.'

"After kneeling in prayer together, this Ingersollite left me. Two weeks later, at the close of service, I gave a similar invitation to inquirers. The congregation was scarcely half out of the house, when this same man came towards me, with both hands extended and his face beaming. 'I have found God and Christ, and I am a happy man!'

"He sat beside me and told me the fascinating story. He had gone home that Sunday night, taken out from his trunk the Bible his mother had put there when he left home; had opened it and knelt before the unseen God. He simply, sincerely asked that if there were a God at all, and if the Bible were the Word of God, and Jesus Christ His Son and the Saviour of man, it might be shown him plainly. As he read and prayed and sought for light, light was given; he humbly tried to follow every ray and to walk in the light, and the path became clearer and plainer and the light fuller and brighter, until his eyes rested in faith upon Jesus."

At about this time—in 1878—another remarkable influence came into Dr. Pierson's life and another teaching of the Scripture was revealed to him. It was in connection with the visit of the sainted George Müller of Bristol, England, to America. These two men who were to be so closely associated in later years had never met. It chanced that, in the providence of God, Dr. Pierson had been invited to accompany a party to the Pacific Coast for rest and recuperation for a severely overstrained body. While in San Francisco he learned that George Müller was on the coast and would start East on Friday or Saturday. He was somewhat astonished, as this would involve travelling on the Sabbath and, as it was his only opportunity for the coveted interview, he was sorely tempted to break his own rule by taking the same train. After prayerful consideration he decided not to do so, however, and was rewarded by discovering on reaching Ogden that Mr. Müller was

First Meeting With George Müller 143

on the same train. He had not travelled on the Sabbath but had rested at Ogden. Together they journeyed to Chicago and afterwards Mr. Müller accepted an invitation to visit Detroit.

Up to this time Dr. Pierson had been an earnest advocate of what is known as the "Post-Millennial" view of the Lord's Second Coming. Many times he had addressed the Presbytery and other bodies on the subject and had set forth what seemed to him unanswerable arguments in the support of this view. Now, however, he was led through Mr. Müller to make a new and more careful study of the subject. He says: "Mr. Müller listened patiently to my objections and then said, with his celestial smile: 'The only thing I can say is that none of your arguments are founded on *Scripture*. It makes no difference what *we* think but *what does God's Word say?*' For ten days he came to my study every day and opened up the truth to me. Ever since that time I have been looking for the Lord's personal return and it has been the inspiration of my life."[1]

This doctrine came to be to him a key with which to unlock many perplexing difficulties in Biblical theology. He says: "Two-thirds of the Book which had been sealed to me were opened by this key, and I was permitted to enter and walk through marvellous chambers of mystery."

Although Mr. Müller was thirty-two years older than his friend and although the days actually spent in each other's companionship through life would not aggregate one year, it is impossible to estimate all that the friend-

[1] Dr. Pierson's views on the Second Coming are given in a small volume entitled "The Coming of the Lord."

ship meant to Dr. Pierson. Mr. Müller came into his life at a critical time and they were irresistibly drawn to each other. Daily for twenty-eight years they remembered each other in prayer until the older man went to his reward. Only those who have studied the prayer life of Mr. Müller and know what power he had with God can estimate the results of this prayer covenant.

Meanwhile God seemed to be stirring the nest and there were thorns that made it uncomfortable. Dr. Pierson was impressed with the thought that he should work more systematically for the masses. Gradually the church work seemed to be getting back into old ruts, and he found that he could not carry out his ideals for simplicity in worship. In spite of the pastor's musical talent, the elaborate anthems by the choir were irksome to him and too often seemed out of harmony with the sermons. He believed in congregational singing and said, "God never intended four or forty people to stand in a choir and do the singing for all the people." He also had an unconquerable aversion to anything that seemed to him like formal ritualism or liturgy in a church service. With characteristic faithfulness he presented his views to his congregation, for he could not endure the bondage involved in shaping his course to meet the preferences of men. Freedom and truth demanded that he deliver his message as he believed it came from God.

It was natural that many, especially among non-Christians, should be offended by some of his outspoken utterances as he declaimed against Sabbath desecration, intemperance, ritualism, rationalism and worldliness. Efforts were made to attack his character and to discredit him in the eyes of the public, but without avail.

A Pastoral Letter 145

His reputation and his character were in the hands of God.

A year before he left the Fort Street Church Dr. Pierson wrote a long pastoral letter to his people which he printed and distributed. This letter set forth the history of God's dealings with him and with the church since his coming. It spoke of his own temptations to ambition and self-glory and the entire revolution in his own convictions and ideals. After rehearsing the story of the fire and the experiences and lessons of the Opera House meetings, he went on to say :

"My conviction was strong that such a church building as ours hinders access to the common people. The very elegance of its architecture, its furniture, the high rate of its pew rents and the air of exclusiveness that seemed to outsiders to hang about it would repel a poor man.

"I do not mean to say that my beloved people are to blame for the impressions, often unjust, which keep the masses out of our place of worship, but it does seem to me that if we are really aiming to reach those who neglect the Gospel we would build and run our places of worship accordingly. Formerly I justified costly church edifices, and when our former house was remodelled, I helped to plan its artistic completeness, but I believe that God has taught me that the present system of building and conducting churches is a real hindrance in saving souls. When, however, the congregation determined to rebuild in the same style as before the fire, I forbore to obtrude my views on the people.

"Next I tried to show that the rental and reserving of pews would repel the poor and I offered to serve without guaranteed salary if the seats were made free. . . . After presenting my views and supporting them on Scriptural basis, I left you, my dear people, to decide without any attempt or desire to fetter your action. . . . You decided to maintain the former system of pew rents but to make them free in the evening. I worked hard, and during the summer after our return to our new church building I took no vacation but maintained the Sunday preaching services, the inquiry meetings and prayer-meetings. Yet, as you know, from the day of entering our new edifice the work of God's grace in conversion has steadily declined. There have been marked cases of spiritual growth among disciples, but the number of converts has become smaller each year.

"With perfect frankness, I wish to lay down plank by plank the platform of Bible principles, as I see them, on this subject:

"1. The Church of God exists on earth in great part to rescue unsaved souls.

"2. The more destitute souls are, the greater is the obligation of the church towards them.

"3. Practical indifference to the salvation of the unevangelized forfeits the claim of the church to God's blessing or even to a place among His Golden Candlesticks.

"4. The twofold work of evangelization and edification must go on side by side.

"5. Everything in the church should be adapted to these two ends—the salvation of the unsaved and the building up of believers.

"Now as a church are we reaching the results that God's promises lead us to expect? . . .

"I write this letter only that I may put you into the full possession of facts, and that I may impart to you any light that I may have received. I could not be faithful to you or to God without telling you how I look on these matters. I have no plans only to follow Him patiently step by step. . . .

"We must stand by each other and by God in the firm resolve to elevate the standard of holy living. I

The Ideal Church 147

am ready to 'cross the stream and burn the bridge behind me.'"

When the large influx of converts received in the Opera House services did not continue, Dr. Pierson grew impatient for contact with the masses. Sermons on the subject of the "Ideal Church" and the "Mission of the Church" were followed by remonstrances from his officers who decided that it was unwise either to erect another branch church or to do away with the ownership of pews. The officers expressed their love and admiration for their pastor and he reciprocated their cordial feeling, but they did not see eye to eye with him in these matters of church policy, and he saw that it would be difficult for either to yield. It was inevitable therefore that he should listen to the overtures of another church that seemed to offer larger opportunities to reach the multitudes. It cost him unspeakable sorrow to sunder ties that bound him to his people, and it was a difficult matter to pull up the roots that had run wide and deep in the interests of city and state, but he felt the call of God to leave, and on July 19, 1882, after thirteen years in Detroit, he resigned his charge to accept a call to the Second Presbyterian Church of Indianapolis.

IX

A YEAR IN INDIANAPOLIS—VICTORY OR DEFEAT?

INDIANAPOLIS, the capital of Indiana, is an important commercial and political centre, with much natural beauty. In 1882 there was among its 75,000 inhabitants the usual amount of worldliness and carelessness in spiritual matters. The Second Presbyterian Church had had for one of its first pastors the famous pulpit orator, Henry Ward Beecher. He had ministered to this people for eight years with marked success and although he had been away from the city for thirty-five years, the memory of his powerful preaching and striking personality was still strong. This perhaps influenced the standard set by the pastoral committee in their search for a minister. A newspaper critic declared, somewhat sarcastically and caustically, that "they went to their task with the honest deliberation of county fair judges deciding upon a prize pig."

Eight points were agreed upon by this committee as those by which they were to judge a pastor's qualifications. These were reasonable enough, but their sequence was somewhat unfortunate. In order they stood thus:

1. Personal appearance.
2. Pulpit manner.
3. Delivery.
4. Voice.
5. Intellectuality.
6. Spirituality.
7. Magnetism.
8. Apparent age.

The same journalistic critic, who perhaps had not had much experience in such delicate work, remarked:

Weighing the Call 149

"We can readily see why 'apparent age' should be taken into account in choosing a beefsteak or a chicken but not in selecting a pastor." The committee, however, reported enthusiastically that the pastor of the Fort Street Church, Detroit, met all their requirements and had some excellent qualifications in addition. A unanimous call was extended to him in June, 1882, but he discouraged these advances and suggested that there were also some qualifications which a church should possess when seeking to obtain the man of their choice.

"I am in no sense 'in the market,'" he wrote. "God put me in Detroit and has kept me here by marked providential signs. I would go anywhere at any cost if I could clearly see His blessed hand leading, but I have made up my mind never to take one step of my own towards a change of field. . . .

"I have fought here a thirteen years' battle against worldliness in the church, against having worldly men in the Board of Trustees, worldly singers in the choir, and worldly spirit in the church management. I have stood for a free church, for the pure Gospel and for a deep Christian experience. God has given the victory —at least in large measure—for fully three-fourths of the church are with me.

"There is only one reason why I think it possible that I may leave Detroit and that is that I have substantially completed the work for which God sent me here. But I dare not trust my own judgment to make a decision. Thousands of ties must be sundered and a hundred sceptres of influence laid down. Every worldly consideration binds me to Detroit where my dearest friends abide. If I go elsewhere it will be only that I may reach more souls. If Indianapolis can assure me freer access to the unsaved and an earnest prayerful church to coöperate with me in the effort to evangelize the neglected thousands, all I can say is 'Here am I, Lord, send me.'"

Again and again the call was repeated and the importunity and arguments of the committee finally persuaded him to visit Indianapolis. Here he was greeted with large congregations and received an enthusiastic welcome. He was assured that what the people wanted was gospel preaching and that the officers would coöperate with him in his efforts to evangelize the non-Christian population. This spirit was all that he could desire, but the building was inadequate. For six weeks he weighed the matter and then with a candour that could not be misunderstood he wrote the committee:

"The Lord seems to restrain me from a decision favourable to your call. In a step so momentous and solemn I have a desire to act with more prayerful and hallowed discretion and deliberation than ever before. Among the causes of hesitation none is more prominent than the exceedingly limited capacity of your church. Your membership alone, if all were present at one service, would fill every available sitting. There is therefore no accommodation for other members of the congregation or for the Sabbath-school. There is no room for outsiders at all, and to my mind this is so serious an obstacle to all aggressive work that it alone overbalances all other arguments and attractions which may be presented in favour of the field.

"An audience room whose capacity is barely equal to the actual membership of the church not only limits the possibility of gathering a proper audience of such as need the Gospel, but is a tacit invitation to those who

may not feel strongly impelled to come to remain away.
. . . What force or even honesty can there be in extending an invitation to the Sunday-school members, which we are not prepared to have them accept? Then, of course, for the real power of the Word we must have an unconverted element to work upon, the larger the better, but where are we to put them? You promise to enlarge or build, but the expectation is not the same thing as the accomplishment."

He explained to the church officers the purposes to which he had devoted his life and the principles to which he was committed, namely, the establishment of free churches supported by voluntary contribution and the evangelization of the unsaved. He gave them copies of his pastoral letters and sermons that had aroused opposition in Detroit and they readily agreed to the positions and opinions expressed. A congregational meeting was called and appointed a committee to prepare plans for enlarging the church building and to secure an opera house until the more permanent and commodious accommodations should be provided.

God seemed to be leading in all this, but the ties by which he was bound to Detroit were not to be broken without an anxious struggle. The roots of friendship had gone deep; the people pleaded with their pastor to remain, and their importunity was difficult to resist. He said, "My heart is aching to have this matter set at rest. Do not censure nor reprove nor even persuade me, but pray, pray for me that I may know the will of God and that my life may be all for His glory."

There was also the delightful friendship with Charles Buncher, a prominent merchant, who had been led into new Christian experience and service during the Opera House meetings. This comradeship with a man rippling with buoyant joyfulness and humour opened up to Dr. Pierson a new appreciation of the ministry of good cheer. These two men loved each other like brothers, and many were the hours they had spent together, sometimes in prayer and conference, and at other times in repartee and the exchange of humorous anecdotes. Such an attachment as that for Dr. George D. Baker, pastor of the First Church, meant much to his spiritual life. This man's clear judgment and calm counsel were invaluable to his friend in many a crisis.

In the autumn of 1882 Dr. Pierson removed to Indianapolis—with the consciousness of God's approval of the step and with the confident expectation of larger victories for the Master. The six months which followed were not without success, but they were a sore disappointment to him. He seemed to fail where he had been strongest before, and this period was for years one of the mysteries of his life.

He began by boldly preaching the Gospel of Christ and its necessary influence on personal character. He had not yet won his people's affection or confidence, and was ignorant of their attitude on certain questions of popular amusements. He had strict views of what a Christian should be and do and appealed strongly for a higher type of piety, for an "other-worldly" life.

"I had not finished my first address," he said later, "before some in the audience began to gnash at me with their teeth, because I had assaulted their idols (not even knowing that they were their idols). It was strongly suggested to me that I should stick to the Gospel and leave men's personal habits alone."

Fearless Preaching

The advice was given to the wrong man, for Dr. Pierson knew not the fear of public disfavour, and he did not hesitate to be an iconoclast in breaking the idols that the world held dear. He could not withhold a rebuke when he made a call one evening unexpectedly after prayer-meeting and found some of his church officers at home playing cards.

While many of the members were stirred to new consecration, others seemed predisposed to misunderstand. The pastor had come from a people by whom he was known and loved and who were therefore ready to receive his rebukes and to welcome his advice. In Indianapolis, on the contrary, he was preaching to those who were strangers and he felt that they did not give him encouragement to preach boldly the truth of God as he believed it. There was no lack of numbers in attendance at his preaching, for the church was crowded. Those who appreciated fearless speaking, high spiritual living and deep teaching were enthusiastic. One of his congregation, the attorney-general of the state, Daniel P. Baldwin, wrote in his letter of appreciation:

"Your sermons are most helpful because they are full of Gospel and Scripture and have little of Pierson in them. We in the pews are weary, *weary* of literary essays in the pulpit. There is nothing like the 'full cup' preaching. After six days of work our spiritual natures are parched and shrivelled. The faithful preacher's sermon is like the rain on the dry earth. We need *a special message from the divine Spirit* to get us ready for the coming week."

The church work was blessed in many departments and there were signs of a coming revival. A weekly meeting which was started for church-members for the promotion of personal holiness soon outgrew the pastor's study and adjourned to the Y. M. C. A. Hall and Christians came there from all over the city for prayer and Bible study.

The power of the pastor's prayers was recognized by many of his people who felt themselves ushered thereby into the very presence of God. One of the church officers, with whom he had had some difference of opinion, afterwards wrote of one of these interviews:

"I hope you will still sometimes pray for me in secret as you did that day in your study. I would not take *uncounted millions* for that prayer uttered by you for me by name. Kneeling sometimes in the secret place, I try to recall the words and to imagine that I hear them again."

During the winter months the Grand Opera House was rented for Sunday evening services and the large numbers who attended were a challenge to the speaker to give them his best. He preached a practical gospel for every-day life. The Y. M. C. A. also inaugurated a series of weekly Bible lectures under Dr. Pierson's leadership and the whole Christian community felt the uplift.[1] Letters came telling of new faith and joy in Christ and new love for His service.

Pastors of the city were also stimulated by their new colleague, in whom they found not a rival but a friend and co-worker. One fellow minister testified that the pulpit tone of the entire city was heightened by Dr.

---

[1] His lectures on Christian evidences were afterwards published in a volume, "Many Infallible Proofs," which has been translated into many languages of Europe and Asia.

Henry C. Mabie's Experience 155

Pierson's public work. "His minute and careful word studies helped to drive us younger ministers back to our Greek lexicons and Testaments to see if the wealth of meaning he brought out was really there."

One who has often publicly acknowledged his debt to Dr. Pierson's ministry and personal counsel is the Rev. Henry C. Mabie, D. D., later the home secretary of the American Baptist Missionary Union. In 1882 he was pastor of a Baptist church in Indianapolis and had been for some time in broken health. He was nervously depressed and had decided to give up the ministry. In his trouble he sought a confidential interview with his neighbour, Dr. Pierson, in whom he recognized a man of positive convictions and spiritual insight. After a conference lasting several hours, Dr. Mabie's faith was strengthened, and as they knelt in prayer he testified that he passed through a profound realization of God's loving attitude towards him and saw the divine meaning of his painful experiences.

"I shall always feel," he adds, "that Dr. Pierson was sent to Indianapolis on a particular errand to me at a time when I needed an elder brother. He led me to appreciate the importance of the salvation of the *life career* of each believer in Christ, not simply the salvation of the *soul*. God wants to save the life to use it in His plan. It was at this crucial point that Dr. Pierson found me in my moment of despair. From that hour I became an expository preacher and determined to risk everything in the work of driving home to men's hearts and consciences the divine truths. This method instantly revealed to my people the change that had taken place in me."

Dr. Mabie did not give up preaching but entered on a

long and useful career of service. A revival began in his church in which many were converted.

But while Dr. Pierson's influence was extending to the borders of the city, it was evident that there was a lack of coöperation in his own church. Six months had passed since his installation, and although there were signs of steady growth, no steps had been taken by the building committee to enlarge the church. To suggest it meant friction, to push it meant rupture. A few influential men strongly opposed it; others, desiring harmony above all things, counselled making no move at all; still others, catching the vision of the church's larger destiny, were eager to follow their leader to new victories. These last also felt that their promise had been given at the time of the call when they had agreed to his conditions.

Dr. Pierson urged enlarging, rebuilding or colonizing—any plan that would give an opportunity for growth—but there was no response. On April 20th he wrote to his session after a night of prayer and mental distress that he felt so hedged about that he was driven to resign. "I wish," he said, "to quietly withdraw and leave the church in peace to pursue what seems to me to be a mistaken—yes, even a suicidal policy."

The resignation was like a bombshell to most of the congregation and for a time threatened to disrupt the church. The pastor therefore consented to withdraw his resignation temporarily until he could explain his position to all the members. A month later a congregational meeting was called together and without making any accusation of unfair dealing or even revealing his bitter disappointment the pastor asked his people to

The Tabernacle Movement

accede to his wishes and to maintain their undivided allegiance to the church organization. With no other church in view and with no knowledge of whence he might expect support for his family of ten, he repeated his request for release and it was granted. A newspaper reporter commented on this action as follows:

"It is not often, in an age so devoted to the pursuit and adoration of wealth as this is, that a person resigns a position with an income of $5,000 a year, and goes out into the world to preach without the least assurance of pay, literally trusting that 'the Lord will provide.' Dr. Pierson's religious enthusiasm has also led him to distribute to religious or charitable societies all, or nearly all, the savings of past years. There is a picture on which Robert Ingersoll may gaze with reverence. While the brilliant infidel is defending the vilest criminals for about $100 a day, the preacher is sacrificing wealth and social position for a precarious existence at the bidding of a call which he believes to be sacred."

When the fact of his resignation became known there was a determined effort on the part of another church in the city to secure Dr. Pierson's services. They promised to build a free tabernacle, and to conform its management in all things to his ideas. A number of leading, spiritually minded men agreed to serve as elders, deacons and trustees, and hundreds of letters followed him to the little retreat to which he had gone to be alone. Details of the plans, which were really of his own suggesting, were laid before him, and he was not only urged to father the new work but many felt that he could not conscientiously decline. This call which seemed to him to present such a longed-for opportunity did not commend itself to his friends. A letter of excellent counsel was written to him by his friend, Charles Buncher, of Detroit, in which he says:

"I am convinced that you stand at the critical period of your life. Either you will be led wisely and will become a greater power for the Master or you will increase in restlessness and so lessen your influence and give your enemies greater opportunity for criticism. . . . I do not believe you can make an independent tabernacle movement a success because no man can. The churches would fight it, the devil would fight it, and your soul would wear out your body for very vexation. Give your best labour to a good earnest church, cultivating that vineyard and from that centre reaching out to the masses."

His diaries and letters to his wife attest the days and nights of struggle through which he passed. His own will was towards Indianapolis, where all that he most wished for seemed so easy of attainment. He looked for signs of external leading, but there were none. He wrote: "I cannot get peace on this Indianapolis tabernacle matter. The friends there press me more and more and every letter wrenches me anew, until it seems as though I should go crazy. My nervous system is prostrated. I can find no rest. . . . There must be something lacking in my prayers or the dear Lord would not fail me. . . ." Later he added: "God has answered. I arose at midnight to ask for light. God showed me that in all this movement I had been willful and stubborn, however conscientious. I had been heedless of consequences. I spent the night in prayer beseeching God to enable me to give up my own will, and He did. I then made an entire surrender of this darling project and cove-

Healing a Breach

nanted with God not to take another step without His manifest leading. It became plain to me that I had been fighting against God, persisting in my own way, blind to providential hindrances. . . . I can see now that the more successful the tabernacle movement might be, the more it might hurt the Second Church and the more it might deplete the weaker organizations of the city."

When the seventeenth of July came, the day on which six years before the father and three children had so narrowly escaped drowning, Dr. Pierson wrote his wife:

"The sweet peace of God is given me to-day—this anniversary day which is sad and yet joyful—this day on which we gave ourselves and our loved ones to the dear Lord. God has laid His hand on me, restraining me, and I have ceased to fight for my own will. I have written to Indianapolis declining the call. I shall be abused and misrepresented, charged with breach of faith, but it is a small thing to be judged of man's judgment since He that judgeth me is the Lord. The only thing that disturbs me is that my work in Indianapolis seems destructive so far and not constructive—a church rent, another in formative state without leader or guide and threatening to fall asunder, the enemy triumphant, reproaches falling on friends for their adherence to me—disappointment in the work begun for the Lord. . . . I feel as though I had been beaten sore and bruised from head to foot. I ache at the very remembrance."

In this spiritual struggle Dr. Pierson's physical strength very nearly broke down, but the decision was followed by tokens of God's approval. From time to time testimonies reached him from members of his former church and Bible classes in Indianapolis. One of them reads:

"To me there is no mystery about the purpose of God in bringing you here. It is being revealed in the lives of many who by you were led into truths that centre in the higher Christian experience and who are now entering into the full enjoyment of them. Your reward will come in the revelation."

Five years later the Second Presbyterian Church of Indianapolis invited Dr. Pierson to attend their semi-centennial exercises and he had great pleasure in doing so. The correspondence with one of the church officers who had been especially antagonistic shows the change that the years had wrought.

"*February 24, 1889.*

"MY DEAR DR. PIERSON:

"The portrait of yourself which came in due time now adorns our pretty chapel. It hangs there in company with other honoured and beloved pastors, reminding us of the precious truths you taught and illustrated during your ministry among us. There were some things, many things perhaps to be regretted—things which would not occur again. Sorrowing over them as I recall them I wish to introduce what I have it in my heart to say to you now.

"Your return at our anniversary time was a most happy event. What you said to us in public was most precious. It went to all our hearts like a benediction. It gave us a foretaste of the language of our Father's house, and of the spirit of love that is to be our own in common with all His children when at home in heaven. Those kind words drew us to you then as we had not been drawn before.

"Now, let me say a more personal word, referring to that time when the cross purposes were going on between us in regard to our church work. . . . I know my faults and that there are in me elements that constantly have to be watched lest they bring me into collision with other earnest and positive natures. But pray for me, pray in the secret place as you used to pray when here. I hope to meet you again in earthly places—and so allow me to subscribe myself,

"Your affectionate friend,
"———— ————."

To this letter Dr. Pierson replied:

"MY DEAR BROTHER:

"The blessed Spirit of God must have had full sway in your heart when you wrote that beautiful letter of February 24th. I have had nothing come to me in the course of twenty years more laden with precious fragrance from God's Garden of Spices.

"My residence in Indianapolis I always look back to with unfeigned sorrow and regret. But I want you and the dear friends in the Second Church to know that it is sorrow and regret for my own deficiencies. I had not the requisite patience to wait for results that from their nature come slowly. I was full of a certain sort of enthusiasm and I fear it gave much heat to my nature. I was not calm and could not be content to gain the confidence and coöperation of the people by slow degrees. But I learned many a lesson that is daily blessed to me.

"Brother, you and I are both rapidly nearing the final change. We both know how insignificant are all those little chafings and frettings that often alienate brethren. I am glad to say, in full and hearty response to your thoroughly Christian letter, that in my heart only a great love burns towards my beloved brethren in the church at Indianapolis. With love to your entire household and many prayers for your good old age with perpetual sunshine.

"Affectionately yours,
"ARTHUR T. PIERSON."

This letter brought the following response:

"From the bottom of my heart I thank you for your letter. It is very precious to me and many times I have thanked God for it. He only could have inspired it. The words linger in my memory and sing to me by day and by night. Notwithstanding the short time you were here, there is much in your ministry for which I am thankful. *You preached the Gospel faithfully and savingly.* I thank God that I was permitted to hear it. I do not know that I ever addressed you as 'my dear pastor' while I might have done so. It is in my heart to do so now. I know of no one at whose feet I would more gladly sit to learn of Him whom you serve and whom I trust I also love. . . . Your letter has made me value my membership in the household of faith more than ever before. The sacred office of the ministry also assumes more real and personal nearness to me."

The story of the breach and its healing, the story of the lesson and its learning is complete.

Without doubt the greatest benefits of the Indianapolis experience were the lessons learned by Dr. Pierson himself—a conviction which he expressed in a letter to former parishioners in Detroit:

"I believe that I was sent here as much for my own instruction as for service. I have learned in these short months lessons as to human nature, and my own nature; in ways to do the Lord's work so as to reap results. I see now how I might have changed my ministry in Detroit so as to double my usefulness, if I had only had another spirit in my work. I have strong convictions and am often impatient for results. I might have drawn those whom I repelled and might have assimilated where I failed to mould; might have led where I drove. I will henceforth try the new force of love and patience and prayerfulness, not urging my own views unduly but putting responsibility where it belongs. My chief work seems to be to bring disciples to a higher level. Oh, that I could with present experience bring back lost opportunities and start afresh with my new knowledge of myself or others and of God."

Dr. Pierson's experience and success in evangelistic work led him to think seriously of devoting himself to general evangelism. He wrote to friends about it but they discouraged any such departure. One faithful adviser wrote:

" I believe your place is at the head of a large flourishing, progressive and aggressive church. God has fitted you to be a teacher rather than an evangelist. Frankly I do not think you are sympathetic enough for a popular evangelist. I do not think you could draw the hearts of these masses as your soul yearns to do."

God had manifestly been preparing His servant for a more educational ministry, and when the lesson of patience and submission had been learned in Indianapolis He opened the door into another field which was more nearly to his mind. Bethany Church, Philadelphia, was a large congregation of middle class wage-earners and with it was connected a still larger Sunday-school, superintended by John Wanamaker. This church now gave him a hearty call but the very size of the church was now a cause for hesitation. Dr. Pierson wrote:

" My desire is to take a small church and mould it to my mind. To have a Sunday-school with Bible models, maps, etc., instead of a library with passing fiction ; an undenominational sort of church, with a font for immersion of those who believe in that form of baptism."

He frankly stated his premillennial views and expressed his desire for inquiry meetings after the preaching services. The reply from Mr. Wanamaker took the arguments he had offered against coming and turned them into reasons for acceptance. "It seemed," he wrote, "as I read your views and your plans as though you must have hovered about us and our church all these years, and stood over the Bethany work to make me and the church so closely akin in spirit and life to what is your ideal. I believe through and through in your plan for a broad Bible church. Strange, isn't it, that builded into Bethany, covered up until wanted, is a baptismal pool waiting for the man wise and brave enough to use it! For years we have taught our scholars to bring their Bibles to Sunday-school. We have no Sunday-school library. We discarded it ten years ago, disgusted with the silly fiction it was distributing, so that the way is clear for any new plan. Your 'after meeting' thought has been one of the plans in our hearts for some time. And I have always held the view of our Lord's Second Coming with you and take comfort in the blessed hope that His day may dawn at any moment."

It was not to be wondered at that Dr. Pierson felt that God had taken out of his way every obstacle, and seemed to have made the work for him and him for the work. After a series of conferences in Philadelphia he accepted the call and entered upon his work in the autumn of 1883, at forty-six years of age—in the prime of life. "The call to Philadelphia," he said, "came by way of the Indianapolis pastorate."

X

THE PHILADELPHIA PASTORATE—THE FIELD AND THE FORCE

"THE Ideal Church" usually exists only in the mind of man or in the plan of God. Arthur T. Pierson had before his mind and heart such a church—ideal not in its attainment but in spirit and purpose. He set as a standard four characteristics:

"(1) Evangelical in faith; one that accepts and adopts the Bible teachings as the rule of life.

"(2) Evangelistic; one that seeks to obey the command of Christ to carry the Gospel to every creature.

"(3) Educative; one that aims to reform and instruct the individual so as to benefit the family, the commonwealth, the nation and the world.

"(4) One that will not tolerate the spirit of caste, and in which the seats are free to all who will come."

Dr. Pierson had heard of Bethany Church and of its founder, John Wanamaker, and was prejudiced against both. He had been given an idea that the Sunday-school was entirely too unconventional. That sometimes it was like a school, at other times like a salvation army meeting, and at others more like a circus. He had thought that the superintendent was an ambitious, adventurous young man who did things, but did them in his own fearful and wonderful way, as though with wind, water and steam all at once. Some of these impressions had been corrected before the first intimation of a call reached him, but when it was suggested that this would be a good field of labour he replied: "I may some day take a pastorate in Philadelphia, but never in Bethany." He said later that he was thankful that kind Providence had pigeonholed that remark along with his wife's statement that she might some day marry—but never a minister.

Philadelphia was then the third city in size in the United States—conservative in social and religious ideas, a city famous for the number of its homes for thrifty wage-earners of moderate means. Bethany Church was composed largely of people of the middle class, earnest and sympathetic. Sittings were rented, but at so low a rate that they were within reach of the poorest. The work was well organized and the evangelistic spirit was strong. The membership was nearly double that of either the Detroit or the Indianapolis church, and the Sunday-school was one of the largest and best equipped in the land.

Bethany had had a unique history. One winter afternoon in February, 1858, John Wanamaker, a young man then twenty years of age, went with a missionary of the American Sunday-school Union, E. H. Toland, to start a mission school in the second story back room of a humble house on Pine Street, Philadelphia. The workers and the few children who came together were soon driven out by rowdies who were terrors to the neighbourhood. Not at all discouraged Mr. Wanamaker found another room on South Street and there began his Bethany mission, with twenty-seven children and four teachers. The work grew and when summer came the school moved into a large tent accommodating four hundred people. Services were

The Beginning of the Work

held on Sunday nights and men and women were converted. Prayer-meetings were added and in 1865 a church was organized with twenty members. Twenty years later there was a church-membership of 1,500 and a Sunday-school of 2,500. The brown stone buildings which housed them were together capable of accommodating audiences of five thousand and they represented an investment of half a million dollars, although most of the members were far from wealthy. In this twenty years that whole section of the city had been transformed. Drinking saloons, and low hovels had given way to well-built but economical homes. Sobriety, thrift and piety were evident where once drunkenness, crime and idleness prevailed.

To this attractive field Dr. Pierson was called on June 27, 1883, before he had ever preached in Bethany pulpit or had even attended the prayer-meeting. When he was offered a salary of $5,000 a year, he replied: "I will go alone with God in prayer for a week or more before I decide." He went to Niagara-on-the-Lake and after a month wrote to the committee:

"I have a divine assurance that I should come to Bethany and have decided to accept the call but not the $5,000 a year. That would be too much more than the average income of the members and would prevent me from getting as close to them as a pastor should. I will come for $3,000 a year. We can live nicely on that and still give our tenth to the Lord."

He entered upon the work in October with a determination to devote his best energies to the development of his new people as a working force for the evangelization of the city, the nation and the world. He found able and consecrated co-workers. Mr. Wanamaker proved a true friend, a generous and loyal supporter of every good project suggested by the pastor, and was a warm personal friend and a wise counsellor.

The first year in Bethany was spent in studying the local conditions and the available forces at close range, in efforts to build up the existing services and organizations and in making 2,000 pastoral calls. The opportunities had not been misrepresented, but there were enough hindrances to call forth all the pastor's energies and to send him to God for wisdom and power.

1. First there was a debt of $47,000 which caused a disinclination on the part of the people to undertake any new work involving expense.

2. The work of ministering to three or four thousand people was too heavy for one man who was to be pastor, preacher and teacher, but there were no funds with which to pay an assistant.

3. There was a lay college in which secular subjects were taught, but it was in debt and added to the financial burden of the church. The secular seemed also to be obscuring the spiritual in the college work.

4. There were cases of open sin in the congregation, which caused unbelievers to blaspheme and hindered spiritual growth.

5. There seemed to be a lack of sufficient material for strong church officers. Among the noble and able men in the congregation comparatively few had leisure, piety, tact and intelligence combined in such proportions as to make them strong elders, trustees and deacons.

6. The church officers were so busy that it was difficult to secure their attendance generally at prayer-meeting or even at session meetings.

7. Some of the minor organizations had been in-

Facing New Problems 169

vaded by a spirit of strife and seemed to be promoting dissention.

As he studied these problems and elements of weakness he wrote in his private devotional diary:

"I must cast myself on God and never let a day begin or end without prayer and *devotional* Bible study. I must be careful to be always on guard against ill-temper or impatience or morbid moods and must do nothing without sanctifying it with the Word of God and prayer. Above all I must make constant supplication for spiritual power and anointing. I must watch for souls as one who is to give account unto God. The Lord is under no restraint to save by many or by few. He can show how to pay the debt and how to meet expenses. We need frequent meetings of the session for prayer and conference. Every sermon must be a consecrated effort to win souls."

The first strengthening of the bulwarks and the training of the working force was in the famous Sunday-school. A teachers' meeting for consecration was held and the class for the exposition of the Sunday-school lessons, which had been discontinued, was revived. The pastor assumed charge of this class and the growth in attendance was so rapid that frequently there were more than one thousand present. With the help of a large blackboard Dr. Pierson taught the international lesson for the coming Sabbath in an informal, practical way that drew many teachers from all over the city. A little later he was petitioned to give these lectures to all the teachers of the city every Saturday afternoon in the Y. M. C. A. Hall. There he continued the work for several years and many testimonies speak of the blessings received in these gatherings. These lesson studies became one of the greatest features of his Philadelphia ministry. He put hours of study, and a large measure of vital energy into this work, planning unique outlines, acrostics and rhymes to help deficient memories.

In the Sunday-school work John Wanamaker was a faithful co-labourer whose letters to his officers and teachers were often inspired by the pastor's words. In one of these letters he wrote:

"Dear Fellow Teacher:

"I have just come from Bethany teachers' meeting and am thinking of the earnest talk that followed the pastor's lesson. It was about winning souls. I wish all the teachers could have heard it. God Himself seemed to be opening a door to each of us for service. Some of us have been 'saying lessons' to our classes. We have been entertaining and friendly with our scholars but is it not possible to do more? Choose one in your class and work and pray for that one to bring that soul to Christ and when God honours your faith pick some one else and see how many souls God will give you by the next communion. . . . 'He that winneth souls is wise.'"

With such a pastor, such a superintendent, and with many consecrated officers and teachers, it is not surprising that Bethany Sunday-school was and is famous the world over. The large, well-lighted building, seating 3,000, is in many respects a model of construction. A fountain plays in the centre; large class rooms open out on all sides; circular seats bring teachers and pupils close together; the platform holds a large orchestra and back of it is space for the platform class.

Bethany was a church school, under the close supervision of the session, and included in its membership those of all ages and conditions from the children just learning to walk to tottering old men and women. The aim of the school was that it should include the whole church in the systematic study of the Word of God. The show of uplifted Bibles each Sunday in all classes revealed the fact that this was indeed a *Bible* school. At the inquiry meetings after the close of the session many hearts have been given to Christ.

One unique feature of the Bethany work was the college which had been founded in 1880 to offer an opportunity to day workers for evening studies. It met twice a week for three terms of nine weeks each. In addition to twelve secular branches Dr. Pierson organized a religious department to include lectures on Christian Doctrine, Church History, and practical work. The tuition fee to members was only twenty-five cents a term and the enrollment was over seven hundred. The entire body of students took the courses under the pastor, and one encouraging result was the linking of the religious with the secular in such a way as to bring God more into daily life. New interest was aroused in practical godliness and many developed a taste for religious knowledge and activity. An "Evangelist Band" of young men was organized, with thirty members pledged to do definite Christian work. On their knees, the members of this band signed a solemn agreement:

"In joining the Evangelist Band, I purpose with God's help to maintain and live, not only a strictly moral and temperate life, but to be an example to all believers in godliness and purity, and to devote such portion of my time as may be consistent with other duties to the direct work of witnessing for Christ and of winning souls to Him."

Then these young men went out conquering and to conquer. They visited houses and established cottage prayer-meetings. They started a branch Sunday-school and mission in an outlying district. They preached in open lots and won men and women to Christ.

The work outgrew the supervising power of one pastor, and Thomas C. Horton, a young business man who had been led into Christian work under Dr. Pierson's ministry in Indianapolis, was called to be assistant pastor. Under his leadership the young men put up a gospel tent in a neglected quarter of the city. They secured the use of a vacant lot, dug post-holes, bought lumber and with their own hands built a high board fence, a platform and benches. There they held Sunday-school and preaching services. So great was the interest that in the autumn they put in stoves and continued the services during the winter. The young men acquired a taste for soul-winning and the whole work of Bethany Church shared in the blessing. The spirit of personal work spread through the congregation; in three months the list of converts reached 538, many of whom were enrolled in classes for further instruction. All this was done without special advertising, paid evangelists or extra services. Of the original Evangelist Band several were led either into the mission field, into the home ministry or into some other distinctive Christian service.[1] The mission itself developed into the John Chambers Memorial Church, now an independent and strong organization.

---

[1] The results of these and former experiences Dr. Pierson put into a volume entitled, "Evangelistic Work in Principle and Practice." This has been widely published and translated and has led to the establishment of similar bands and training schools in London and elsewhere.

An Ideal Charge to a Pastor 173

When Mr. Horton was ordained and installed as assistant pastor, Dr. Pierson gave to him an impressive and unique charge, the outline of which is worth quoting as a model for such an occasion:

" You have crossed a line which you cannot recross from simple membership in the church into its ministry.

" You are a minister of the Word and your great work is to study and unfold that Word.

" You are a minister of Jesus Christ. The Word is mainly precious as the casket which enshrines this priceless jewel. 'In the Volume of the Book it is written of Me.'

" You are a minister of the Holy Spirit. The application of the Word of God and the blood of Christ is solely committed to Him. . . . My brother, you are to be a Bible man, a Christ man, a Holy Spirit man.

" You are a minister of the Church. For the sake of the Church the ministry exists. You are to be a winner of souls, a keeper of souls, to gather God's penitent believers out of the world and gather them into His fold.

"The pastor is literally a *shepherd*, which implies a flock. The pastoral duties are to lead, to feed, to guard, and to govern.

" 1. Leadership. The Good Shepherd 'goeth before' his sheep. He leads rather than drives. He goes before by voice and by example.

" 2. Feeding the flock. The sheep and lambs have every variety of spiritual need and you are to search for the variety of food adapted to these needs.

" 3. Guarding the flock. David slew the lion and the bear lest a kid might be lost. He risked his own life to save the humblest of the flock.

" 4. Governing the flock. The pastoral staff is a symbol of authority. Church government and discipline are sadly in danger in these days. Take firm hold of your pastoral staff, for you will need to use it in loving but faithful correction.

"In all these duties you will need to follow the Chief Shepherd. With your eye on Him, you cannot go far astray. . . .

"Your *pulpit* will, I hope, be not only in the church but in any place where you can, by tongue or pen, appeal to men in the stead of Christ—a street corner, a dry-goods box, a green hillock or a stone by the wayside.

"Your *library* will, I hope, be mainly composed of four books, constantly and carefully studied—the book of God's Word, the book of God's works, the book of God's providence or history, and the book of human nature. To understand these four volumes is to be a master workman.

"Your *sermons* will, I hope, be largely living epistles composed of your own beautiful example and the lives of those converted through your instrumentality,—living sermons.

"Your *weddings*, may they be many! joining penitent believers like chaste virgins to Christ the heavenly bridegroom.

"Your *funerals*, may they be equally numerous! burying the sins of transgressors out of sight—the doubts, vices, inconsistencies of professed disciples in the sepulchre of a forsaken past.

"Your *vacations*—may they be frequent in the relief and refreshment of daily prayer and communion with God, resting in Him and with Him.

"Your *parish* is broader than this church and will be found wherever there is a soul to be saved.

"Your *monument* will be found in the hearts and lives of disciples whom you have benefited."

Mr. Horton proved to be a noble helper in the work of the church. His cheerful optimism and his hearty response to any plan suggested by the pastor levelled the mountains and exalted the valleys to prepare the way of the Lord.

A Vision of the Future 175

The White Ribbon Army was organized in Bethany on December 7, 1884, with Dr. Pierson as its first president, and soon had five hundred pledged to temperance in the church and Sunday-school. This organization afterwards spread to practically every state in the Union and in a few years enrolled thousands of members.

Other plans suggested by the pastor were adopted —some of them with temporary and some with permanent success. There were organizations covering numerous interests for all classes and all ages. A partial list includes :—the Ladies' Prayer-meeting, the Ladies' Foreign Missionary Society, the Dorcas Society, Young Ladies' Aid Society, Evangelists' Band, Young Christians' Association, Young Ladies' Prayer-meeting, Young Girls' Association, Busy Bees (for children), Young People's Society, Male Choir, Converts' Class, Bethany Aid, Door Men's Association, and Bethany College.

In connection with the twentieth anniversary of Bethany Church in 1885, the pastor outlined in his sermon on "The Vision of the Future" more of his conceptions of the standards a church should seek to attain. Much is worth quoting, but there is space for but a few paragraphs:

"I. *Financial Outlook*. Money is at the root of most good things in the world as well as of a great many evil things. I say without hesitation that the basis of church prosperity is largely a financial basis. When Aaron and Hur held up the hands of Moses they first seated him on a *stone*. He had a firm place on which to rest. How can a pastor or church work for Christ when in the miry clay of debt? Let there be a solid material basis and then the work of evangelization can go forward. Money is a stepping-stone to good or a stumbling-stone to ruin. But in addition to the removal of the debt we need to cultivate habits of systematic, proportionate giving. Hundreds of people come and go week after week without taking any real share in the financial burden of the church. If there is anything I seek to secure it is that every man, woman and child shall be a giver in the house of God. . . . So here is my financial outlook—the debt paid off, every bill honoured, every repair and improvement necessary completed, and all members of this congregation conscientious givers as God has prospered them, by pennies, dimes and dollars, for the purposes of the kingdom of God.

"II. *The Social Outlook.* The church is a society and needs a spirit of fellowship and union. In a large church it is difficult to maintain acquaintance and so there often develops a spirit of caste. Everybody who comes should be welcomed, whether he comes with ragged clothes and an unwashed face or rolls up to the door in a carriage. . . .

"III. *The Educational Outlook.* It is a great mistake to undervalue culture. One with the grace of God in his heart and an educated mind can do more than one without trained intellect. Culture elevates the whole sphere of our employments and amusements. The college, with its growing power over the young people, will do an educative work that is not to be despised; for years, perhaps for generations to come, the influence will be felt.

"IV. *The Spiritual Outlook.* This is the most important of all, for spirituality lies both at the bottom and top of all true living. . . . God must be magnified in the whole service. . . . The singing and preaching must not exalt human art. . . . Prosperity does not consist in numbers. Sensationalism may draw a crowd but the greatest power is in the consecrated few. . . . Do not mistake the enthusiasm of numbers for the influence of the Holy Spirit.

. . . Magnify the power of the prayer of faith and the spirit of evangelism. . . . The church that does nothing for outsiders will do poorly by insiders."

At the first anniversary of the church after he had assumed the pastorate, Dr. Pierson asked his people to undertake to lift the load of the $45,000 debt, the $2,000 floating indebtedness having already been paid. His friends urged him to let it alone on the ground that it had been incurred previous to his pastorate and that the business conditions and poverty of his people were not favourable to such an undertaking. One friend wrote:

"You are treating yourself as if you were the same Goliath in *body* that you are in *spirit*. But you are not. I wish I could push you into an easy chair and make you stay there. You're burning the candle at both ends."

But he was not to be deterred from the effort to remove what he believed to be an incubus on the church. He began a systematic endeavour to educate the people into a higher standard of giving and to teach them the joy and blessing of it. Sermons and midweek prayer-meetings considered the Bible standards of benevolence. It was shown that among the Hebrews the people were required to give a poll-tax, tithes and first fruits. In addition to that there were free-will offerings and jubilee gifts. The pastor explained that the New Testament standard is even higher and that a Christian's gifts are judged, not by the amount he gives, but by the amount and proportion he keeps. Selfishness grows by indulgence; so does liberality. A careful estimate was made of the resources of the congregation and it was found that the total yearly income of 500 families would be not less than $300,000. One-tenth of that sum would yield a revenue of not less than $30,000. Next he called the congregation together and explained the need of paying the debt and his own conviction that the way to do it was not to get up entertainments and sales but to honour the Lord with their substance, little or great, and with the first-fruits of all their increase. He told of a woman who was asked to be one of one hundred ladies to give a small gift of $2.00 each to missions. She declined on the ground that she was already giving all that she was able. The subscription plan failed and then this woman suggested a Missionary Supper, with contributed articles of food and tickets at fifty cents each. She was interested in the success of the plan and agreed to give two turkeys and to buy five tickets. Thus she spent her time and paid six dollars in money, whereas she had thought she could not afford to *give* two dollars outright. Even though such methods may at first realize more money, giving brings more satisfactory results in the end. In the "Supper Plan," also, the money did not all go to missions and the givers were not trained in unselfish benevolence.

The Bethany people caught the pastor's enthusiasm and a few prosperous members gave largely on condition that the whole amount should be raised. The poor also gave generously. A self-denial society was started, every member of which promised to pay ten cents a week extra saved from personal expenditures. The payments were made to authorized collectors and were entered in a pass-book. Jugs were furnished in which additional sums could be deposited. There were quarterly meetings of the society, open to members only, and at the annual meetings reports were given and jugs were

Burning the Mortgage 179

broken. The members were divided into sections as follows:

1. *Tobacco section.*—For smokers and chewers. It being conceded that any one who used the weed could easily deny himself the worth of a dime a week.
2. *Anti-tobacco section.*—For abstainers. If some can spend money on the luxury of tobacco, those who do not can give at least ten cents a week.
3. *Nicknack section.*—For ladies who can save from sweetmeats, ribbons, pin money.
4. *Housekeepers' section.*—For housewives, to encourage economy in table expenses and luxuries.

The result of the pastor's teaching and of the self-denial society was seen in many members and yielded during the next year an income of $25,000 for church expenses and benevolence. In four years the happy result was that the whole amount of the debt was subscribed and one Sunday morning the gifts were brought and laid on the communion table as an offering to God. None were impoverished by the experience but many were enriched in their spiritual lives.

The occasion of "Burning the Mortgage" was a memorable one. It was planned to resemble a funeral with a joyous conclusion and notices were sent out as follows:

"NOTICE. *Died*, after a lingering illness, by violent collapse, Bethany Mortgage, last survivor of the church debt. As his life was only a curse, his death is only a blessing. Consequently there are no mourners. The funeral ceremonies will be observed as an occasion of thanksgiving and congratulation."

Some of the daily papers found only occasion for criticism, so that Dr. Pierson prefaced his original

"Poem on the Burning of the Mortgage" by a few words of reference to their attacks.

"I beg to say in behalf of the Committee that in the joyful rebound from the bondage of many years, we have felt that it would be entirely in keeping to call our neighbours and friends together to rejoice with us. This old debt seemed to us like some vampire that had been sucking our very blood and threatening our very life. And as it was believed that vampires had some strange life that could only be destroyed by cutting off their heads and burning their hearts, we thought it entirely innocent on our part to cancel the face of this mortgage and then reduce it to ashes. . . . This death was no occasion for mourning, but rather for rejoicing. The idea of death suggested the kindred idea of a final disposition of the carcass of this vampire. That we might avoid offense to propriety, we chose not burial, which is a Christian custom, but cremation or burning which is a modern and scientific method of preventing unhealthy results from natural decay.

"It is a matter of regret to us that our program has attracted the adverse criticism of the public and especially of the newspapers. A proper consideration of the delicate taste and tender conscience of the press would have led us to avoid all such breaches of propriety. The newspapers are themselves very particular never to spread in their columns needless, disgusting details of crime to poison the imagination of young readers; they never issue Sunday editions to interrupt the spiritual worship and service of the Lord's day; they never retail jokes and jests which turn Holy Scripture into ridicule, or repeat anecdotes which contain profane and blasphemous allusions to divine things. . . . So we are especially sorry that our program should have been open to the criticism of these sensitive educators of public taste and conscience.

"Hereafter we shall be doubly careful of our use of terms and never speak of a debt as *expiring*. We shall

Private Prayer Life 181

undertake to be as *grave* as the subject demands, and not travesty solemn realities. It shall be henceforth unlawful to speak of *burying the hatchet* or of burying animosities in the *grave of oblivion*. Suffice it that we have *appalled* the public for once, by venturing to speak of a *dead debt*, whose departure no one mourns, and whose remains we propose to get out of the way."

Among those who took part in the services were John Wanamaker, Dr. J. R. Miller, Dr. Theodore L. Cuyler, Rev. John Hall, D. D., and Dr. Samuel T. Lowrie. The program included the tolling of the bell, a funeral march by the orchestra, a humorous funeral oration and dirge, and a cremation. The joy was as universal as the self-denial had been and every member of the church entered fully into the spirit of the unique program.

It may be well here to turn aside again to study Dr. Pierson's own prayer life and habits. He was slender in body but vigorous in mind and almost reckless in his expenditures of physical energy. At one time he was ill in bed for a week and remarked to a friend who visited him, " No doubt the Lord had many things to say to me that I was too busy to hear, so He put me on my back that I might listen."

His habit of excessive introspection is noticeable throughout his diaries and the extreme sensitiveness of his nature made his body subject to many more than necessary ills. Anxiety about himself, his family or his church would often rack his sympathetic nervous system and bring on a severe attack of fever or exhaustion.

It was by prayer that he sought relief from the anxieties of his work and endeavoured to regain his spiritual poise and vision of God's will. He kept a

Prayer Record[1] in which he noted the date when each special request was begun, the promise pleaded, the petition made and the answer received. A few of these entries are quoted to show the range of his supplications.

Prayer Begun	Promise Pleaded	Request	Answer
Nov. 1, 1883	Phil. iv. 6	Restoration of MS.	Nov. 7, 1883
" " "		Assistant in Bethany	T. C. Horton
Jan. 29, 1884	James v.	Conversion of R. B.	Died in hope
" " "		Illness of Wm. McC.	Recovered
" " "		Harmony between W. and L.	Adjusted
Feb. 15, 1884		Revival in Princeton	Answered
Mar., 1884		Removal of Debt	Feb., 1888
May 1, 1884		Home for Summer use	May 7, 1884
Feb. 6, 1885	Matt. vi.	Banishment of Anxiety	1888
May, 1886		New Power in Pulpit	1888–9
Mar., 1889	Ps. cxlv. 18, 19	Personal Holiness	

The man himself is best disclosed in these private diaries. His strong individuality had many failings which he himself recognized but which he was slow to acknowledge to others. One who knew him well for many years remarked: "He was humble before God but not always before man."

A single prayer recorded in his devotional diary will reveal the spirit of the man's supplications for himself. There are other prayers for his family, his friends, his church and the world.

"O God, my Father, help me to be *wholly* Thine. My temper consecrated so that my whole disposition may accord with Thy will and reflect Thy love; my tongue consecrated that a double watch may be kept especially from saying what is not perfectly accordant with truth, purity and charity. My pen consecrated that every line I write may bring glory to Thee. Es-

---

[1] This plan was so helpful to him that he later published a little record book with lined spaces and with appropriate Bible verses encouraging to prayer.

pecially help me to promote the coming of Thy kingdom—to set myself apart to the great work of a world's evangelization—to save money on self that it may be spent on Thee and Thy cause; to sacrifice superfluities and luxuries to supply the poor with the necessaries of life and the heathen with the bread of life; to live simply and inexpensively that we may give abundantly.

"Teach me to pray believingly and prevailingly to know that Thou art mine and I am Thine. . . . Let the products of my entire thinking be laid at Thy feet and help me to be unconsciously humble lest I be betrayed into the worst of all forms of pride—the pride of humility. Particularly help me not to seek great things for myself but all for Thee."

He devoted an hour to devotional Bible study before breakfast. After family worship he spent an hour (8:30 to 9:30) with his letters and answered all his correspondence by hand. He never could accustom himself to a stenographer either for personal letters or literary work. The remainder of the morning he spent in creative work or study for sermons, lectures, books or articles for the press. After luncheon he usually took an hour (2 to 3 P. M.) for reading books and papers and covered an immense territory in almost every branch of literature. Popular books were reserved for evenings with his family.

The hours from 3:00 to 5:30 in the afternoon were occupied with pastoral or friendly calls, with shopping or outside speaking engagements, or with recreation when possible. The evenings were usually filled with committees, addresses and other church or outside work, but at least one or two evenings a week were reserved for his family.

One habit formed in Philadelphia was ever afterwards a source of strength. Before retiring he was accustomed to sit in a chair for half an hour reviewing the day, its failures, opportunities and victories, that he might gain, if possible, God's view-point. Then he would spend a brief season in *audible* prayer, presenting definite petitions for himself, his family, his parishioners and the world-wide work that had been laid on his heart. When engagements permitted he retired early—not later than ten o'clock—that he might have at least eight hours sleep and be ready for a new day's toils and battles.

Many have remarked on Dr. Pierson's fluency and power in public and in private prayer. They have coveted the same gift but knew not the rough and thorny path that led to victory. We find in his private diary some intimations of the school of prayer in which he was trained. There was a careful study of the prayers of the Bible, and the words of praise, of adoration, of petition were written out and memorized so that they became a part of the very fibre of his being. In his church and family prayer-records the definite needs, difficulties and temptations of individuals are named and portions of their history are given to present before the Throne. The whole world was included in the scope of these prayers which show an intimate knowledge of the progress and problems of the Kingdom.

This private prayer life, of which the world knew nothing, was the secret of the man's victories over himself, his influence over men and his power with God. Like Jacob he met Jehovah alone in the early hours of the day and learned how to prevail. This was of especial importance in view of the new and larger field of service that was about to open before him.

XI

CONFERENCE AND MISSIONARY WORK—A WORLD-WIDE CAMPAIGN

WHILE Dr. Pierson was devoting his energies to the training of his people at Bethany and in his own prayer life was seeking earnestly for new power and new victories, he himself was being trained, in unseen ways, for a new campaign. His preaching, writings, and Bible lectures had caused his name to become widely known in America and he received many invitations to address colleges, conventions and conferences. While pastor at Detroit and Indianapolis his work had been local, now it was national and was soon to become international. The era of missionary and Bible study conferences was dawning all over America, and Dr. Pierson was recognized as a man peculiarly well fitted for inspiring and teaching such gatherings by reason of his exhaustive study, his wide reading, his retentive memory and his fluent, fiery utterance.

For several years he addressed the Prophetical Bible Conference, conducted by his college friends, Drs. William and Albert Erdman, at Niagara-on-the-Lake, Ontario. Here he came into close fellowship with such Bible students and teachers as Drs. James H. Brookes of St. Louis, Nathaniel West, William G. Moorehead of Xenia, Ohio, and H. M. Parsons of Toronto.

These were the days of warm and even bitter discussion relative to "The Lord's Second Coming."

Pre-millennialists and post-millennialists could scarcely come together for prophetical Bible study without sharp controversy on the subject. Since Dr. Pierson's views had undergone a change, through his interviews with George Müller and his later Bible studies, he held the decided and unyielding conviction that Christians must be ready and looking for the return of the Lord at any moment. He was not prepared, nor did he think it right to prophesy as to dates "since," he said, "the only date given for the Lord's return is 'In such an hour as ye think not, the Son of Man cometh.'" He believed that the world was to be "evangelized" but not necessarily converted before the Lord should come.

His understanding of the teaching of Old Testament prophets and of Christ and His apostles left no possibility of the interposition of a millennium of peace and righteousness before the Second Coming. He was attacked for this belief, and some even maintained that it was incompatible with the evangelistic spirit, injurious to missionary enterprise and deadening to Christian life. His addresses on the subject made a deep impression on many who heard them and sometimes converted even his opponents. Dr. W. G. Moorehead writes: "Some of us will never forget his addresses on 'The Lord's Second Coming as a Motive to World-wide Evangelism' and 'The Comings of our Lord as the Doctrinal and Practical Centre of the Bible.' He spoke without notes and used the blackboard to illustrate the chief points. He pictured to the eye the three great dispensations: The Altar of Sacrifice to represent the Mosaic Age, The Lord's Table to indicate the Christian or Gospel Age, and the Throne and Crown to represent the Millennial Reign."

A Message at Niagara-on-the-Lake 187

Dr. Pierson's positive convictions at this time made him a sharp antagonist but in his later years he came to hold a less militant attitude towards Christians who differed from him on non-essentials. This change is shown in a letter written a few years ago, in which he says:

"I habitually avoid controversy, except on *major* points. . . . After all it is the heart that makes the theology. Let us maintain our witness but not fight too fiercely about minor issues in a day of such awful heresies."

At these conferences he came into contact with Christian teachers and leaders from all over the world and through his addresses and words of counsel influenced the lives of men and women of all ages. Scores were sent to the mission fields; many hundreds were led into deeper spiritual experience and more consecrated spiritual life; and thousands gained new confidence in the Bible and clearer understanding of its mysteries.

It was at the Niagara conference that Henry W. Frost heard in one of Dr. Pierson's addresses the call of God to consecrate his life to foreign missions. Mr. Frost, now for many years the American Home Director of the China Inland Mission, writes:

"What I owe to Dr. Pierson in the dedication of my life to God and in obtaining inspiration for missionary service, seems to call for more than a formal letter. It was he, by an address at Niagara in 1886, who confirmed me in the determination to give myself to God for service in behalf of foreign missions. Although I had been brought up in a Christian family, and had attended many churches, I had never heard a strong address on the subject of foreign missions. In 1885 1 heard two addresses at Niagara-on-the-Lake, one by William E. Blackstone and the other by Mr. Goforth, on this theme. The charts they exhibited and the facts they gave were a revelation to me. I determined to give myself to alleviating the woes of these perishing millions. But before many weeks had passed other interests returned and I forgot the peoples who were far away. I came again to the conference in 1886, seeking Bible teaching. When it was announced that Dr. Arthur T. Pierson was to speak on foreign missions I was tempted to stay away, but finally compromised, deciding to sit outside the pavilion and so avoid being unduly affected. I did so, but, happily for me, could not hear well and finally moved inside. Soon I became absorbed in the speaker and his message as he spoke with soul aflame with compassion for the neglected millions. Under this influence a great soul transaction went on within me and I felt that the One who commanded me to go was waiting for my answer. By God's grace I gave myself to missionary work."

All through his life some of the richest and most abiding fruits of Dr. Pierson's ministry came from the words, winged with prayer, and directed by the Holy Spirit, that found lodgment in men's hearts and transformed their convictions and their destinies. It was an address at New Brunswick, N. J., in 1888, that first gave Samuel M. Zwemer, of Arabia, a sense of the urgency of the missionary task and a conviction that only unbelief and selfishness hindered its accomplishment.

On the day of Prayer for Colleges, in 1886, Dr. Pierson was asked by President James McCosh, of Princeton, to preach in the College Chapel. In the after-meeting a young man arose, in answer to an appeal, and dedicated his life and his energies to Christ. Twenty-five years later, on the occasion of the preacher's golden wedding anniversary, that young man wrote:

"MY DEAR DR. PIERSON:

"There are many throughout the world who are under spiritual obligation to you but there are few who can feel towards you the same grateful and filial love which I feel. Although I grew up in a Christian home and was not unidentified with Christian work in school and college it was in my freshman year at Princeton, on the day of prayer for schools and colleges, after your sermon in the afternoon and at the after-meeting which you conducted in the evening, that I first publicly acknowledged Christ and resolved to join myself openly to His Church. During all the years since, I have owed much to your unfailing interest, encouragement and confidence. For all this I thank you and thank God.

"Ever affectionately yours,
"ROBERT E. SPEER."

In the year 1891, when Mr. Speer was still a student in the theological seminary preparing for his missionary career, Dr. Pierson suggested his appointment to the position of Secretary of the Presbyterian Board of Foreign Missions—a position which he has since filled with such manifold blessing to the cause of missions throughout the world.

In like manner the souls of many other less prominent men were set on fire and their energies were directed into Christian work by contact with Dr. Pierson. One missionary father of world-wide fame wrote from India, in 1884:

"With all the earnestness of my soul I write to thank

you for your kindness to my son, who in a time of great spiritual darkness appealed to you for advice. Poor boy, he had been through a terrible spiritual conflict but, largely through your most excellent advice, he has emerged from the intense darkness into light. . . . He feels much drawn to you and looks upon your counsel almost as a message from above."

This young man afterwards became a missionary and has led hundreds into the kingdom of God.

Another fellow minister's life was brought into line for missionary service by a remark passed on a short railway journey. In the course of the conversation Dr. Pierson said to his seat-mate: "My brother, remember that your parish is not your field. The 'field is the world.' Your parish contains a force committed to you by God to train for Him, that through them He may reach the world field." That remark turned Dr. D. M. Stearns into a missionary and Bible teacher who for over twenty years has conducted weekly Bible classes in many cities. Another indirect result has been the turning of a stream of $650,000 into missionary channels—the gifts sent through Dr. Stearns' church and Bible classes.

"Up to that time," says Dr. Stearns, "I had supposed that my parish was my field, and that to win souls there, and to feed them with living bread publicly, and from house-to-house in pastoral work, was about all that was expected of me; but this quiet message was a word in season, which has borne much fruit, in which we will rejoice together in the kingdom."

During the years of his busy Philadelphia pastorate Dr. Pierson also became linked with Northfield and the Bible conferences inaugurated by D. L. Moody. This union continued to the end of his life and led to the formation of some of his most delightful fellowships with such men as Dr. A. J. Gordon and Joseph Cook of Boston, Marcus Rainsford, F. B. Meyer, Campbell Morgan and George H. C. MacGregor of Great Britain, and others.

Northfield is a spot blessed with great natural beauty. The green slopes of the rolling hills are covered with woods and farm lands. The winding waters of the Connecticut add beauty and freshness to the valley that is noted for the picturesque villages and the schools of learning along its banks. In 1885 the town had already become famous as the home of D. L. Moody and as the centre of his educational work for young men and young women. It has since become a New England Jerusalem to which students go up for preparatory education in autumn, winter and spring, and where Christian workers gather for Bible study in the summer. Dr. Pierson wrote of his first experience at a Northfield Conference in 1885:

"The power of God pervaded the assembly from first to last. At times His presence seemed almost visible. Mr. Moody rang out the motto: 'My soul wait thou only upon God for my expectation is from Him,' and from that moment all eyes seemed turned upward in expectation. Think of it! no program—yet hundreds of believers hanging with deep interest on the lips of speakers. The leader simply looked to God from day to day for guidance and called on such speakers as he felt led to select. At the close Mr. Moody said to me: 'I have attended hundreds of conventions but never one like this for power.' The Spirit's presence was felt in prayer, in song, in speaking, in hearing; not a break nor a blunder nor an inharmonious note nor an infelicitous speech."

Here Dr. Pierson learned new lessons in the Spirit's guidance and here began the warm affection for Dr. A. J. Gordon of Boston, who was for the next decade his intimate friend. The energetic, practical spirituality of Mr. Moody and the quiet, unselfish strength of a man like Dr. Gordon drew, with resistless power, the man who was himself so full of the fire of the one and who longed for the outward evidence as well as the inward experience of the meek and quiet spirit of the other.

This conference not only exerted a deep influence on Dr. Pierson's life but it was destined to produce worldwide results in the missionary cause. The day, August 11th, was given up to prayer for world-wide missions, and Dr. Pierson was asked to deliver a missionary message. The thousand hearers were moved by the masterly presentation of facts and the strong appeal for advance in God's name.

"What is needed," he said, "is a world missionary conference. Let witnesses come from all parts of the world to tell what the Lord is doing, so that we may light upon the altars of our hearts new consecrated fires. Let the missionary societies of all the denominations take part, and let them agree to follow principles of courtesy and comity, so that wherever one denomination has a successful work, other denominations will not interfere, but look farther, and go into the destitute places. At this great council let it be resolved that there shall not be one portion of the earth without some responsible Christian denomination to take charge of its evangelizing. Let the missionaries multiply. Let them be not only educated clergymen, but let them be taken from every walk of life. Let them go through short courses of training in the history of missions, and in the knowledge of the Word of God and Christian doctrine. Then let them go into those great fields, and continue their studies in the language of the heathen among whom they labour. While they are getting acquainted with the people and the language, let them do such work as they can in connection with the mission—setting type, etc., or even menial labour."

He suggested that a call be sent out to Christian disciples of every name to unite in prayer for a mighty outpouring of the Holy Spirit, and further that in some great world centre, at an early date, a world conference be called to consider the immediate evangelization of all peoples.

"Let us have," he said, "an ecumenical council, representing all evangelical churches, solely to plan this world-wide campaign and proclaim the good tidings to every living soul in the shortest time! Let the field be divided and distributed with as little waste of men and means as may be. Let there be a universal appeal for workers and money, and a systematic gathering of offerings that shall organize the mites into millions."

Mr. Moody jumped to his feet and enthusiastically asked the assembly to express their approval of this plan by a rising vote. He appointed a committee of seven, including a Presbyterian, a Methodist, two Baptists, two Congregationalists and a Church of England clergyman with Dr. Pierson as chairman to draw up the "call." In the following form it was ratified by the conference and sent abroad on its mission:

An Appeal to Disciples Everywhere

"*To Fellow-believers of every name, scattered throughout the world, Greeting:*

"Assembled in the name of our Lord Jesus Christ, with one accord, in one place, we have continued for ten days in prayer and supplication, communing with one another about the common salvation, the blessed hope, and the duty of witnessing to a lost world.

"It was near to our place of meeting that, in 1747, at Northampton, Jonathan Edwards sent forth his trumpet-peal, calling upon disciples everywhere to unite in prayer for an effusion of the Spirit upon the whole habitable globe. That summons to prayer marked a new epoch in the history of the Church of God. Prayer bands began to gather in this and in other lands; mighty revivals of religion followed; immorality and infidelity were wonderfully checked; and, after more than fifteen hundred years of apathy and lethargy, the spirit of missions was reawakened. In 1784, the monthly concert of prayer for missions was begun, and in 1792, the first missionary society formed in England; in 1793, William Carey, the pioneer missionary, sailed for India. Since then, one hundred missionary boards have been organized, and probably not less than one hundred thousand missionaries have gone forth into the harvest-field. The Pillar has moved before these humble labourers, and the two-leaved gates have opened before them, until the whole world is now accessible. . . .

"God has thus, in answer to prayer, opened the door of access to the nations. Out of the Pillar there comes once more a voice: 'Speak unto the children of Israel, that they go forward.' And yet the Church of God is slow to move in response to the providence of God. Nearly a thousand millions of the human race are yet without the Gospel; vast districts are wholly unoccupied. . . .

"Christ is waiting to 'see of the travail of His soul;'

and we are impressed that two things are just now of great importance; first, the immediate occupation and evangelization of every destitute district of the earth's population; and, secondly, a new effusion of the Spirit in answer to united prayer.

"If at some great centre like London or New York, a council of evangelical believers could meet, to consider the wonder-working of God's providence and grace in mission fields, to insure fields now unoccupied from further neglect, and to arrange and adjust the work so as to prevent needless waste and friction among workmen, it might greatly further the glorious object of a world's evangelization; and we earnestly commend the suggestion to the prayerful consideration of the various bodies of Christian believers, and the various missionary organizations. What a spectacle it would present both to angels and to men, could believers of every name, forgetting all things in which they differ, meet, by chosen representatives, to enter systematically and harmoniously upon the work of sending forth labourers into every part of the world field!

"But, above all else, our immediate and imperative need is a new spirit of earnest and prevailing prayer. The first Pentecost crowned ten days of united, continued supplication. Every subsequent advance may be directly traced to believing prayer, and upon this must depend a new Pentecost. We therefore earnestly appeal to all fellow disciples to join us and each other in importunate daily supplication for a new and mighty effusion of the Holy Spirit upon all ministers, missionaries, evangelists, pastors, teachers and Christian workers, and upon the whole earth; that God would impart to all Christ's witnesses the tongues of fire, and melt hard hearts before the burning message. It is not by might nor by power, but by the Spirit of the Lord, that all true success must be secured. What we are to do for the salvation of the lost must be done quickly; for the generation is passing away, and we with it. Obedient to our marching orders, let us 'go into all the world, and preach the Gospel to every creature,' while from our very hearts we pray, 'Thy kingdom come.'

"Grace, mercy and peace be with you all.

"Done in convention at Northfield, Mass., August 14, 1885, D. L. Moody presiding.

Committee
- ARTHUR T. PIERSON, Philadelphia, *Chairman.*
- A. J. GORDON, Boston,
- L. W. MUNHALL, Indianapolis,
- GEO. F. PENTECOST, Brooklyn, N. Y.,
- WM. ASHMORE, Missionary to China,
- J. E. K. STUDD, London, England,
- MISS E. DRYER, Chicago,
- D. L. MOODY.

Three years later (in 1888) this call found its answer in the great centenary missionary conference held in London, which Dr. Pierson attended as a delegate, and which introduced him to British Christians as a spirit-filled apostle of modern missions.

This Northfield gathering produced other immediate and far-reaching results. The year following this missionary call, the students of American colleges were invited to gather at Mount Hermon, in the buildings of Mr. Moody's school for young men, and there to spend a month in Bible study and conference. As a result in July, 1886, two hundred and fifty students from ninety colleges came together and inaugurated the first World Christian Student Conference. The mornings were occupied with Bible addresses and talks on Christian work and the afternoons and evenings were devoted to recreation. It was a wholesome summer vacation. The young men were inspired with a new conception of what the Bible was, they saw new visions of the whitening world fields and they were prepared for aggressive, efficient work among their college mates.

Strong speakers were in attendance but Mr. Moody telegraphed to Dr. Pierson in Philadelphia: "I want you at Mount Hermon. Can you come?" He had made arrangements for a western trip, but on the very morning of the telegram's arrival, he received word which caused a change in his plans and all his engagements were cancelled. God had decided the matter and the dispatch went back to Mount Hermon, "God helping me, I will come."

He went North with his family and delivered at the conference a series of addresses on "The Bible and Prophecy"—but this was not the particular message for which God had called him there. There were other plans not in the program. One day, a Princeton student, Robert P. Wilder, came to him and said:

"Dr. Pierson, there are ten or twelve of us who have decided to devote our lives to God as foreign missionaries. We have been meeting every day to pray that others may see the vision and we want you to give us a missionary address."

The regular sessions of the conference were already provided for so that arrangements were made for an extra evening session. The room was crowded, and Dr. Pierson spoke for an hour on "God's Providence in Modern Missions." There was no large missionary map available but the speaker drew a rough outline of the countries of the world on the blackboard and with this he illustrated the divine strategy in modern missions. He voiced the Macedonian call to young men of the Church to give their lives for "*the evangelization of the world in this generation.*" The impression was profound and immediately after the address the students held a consecration meeting. One who was present says: "The sense of the Spirit's presence was so vivid as to be almost visible. Before that week ended the number of volunteers had doubled. Other addresses and conferences followed; the tide of interest rose higher, and before the conference closed one hundred young men had signified their intention, God permitting, to become foreign missionaries. A meeting of nations was called and ten young men representing China, Japan, Siam, India, Denmark, Norway, Germany, Turkey, and the North American Indians voiced their nation's needs in five-minute addresses. It was like a new Pentecost in which the order was reversed and American students heard men of other nations speaking in their own tongue of the wonderful works of God."

Thus was born the Student Volunteer Movement for Foreign Missions, with the inspiring battle-cry, "The evangelization of the world in this generation," which was sounded the next year by Robert P. Wilder and John N. Forman of Princeton in colleges all over the land.

In the summer of 1911 the twenty-fifth anniversary of this Movement was held at Mount Hermon and it was reported that the crusade had spread to Europe and South Africa and that from America alone five thousand Student Volunteers had sailed for foreign fields under the direction of their denominational boards and societies.

Many of the present leaders of the World Student Christian Federation attended this first conference and felt the impress of Dr. Pierson's missionary messages. Among those who volunteered were John

First Student Volunteer Movement 199

R. Mott, now chairman of the Continuation Committee of the World Missionary Conference; Robert P. Wilder, missionary to India and Student Volunteer Secretary in Great Britain; George L. Robinson, for three years teacher in the Syrian Protestant College, Beirut, and now professor in McCormick Theological Seminary; Boon Itt, who returned to Siam to become a Christian leader to his own people; Robert M. Labaree, missionary to Persia and his brother Benjamin Labaree, missionary martyr; and Lewis B. Chamberlain, and John N. Forman, missionaries to India.

God was thrusting out His servant, more and more, into the field of world-wide missions. The year following the Mount Hermon Conference, Dr. Pierson was importuned to undertake the editorship of the *Missionary Review*. This magazine had been founded in 1878 by Rev. Royal G. Wilder, a returned missionary from India, as an independent review to advocate world-wide evangelization. The hands of the pastor of Bethany Church were more than full and opportunities, yes importunities, to deliver addresses all over the land were increasing, but he could not turn a deaf ear to what seemed to him a call of God. He had been well trained for the position of editor by his careful mastery of facts, his literary culture and his wide and growing reputation as a missionary advocate. His book, the "Crisis of Missions," which set forth in a convincing manner the providential openings in the mission fields, had had a wide circulation and exerted an immense influence on the Church. Rev. Donald MacGillivray, now of Shanghai, gives one testimony that might be multiplied many fold, when he says:

"It was Dr. Pierson's 'Crisis of Missions' that so

tremendously stirred up Jonathan Goforth and myself before we ever came to China. So inspiring did we find the book that we gave away hundreds of copies in Canada and I think that book chiefly responsible for the great revival of missionary interest which took place about that time."

On the very day on which Dr. Pierson signed the agreement to undertake the joint editorship with Dr. James M. Sherwood of New York, Mr. Wilder passed away. In the leading editorial a year later (January, 1889) Dr. Pierson wrote:

"We undertook the work because we heard a loud call of God and saw a great need of man. Now it has been clearly demonstrated that just such a review of universal missions is an imperative need of our day; and that in seeking to supply this need we were simply falling into our place in a divine plan. . . .

"No greater need exists than that of the *universal diffusion of information* as to the facts of past and present missionary history. To know those facts, to be informed and to keep informed and fully informed, as to the march of God and His hosts in all the earth, is, in effect, to quicken the pulse of the whole Church of Christ. In missions, Love is the skillful alchemist that turns knowledge into zeal and out of intelligence distils inspiration. If we would have more prayer we must know what to pray about; if we want more money we must know what open doors God is placing before us for the investment of consecrated capital, and what wondrous results He has wrought and is working with the merchant's millions, and the widow's mites; if we want more men and women as workers, the mind and heart and conscience of disciples must be awakened from sleep and aroused from sluggishness, by the electric touch of thrilling facts. If we want more zeal, all true zeal is 'according to knowledge' and consequent upon it. If we want the spirit of holy enterprise, doing and daring for God, missions must be exhibited as the enterprise of the Church, and it must be shown that no equal or proportionate investment of men, means and money ever brought returns so ample—all of which the logic of events stands ready to prove by the most overwhelming of arguments."

Under his editorship the *Missionary Review of the World* set a new standard for missionary periodicals. In those days missionary literature was considered dry reading and appealed only to those of large vision and deep consecration. Dr. Pierson's presentation was picturesque and popular. The artistic sense which he had developed in drawing and painting, with crayon and brush, he now used to portray with vivid, realistic touches the great scenes and heroes of missionary history. He was gifted with the journalistic sense that enabled him to discover obscure characters and little known events and to bring them to public notice. It was he who brought into wide publicity such impressive stories as those of Moravian missions, Thomas Barnardo's work for London orphans, the China Inland Mission victories of faith, the remarkable achievements of Pastor Harms, the Deep Sea Fishing Mission of Dr. Wilfred Grenfell, the romantic stories of Pandita Ramabai, of William A. B. Johnson of Sierra Leone, of William Duncan of Metlakahtla and many others.[1] At the same time he emphasized the Biblical and spiritual basis of missions, the need of generous and sanctified giving and suggested the best methods for awakening the Church to accept her responsibility.

[1] Many of these stories were collected in his four volumes, entitled "Miracles of Missions."

The *Review* also was the first missionary magazine to present a view of the world field and to give an account of the work of all denominations. Thus it became an invaluable help to pastors and to missionaries and referred them to original sources from which they could further satisfy their newly awakened appetite for missionary facts.

The history of the *Review* has thoroughly justified the principles of the editor in its management. In its pages Dr. Pierson advocated and defended many a new or unpopular cause. Years before missionary expositions had been started he urgently called for some one to establish such an ocular demonstration as an unanswerable argument against the assertions of ignorant critics that there were no adequate results from missionary expenditures. He advocated the "living links" between the individual church and the field before any such plan had been adopted by missionary societies. He pleaded for coöperation and union on the part of different denominations and presented a view of the world field without distinction between city, home and foreign missions.

Dr. Pierson's power and authority as writer and speaker in the cause of foreign missions were widely recognized. One admirer remarked that he was "as much a working force in missions as gravity is in the domain of physics" and that he "occupied a field as naturally his own as if he had secured an absolute title deed from the government."

The next step forward was his departure for London as a delegate to the great World Missionary Conference in 1888. This was, in large measure, the culmination of his planning and his prayers. He wrote in his devotional diary in 1887: "My thought and prayer of years have been centering upon the world-wide work of missions and the need for a world council to map out the field and to plan to occupy every part of it. It was laid on my heart in Detroit, and I voiced it there. Again at Northfield, it met with cordial response. This council is now called to meet in London next June and I am asked to go."

On Saturday, May 26, 1888, Dr. and Mrs. Pierson set sail from New York on the 6,000-ton steamship *Umbria*, then one of the largest afloat. This was to be a momentous journey. Dr. Josiah Strong, author of "Our Country" and Dr. Young J. Allan, of China, were fellow passengers, and with them he arranged a series of missionary services on board. This eagerness to advance the cause of Christ marked the whole journey, for, like all his other holidays, it was a tour of service, not a furlough from work.

The first representative World Missionary Conference, which opened in Exeter Hall, London, on Saturday afternoon, June ninth, was in some respects unique in the history of the Church. When before had Christians met, without regard to geographical or denominational lines, to represent a united Christendom seeking to plan a world campaign? There had been other missionary conferences of an informal nature in America and Great Britain but none to which practically all the Protestant Foreign Missionary Societies of the world had sent delegates. The conference of 1860 in Liverpool and of 1878 in London had been comparatively small. The centenary conference of 1888 on the other hand brought together sixteen hundred men and women—leaders in the world-wide missionary campaign. It was an object lesson to the world.

The crowds that sought admittance surprised even the committee and many of the well-planned arrangements needed to be readjusted. The program presented a general survey of the world field and a careful consideration of the efficacy of the various methods of work. Lord Aberdeen presided as chairman and among the distinguished delegates and speakers we find the names of Dr. Robert N. Cust, Dean Vahl of Denmark, Henry Drummond, Dr. Kalopothakes of Greece, Lord Kinnaird, Dr. Alexander McLaren, Sir Monier-Williams, Bishop Crowther of Africa, Cav. Matteo Prochet of Italy, Dr. George Smith of Scotland, Eugene Stock, J. Hudson Taylor, Dr. F. F. Ellinwood of New York, Dr. George E. Post of Syria, Cornelius Vanderbilt, Mrs. Isabella Bird Bishop, and Dr. Gustav Warneck of Germany.

In spite of the presence of men recognized as leaders in Church and state the secular press was inclined to cast stones at the enterprise and so well-informed a journal as the *London Times* said in its issue of June 15, 1888:

"Before the promoters of missionary work can expect to have greater resources confided to them, they will have to render a satisfactory account of their trust in the past. Their progress, it is to be hoped, is sure; indisputably it is slow. A congress like the present would be better employed in tracing the reasons for the deficiency in quantity of success than in glorifying the modicum that has been attained. . . . The cause of missions marches at a pace which appears little more than funereal."

In one of his addresses before the conference, Dr. Pierson set himself to answer this challenge by showing some of the "Triumphs of Modern Missions." The facts which he gave, and his masterly method of mar-

A Challenge Accepted

shalling them, carried conviction and from that hour his fame as a missionary advocate was established in Great Britain. Among other things he said:

"It behooves not Christian nations, which owe all their civilization to Christianity, brought to them by missionaries, to depreciate missions. St. Jerome says that when he was 'a boy living in Gaul, he beheld the Scots, a people of Britain, eating human flesh.' . . . When Julius Cæsar landed at Deal, he found the Britons a mere horde of half-naked savages. It is Christianity that has lifted Britain to the foremost place among the nations of the world."

In twenty minutes he had surveyed the world field in a manner which left no echo of a "funeral march."

This World Conference came in the fullness of time. Thirty years before, many lands were closed to missionaries and men were praying for open doors. Now practically all countries of the world were open to messengers of the Gospel and the work of men, women and young people had been organized to enter the world field. The great need of the hour was a closer coöperation and a spirit of comity between the missionary workers of different denominations. Dr. Pierson urged with all his power that some steps be taken towards such unity of effort, but this convention did not accomplish all for which he hoped and prayed. He said:

"In the presence of the gigantic foe that unites all its forces against the kingdom of Christ it behooves all disciples to stand shoulder to shoulder. . . . We would better stop throwing up defenses and carry the war into the enemy's camp by a united aggressive policy. The voice of God to-day commands *active* coöperation from all disciples in mission work."

But the Church had not yet fully awakened and the various divisions of the missionary army were not ready for union or even for comity. With the foresight of a true seer Dr. Pierson advocated other aggressive steps, many of which have since been taken.

"I am fully persuaded," he said, "that the hope of permanent adjustment of missionary comity is by a missionary committee. The blessed contact here experienced with such overflowing charity should not be broken and lost. . . . What if a committee were appointed consisting of such representative men as Sir John Kennaway, Eugene Stock, Wardlaw Thompson, A. C. Thompson, F. F. Ellinwood, A. J. Gordon, Hudson Taylor, William M. Taylor, Bishop Wilson and Bishop Ninde, which could be organized into an interdenominational committee not for legislation but for counsel. . . .

"Such a committee might be of service (1) in keeping up a living fellowship between denominations; (2) in adjusting matters of difficulty and promoting true comity; (3) in providing for the proper division of fields and forces." Although there was a strong feeling in favour of such action, to Dr. Pierson's great disappointment the rules of the conference did not seem to permit even the passing of a resolution in favour of such a committee.

He lived to see his desire an accomplished fact, but it required twenty-two years more of education before this was brought about. At the Edinburgh Missionary Conference in 1910 a permanent "Continuation Committee" was appointed to represent all the denominations in matters of common interest to the kingdom of God.

The London conference was nevertheless a notable

The Next Step 207

success. The last day was devoted to an all day prayer-meeting. A spirit of harmony had prevailed throughout that might not have been possible at that time had they attempted to pass any radical resolutions. The greatest benefits of the gathering were perhaps that it prepared the way for closer fellowship among those of different denominations, it gave men a broader vision of the field and a clearer conception of the magnitude of their task and of the power of the Gospel. Above all it emphasized anew the need for prayer and dependence on the guidance of the Spirit of God.

Later in the summer Dr. Pierson went into Scotland with Dr. A. J. Gordon, of Boston, to plead the cause of foreign missions in the land of martyrs and missionaries. The success of this tour was so marked that he was invited to return the next year, and to conduct a wider campaign.

He had felt that God was loosing his moorings from Bethany Church and he had offered his resignation to the officers on his departure as a delegate to the missionary conference, but at the earnest solicitation of the church he had withdrawn it. Now, however, this call to Scotland seemed to be the voice of God and after much prayerful consideration he wrote his final letter of resignation.

" I feel myself called to a somewhat peculiar work in behalf of world-wide missions. If I accept a call to any other pastorate it will be to a smaller church where the labour would be compatible with what more and more impresses me as my peculiar mission—to advance the speedy evangelization of the world. At present I have no definite plans save to hold myself open to divine leading and to go where God shows me the way."

The six years at Bethany had been happy and fruitful. The work was well organized and aggressive; the mission was prospering, the Sunday-school was in its usual flourishing condition, missionaries had been sent out and over six hundred members had been received into the church. John Wanamaker and other officers and the people were loath to have their pastor go, and proposed to give him an extended leave of absence or to appoint him their pastor-at-large with a missionary commission, but he replied:

"Let me go, sent in your name as Paul went from Antioch on his missionary journey, but let not my dear people feel they must assume any pecuniary burden which may cripple their benevolent work in other directions."

This step marked another crisis in Dr. Pierson's life. He was conscious of God's call to a wider ministry but he had no human promise of support for himself and his family. A wife, six growing children and an aged mother were dependent on him. His eldest daughter, Helen, had recently gone to Japan as the wife of a missionary, Rev. Frederick S. Curtis. Two sons and two daughters were still in school, the other two daughters were at home. Friends offered to guarantee a definite income if he would remain nominally connected with the church, but this did not seem wise.

For the third time in his life he set out, not knowing from whence his support would come, but he had confidence in the fact that his Father knew what things he needed, and that he could depend on Him for his daily supply. He was not without temptations to accept positions which offered earthly comforts and called for a less heroic exercise of faith in God. On

A Venture of Faith

one such occasion when he had found his financial responsibilities heavy he recorded in his dairy:

"I was approached to consider a call to the ——— church but I felt moved to discourage it. The temptation was the greatest I remember to have undergone. Here are riches, a soft nest, a kind people, a life tenure and provision for disablement or for widowhood of wife. But over against this is my long testimony against large salaries, wealth and worldliness in churches and the conviction that this ease would be purchased at the cost of my wider work for missions. I feel called to self-denial for Christ. . . . I purpose to separate all considerations of money, so far as is possible, from the interests of the kingdom of God. I record my confidence that all needful good will be added to us according to God's promise. I do not desire a large income, as it is too often a hindrance to spirituality and endangers family life by many snares. While I have been living without stated salary I have never lacked any good thing and I believe I never shall."

At this time Dr. Pierson was over fifty-two years of age, a period when many men have laid aside something for old age and begin to think of retiring from active service. The next twenty years were the most widely useful of his life and though he never again undertook a regular pastoral charge and had no invested means of support, it was his frequent testimony that the needs of himself and his family were never before so fully supplied nor was he himself ever so free from anxiety nor was he ever able to give away so much money as after he took this step in faith. God was indeed a bountiful provider.

XII

SCOTLAND AND THE CONTINENT—MISSIONARY CRUSADES

THE visit to the Centenary Missionary Conference in London in June, 1888, was an event that changed the whole course of Dr. Pierson's life. He planned only to attend the conference, present some letters of introduction to prominent men and then to spend a month or two in rest and travel on the Continent; but furlough time for him had not yet come. On sailing for England he entered in his diary,—"Wife and I especially asked of God to-day that this might not be a mere pleasure trip, but that rest and recreation might be combined with service—especially to missions." No prayer was ever more abundantly and literally answered. From the time he boarded the vessel, opportunities for testimony began to present themselves and before he returned four months later he had addressed over a hundred and twenty-five gatherings.

His addresses at the missionary conference bristled with facts, sometimes startling, sometimes distressing, sometimes encouraging, but always unimpeachable. Fires of enthusiasm were lighted and spread over the Continent and the British Isles. At the close of the meetings in Exeter Hall he was invited to address Mildmay and other conferences. Then having no further engagements, his interest in the McAll Mis-

In the Scotch Athens 211

sions led him to visit Paris, in company with Dr. and Mrs. A. J. Gordon of Boston; but their stay was brief, for a call came from Edinburgh which opened the way to definite service. The University students had not yet scattered for the summer and the Scotch delegates from the London conference longed to bring these young men into touch with the forceful facts which had gripped them. They arranged a series of meetings and telegraphed Dr. Pierson and Dr. Gordon asking if they would come over immediately and help Scotland. This meant the giving up of a coveted visit to Switzerland and Rome, but they straightway set out for the Scotch Athens.

An enthusiastic reception awaited them. The initial meeting—a delightful garden party—brought together a large number of leading people of Edinburgh at St. Oswalds, the charming home of Mr. and Mrs. Duncan McLaren. Then followed meeting after meeting and the tide of interest rose higher and higher. The two Americans found a people prepared and waiting, for the large synod and assembly halls were crowded and at times hundreds were turned away.

The Scotch people are able to relish an unlimited amount of religious instruction of the right flavour and meetings four hours in length did not overtax their patience. The speakers were beset with requests to make a missionary tour of Scotland. It was summer and many ministers and their people were on their vacations, but the signs of God's working were so clear that the invitation was accepted. In company with Rev. James Scott of South Africa and Mrs. Stott of the China Inland Mission, Dr. Gordon and Dr. Pierson visited twenty-one of the leading cities of Scotland, and everywhere their progress was like a triumphal march. Not only were there crowded audiences on the Sabbaths but even on damp cold evenings in the week large numbers gathered. In six weeks, Dr. Pierson's voice reached not less than 35,000 people. He presented the facts of missions with map and word pictures, and completely captured the minds and hearts of the Scotch people. If he could not "strike while the iron was hot" he made it hot by repeated blows until the impact of facts and his own fire produced heat. Dr. John Lowe, secretary of the committee, wrote six months later that the results of these meetings had been marked by intensified interest in missions throughout the churches and by the enlarged giving which, he said, "bids fair to place the good old Kirk of Scotland in the forefront of the Evangelical army." The Medical Missionary Society, of which Dr. Lowe was secretary, reported a hundred per cent. increase in the number of candidates offering themselves for the mission field.

This tour had been impromptu, but a committee of influential men, including Principal Cairns of the United Free Church College, Rev. John McMurtrie, convener of the Established Church of Scotland, Sir William Muir, Dr. George Smith, the missionary author, Dr. Alexander Whyte, pastor of Free St. Georges, Duncan McLaren, Esq., with John Lowe, drew up a letter expressing the appreciation of the Scotch people of the help received from Dr. Pierson's and Dr. Gordon's messages and asking them to return the next year for a six months' tour in the interest of missions. They also wrote letters to the Boston and Philadelphia churches, asking them to spare their pastors for a time, and lovingly to set them apart as a modern Paul and Barnabas for an extensive missionary crusade in Scotland.

This crusade of missions called for some Peter the Hermit. A reform of missionary methods was likewise needed under the direction of some Luther, or Wesley. A reconstruction of the people's habits of giving might be accomplished if only some Zinzendorf could be found to lead the way to a higher level of consecrated beneficence. To Dr. Pierson this call was evidence that "a wide door and effectual was opened before him," and there were *not* many adversaries. The result was—as narrated in the previous chapter—that he resigned his pastorate and with his wife sailed once more for Great Britain in November, 1889, preceded by the prayers of the Christians in Scotland and followed by those of his people in Bethany and his brethren in the Philadelphia Presbytery.

The voyage was one of the roughest Dr. Pierson ever experienced on the Atlantic. On the fourth day out, the *Etruria* was struck by a most violent storm and for four days she ploughed through a tumultuous sea, so that she could land neither passengers nor mail at Queenstown. There was need of a bit of cheer in the way of an entertainment in mid-ocean. A program was prepared and Dr. Pierson, never a steady sailor himself, presided and recited an original poem born of most recent throes of *mal de mer*. He began:

> " No doubt it's delightful,
> This sailing the sea !
> Essaying to wash you
> In some heavy 'roll';
> And pitching head foremost
> Straight into the bowl !

> Giving orders for beef tea—
> Just waked from your nap,
> And suddenly finding it
> Overturned in your lap!"

From the hour of landing at Liverpool, when he was hurried off in a cab to meet his first engagement, until his sailing for home seven months later there were countless indications that God was going before His servant. That year influenza first made its appearance in Britain and caused much illness everywhere, but in some cities in Scotland from four to six thousand people crowded in to hear the missionary message.

As a rule two meetings a day were held in each of the cities visited. The leading Christian man in each place presided, and the largest halls were secured for the occasion. When he accepted the invitation to Scotland, Dr. Pierson made only two requests of the committee: first, that the usual formal addresses of welcome and votes of thanks should be dispensed with in order that all the time might be devoted to the message; second, that no collections for his expenses should be taken at the meetings. This would embarrass the speaker and might keep away some who were not already thoroughly interested in the subject. These wise restrictions added greatly to the success of the campaign.

The necessary funds were secured from the churches and through private subscription. Hundreds of pounds additional were sent in as free-will offerings for various forms of missionary work, and there were many evidences of self-sacrifice in these gifts. Jewelry and luxuries of other kinds found their way into the offering plate, and the joy of giving took such hold on some that for years they continued to send through the *Missionary*

Review of the World their "extra" for the Lord's work. A diamond ring was given with the remark: "I can do without it." Men gave up tobacco and other superfluities and put the money into service.

The prime object of the crusade however was not to raise money but to give Christian men, women and churches a vision of the world in the light of the Great Commission and to enlist their interest and coöperation in missionary work. This question of foreign missions was presented in its true place in the spiritual life of the Church and of the Christian. The addresses delivered were on such themes as "The King's Business Requireth Haste," "The World Field," "The Needs of the Hour," "The Fruits of Missions," "The Unity of the Human Family," "The Strategy of God," "The Appeal for Labourers," "The Power of Medical Missions," "The Individual Responsibility," etc. In many of the meetings the sense of the divine presence was almost overpowering. Men and women were bowed in prayer and sometimes in tears. No *man* could have produced such an impression; it was manifestly of God.

Dr. Pierson could not but be impressed with the energy and money that was often wasted in arousing churches to a sense of duty when that power might have been used in direct missionary work. This conviction he expressed forcibly when he said:

"Themistocles, at the battle of Salamis, delayed a naval engagement until the land breeze blew which swept his vessel towards the foe, and so left every oarsman free to act as bowman and spearman. What new power would be available if the *energy expended in propelling the vehicle of missions could be left free to do the work of missions*. Imagine the result if the Spirit of God should sweep the Church towards the crisis of the engagement instead of our toiling hard to bring up God's people to the encounter."

The zeal of the speaker could not but communicate itself to the audience. Once when he was speaking with great earnestness on the necessity for evangelizing the *present generation* of men, in his vehemence he broke the pointer which he held in his hand. After an apology he remarked, "I wish I could as easily break in pieces the apathy that prevails to-day in the Church of Jesus Christ." The applause that followed proved that the application of the accident was appreciated.

One of the incidental benefits of the tour was the union of various denominations on one missionary platform. The differences between Established, United and Free Presbyterian Churches, and the conflicts of opinions as to work and worship were lost sight of in the great common purpose to advance the kingdom of Christ throughout the world. The hearty coöperation of strong men in the large cities is evidenced in the names of those who, in the great Scotch metropolis, showed their deep interest in the series of meetings in the interest of missions.

The success of these meetings Dr. Pierson ascribed to the spirit of prayer in which they were conceived and conducted. In various centres of Scotland many had been regularly praying in secret and in small circles for a mighty manifestation of God's presence and power. Instead of looking to man for victory they looked to the great Commander-in-Chief and God honoured their prayer. This spirit of prayer also characterized the speaker. In the midst of his crowding engagements and busy hours of study we find such entries in his diary as the following:

"Met Major Whittle to-day for prayer and dedicated myself anew to God and His work."
"Much humbled in prayer. . . . New surrender."
"Rose at daybreak for a season of uninterrupted prayer."

The results of the crusade were lasting in the Scotch churches. New interest in missions was awakened and nearly three hundred volunteers offered themselves for the foreign field, and missions came to have a larger place in the programs of pastors and their churches.

It had long been a desire of Dr. Pierson to visit the birthplaces, parishes and familiar haunts of God's great and good men whose lives had been an inspiration to his missionary zeal, and this visit to Britain furnished him that opportunity. The grandeur and beauty of the Scotch Highlands and the Trossachs and the English Lake region impressed him as a lover of nature, but he enjoyed even more his visits to the homes of David Livingstone, John G. Paton, William Carey, John Bunyan, John Howard and others. "You have," he said to the British people, "no excuse for not being heroic, for you are treading amid the very scenes that are consecrated by heroism on every side. I stood by the gateway of Dundee where George Wishart spoke to the plague-stricken people. I visited the hamlet where David Livingstone first saw the light. I entered the little shop in Hackleton where Carey used to cobble, and there, as if to make the picture more vivid, sat a man mending a boot. I said in my heart, All the organized missions of the Church of modern times were, in a sense, born in that shop. In Strathaven I felt the inspiration of that little home from which went out William and Gavin Martin to India, James Martin to Jamaica, a son to the East Indies, a daughter to the West Indies, and which has two more consecrated sons in preparation for the same work—seven missionaries from one home,—we might almost say from one cradle! Have you felt the inspiration of it?"

The Scotch people crowned their acts of appreciation of Dr. Pierson's service by appointing him, at the close of his crusade, to deliver the next series of Duff lectures. These lectures were founded in memory of the great Scotch pioneer missionary, Dr. Alexander Duff, and covered a period of four years, three for preparation and one for delivery in the leading university centres of Scotland. Many distinguished men, like William Fleming Stevenson and Sir Monier-Williams had filled the office, and Dr. Pierson put some of his best thought and genius into these lectures.[1]

From Scotland Dr. Pierson went to London, where he addressed large assemblies and thus gained the ear of all England. One of these gatherings in the metropolis was convened by the missionary secretaries of the Congregationalists, Baptists, Presbyterians and Wesleyans acting together and the meetings were held in the Westminster (Congregational) Chapel, the Marylebone (Presbyterian) Church and the Down (Baptist) Chapel.

At the invitation of Pastor Charles H. Spurgeon he preached in the Metropolitan Tabernacle. Twenty-two

---

[1] These lectures were published in a volume entitled "The New Acts of the Apostles."

years had passed since his first visit to that church, and he had never lost the influence of that service, nor had he forgotten the message delivered by that servant of God. He had visited Mr. Spurgeon in his home and had assisted him at minor services but it was with a peculiar feeling of a sacred mission that Dr. Pierson stood beside him in his pulpit and preached to his people.

"Before I went upon the pulpit platform," he said, "a score of devout church officers met me in the retiring-room, and for fifteen minutes there was such praying for me as would suffice to help any man to preach with Holy Ghost power. Somehow Mr. Spurgeon has trained his people to *devout hearing;* and whoever preaches there, if he be at all susceptible to the influence of an audience, feels that atmosphere encircling him, and he breathes spiritual ozone that gives energy and vitality to his utterance."

The letter from Spurgeon the next week was characteristic of his great heart.

"Our people have had nothing to compare with your sermon. It fired the whole mass. God bless you and make you of more use than ever. My men meet in conference Tuesday at the Orphanage. Could you speak to them? You could do the men great good, but do not be worried by my request if it is unsuitable. I will rejoice if you can come. I shall know if you cannot that it is really so.

"What you say of special love to me I echo to yourself. The Lord Himself be your exceeding great reward. Pardon brevity. I have some little gout in my 'write' hand.

"Yours lovingly,
"C. H. SPURGEON."

A visit to the Continent in the spring of 1890 afforded a long-waited-for opportunity to examine more carefully into the methods and work of the McAll Mission in France and to see the conditions in Papal and Protestant districts of Italy. "Many a church," he wrote, "might well send their pastor abroad to carry cheer to the missionaries on the field and at the same time to come into personal vital contact with the mission fields and mission workers. If all travellers would visit the missions they would be fired with a new enthusiasm." Dr. Pierson's interest in the McAll Mission had already helped to carry it over a crisis. He was greatly impressed with the crowds of French working men that eagerly thronged the Salles in Paris, with the earnest, self-forgetful spirit of the workers, with the evangelical tone of the preaching and with the solid character of the converts.

An interesting scene occurred at one of these Salle meetings during Dr. Pierson's address. It reveals at once his ability to adapt his message to an audience of uneducated foreigners and his graphic way of presenting truth. He was speaking from the fifth chapter of second Corinthians concerning the relation of God to the sinner and of the sinner's relation to God and wished to illustrate the word "reconciliation" so that a child could understand. He asked a friend to stand up with him on the platform and as they stood back to back he pointed out that this was the attitude of complete alienation. "But in Christ," he said, "God becomes reconciled to the sinner and turns about to face him with hands outstretched. Still it remains for the sinner to be reconciled to God. When the sinner learns of God's attitude and is ready to do his part he turns towards God face to face (is converted), and the reconciliation is complete." As he gave this graphic illustration through an interpreter, the Frenchmen clapped their hands and stamped their feet and many of them turned to God that night.

From Paris Dr. and Mrs. Pierson travelled to Italy where they visited the Waldensians in the Vaudois Valley. This was the historic spot where saints were bound and hurled from precipices, and where others escaped by hiding from their implacable foes in the recesses of a cave. Dr. Pierson crawled into the low opening on his hands and knees and was thrilled with the thoughts of the days of persecution when streams ran red with the blood of martyrs.

In Rome, Florence, Piza, Venice, Milan, and Naples he saw the monuments of past ages, the ruins of pagan and the palaces and cathedrals of papal Italy but what impressed him most was the need for chapels and missions where the Gospel might be preached in truth and simplicity. The ignorance and open sin of the people was strangely contrasted in his mind with the prevalence of outward forms of religious observance.

Humorous experiences of travel were always appreciated and served to brighten what might otherwise have been a sombre experience to one so keenly sensitive to the spiritual darkness around him. One of the events that enlivened the tour occurred during his visit to Naples and is described in his letter home:

"Our charming companion in European travel has been our beloved and intimate friend, Major D. W. Whittle. We left him at a restaurant near the *Musee Bourbonico*, while we went a-shopping. The Major happened not to know any Italian, beyond a few phrases; but it occurred to him he would take a cup of coffee, so he called the waiter and asked for '*café*.' That was successful; it brought the rich, brown decoction; but the Major likes milk in his coffee and no milk was forthcoming; so, beckoning to the waiter, he asked for 'milk.' But milk was not an Italian word, and the waiter was at a loss. The Major did not know the Italian word, *del latte*, and he was equally at a loss. Remembering that Professor Gillette, after his long experience with the deaf mutes, declared that sign language would render a man intelligible in any part of the world, he ventured to use the language of signs. He made his first sign by imitating the act of pouring from a pitcher into his cup. The waiter smiled and ran to bring a brandy bottle. The Major shook his head and the waiter tried again; he brought some hot water. This would not do. Major Whittle shook the end of the table cover that its whiteness might suggest the milk. The obliging attendant brought him a napkin. But again both were disappointed. By this time the other persons at the restaurant had become interested, and the proprietor ventured to come to the rescue. He suggested one thing after another, bread and buns, etc., but without success, and all took it good-naturedly and laughed at the mutual discomfiture of the Italian servants and the American guest.

"At last a brilliant idea struck the Major, who is not easily discouraged. He put up his hands to imitate horns, he motioned with them as though milking a cow, he imitated with his voice the lowing of a heifer, and crowned all his attempts by a sketch with his pencil, on the corner of his newspaper, showing the outline of the very animal itself. Ah, yes, the proprietor laughed at his stupidity. He now had caught the evasive idea. He bowed profusely, and intimating that the desired article was not at hand in the restaurant, despatched an errand boy to fetch it. The Major waited full five minutes, and then the proprietor came to conduct him to the door. Why he was to be led to the door was a mystery, unless he was expected to milk the cow. But when he came to the door the mystery was solved. There was a donkey all ready to mount. The Major's hands had been put up to his head, that meant ears; then the motions he meant for milking were interpreted for jerking reins; the lowing of the cow was thought to be the braying of an ass; and, last but not least—oh, cruel sacrilege upon our friend's artistic sketch—his drawing had been mistaken for a donkey.

"Again, amid roars of laughter, the Major declined the donkey, and tried his hand at another sketch. This time, by greater care, and by outlining the udder of the milk-giving mammal, he managed to convey to the proprietor the idea that not a donkey but a cow was wanted; and with a lavish apology in Italian, amid the intense amusement of the spectators, a pitcher of milk was brought. Later when we saw the first sketch we all agreed that no blame could be attached to the proprietor for ordering that donkey."

We can well understand with what intense interest Dr. and Mrs. Pierson and Major Whittle read again passages from the Bible as they traversed the Appian Way along which the Apostle Paul walked into Rome, and as they visited the Mamartine Prison in which he is said to have been confined, or gazed at the huge Coliseum where the early Christian martyrs were torn to pieces by wild beasts. With Dr. James Gordon Gray, pastor of the Scotch Church in Rome, and others they visited the Catacombs of St. Calixtus, outside the walls and there held a meeting for prayer and consecration.

The experiences and the friendships formed in Great Britain greatly enriched Dr. Pierson's life and were a preparation for a still wider ministry. After having held one hundred and fifty meetings in England and Scotland from Bristol to Aberdeen and from London to Glasgow there were more applications unfilled than had brought him across the water six months before. On his return home he made the following entry in his devotional diary:

"The whole experience of the year since Nov. 9, 1889, when we set sail for Liverpool, has been one of God's unfailing goodness and mercy. No want unsupplied—not a day of sickness or suffering or special weariness, gracious provision for daily wants. . . . Never felt the need of believing and prevailing prayer as now. Only constant fellowship with God can suffice to make us victors over present perils, temptations and trials. . . . I especially ask God for personal victory over besetting sins, whatever they may be—impatience, uncharitableness, to which I am very prone. 'Watch and Pray.'"

Plans were laid for a visitation of churches in America, under the auspices of the Presbyterian Board of Foreign Missions, similar to the crusade in Scotland, but there were no special funds available for the support of such a work. After a few months devoted mostly to local conventions, Dr. Pierson withdrew from this campaign as he was unwilling to accept for the supply of his own commissary department money contributed for foreign missionary work. In response to a request to deliver the Graves Missionary lectures at New Brunswick before the Rutgers Theological Seminary, he gave the series entitled "The Divine Enterprise of Missions."

The death of his colleague, Dr. James M. Sherwood, in October, 1890, cast the entire responsibility of the *Missionary Review* upon Dr. Pierson, and this extra work together with writing and preaching rounded out another busy year of life for him. Several calls came to vacant churches on both sides of the water, but he was conscious of a more urgent summons to serve the church at large in the stirring up of missionary interest. In the midst of this work, however, he was being prepared for another line of ministry in behalf of deeper Bible study and higher spiritual life—but that is another chapter in the story.

XIII

AT SPURGEON'S TABERNACLE—TWO YEARS AS A SUBSTITUTE

IT was a remarkable chain of circumstances that led Arthur T. Pierson, for thirty years prominently identified with the Presbyterian Church in America, to leave his own country for the pulpit of the leading Baptist Church in the world. The Metropolitan Tabernacle of London had become famous under the unique ministry of Pastor Charles H. Spurgeon. Not only did he preach each Lord's Day to audiences of five or six thousand people, but his sermons were printed and sent to the farthest corner of Christendom; his Orphanage, his Pastor's College, and other enterprises, formed a vast organization which required skillful management and a large income. When therefore, in the spring of 1891, the sad news became known that Pastor Spurgeon was stricken with Bright's disease and was dangerously ill, the whole Christian world was deeply moved. Many were praying for his recovery and all were perplexed to know where a successor to such a man could be found.

On the sixteenth of July word was cabled to America, and reached the Bible conference at Niagara-on-the-Lake, that Mr. Spurgeon was dying. Immediately a group of Christian men met for an hour to pray that God would spare this great man for further service. The next day cablegrams announced his

Invitation from Charles H. Spurgeon

improvement and a praise service was held. One of this group was Arthur T. Pierson. He wrote a few days later to Pastor Spurgeon to tell him of the prayer-meeting and to express his sympathy and the earnest hope of all American Christians that his health might be fully restored. In reply he received the following letter:

"*Westwood, August 7, 1891.*
Upper Norwood, London.
"DEAR DR. PIERSON:

"You can hardly imagine what joy Mr. Spurgeon felt this morning when I read to him your loving letter. Only last night he asked me to ascertain if you were still able to carry out the kind offer of help that you made many months ago. Truly you must have been inspired to write just at this time. I am thankful to say that prayer has been heard in Mr. Spurgeon's behalf and that he is spared to us, but under the most favourable circumstances it must be many months before he will be able to preach. Mr. Spurgeon is not yet well enough to enter into the details of any arrangements but he wishes to ask if you are free for three, four, five or six months, beginning with October, to 'come over and help us.' . . . Mr. Spurgeon's illness has evoked such a spirit of prayer and caused such Bible searching on the part of the members that we believe the Tabernacle Church is being prepared for a great revival. Mr. Spurgeon's confident hope is that you may be used greatly to this end. He sends you his heart's love.

"Yours very truly,
"J. W. HARROLD,
"*Private Secretary.*"

Just twenty-five years before the day on which this letter came the recipient had sat in the Metropolitan

Tabernacle and for the first time had heard Mr. Spurgeon preach. The influence of that sermon and service had transformed many of his ministerial ideals. This is his testimony:

"I often look back to the nineteenth day of August, 1866, when I sat in the gallery of the Tabernacle and for the first time heard Charles H. Spurgeon speak. His text was taken from the closing verses of the third chapter of Ephesians. . . . I made up my mind to imitate that man in the simplicity of his preaching, in his passion for souls, and in the boldness of his faith that dared to do everything for God. . . . Thus began that war for the truth, for a simple worship, and for entire dependence on God for which I have been fighting ever since."

Mr. Spurgeon's invitation came as a surprise to his American friend, for though the offer of help had been given genuinely it was made with reference to general service and without any expectation that it would involve preaching at the Tabernacle. Dr. Pierson's answer was characteristic:

"East Northfield, Mass.,
August 18, 1891.

"MY DEAREST SPURGEON:

"Please don't 'Reverend' or 'Doctor' me. I am not as reverend as you are for I am fifty-four and you are a little more venerable; and as to 'Doctoring,' you unhappily have more need of it than I. . . .

"Now as to the contents of your loving letter. I fell on my knees. There was a touch of the supernatural in all this and I was overawed. First of all, when I was unexpectedly called to preach in the Tabernacle in December, 1889, never did I feel such divine uplifting. . . . I felt that nowhere on earth would I so gladly hold forth the Word of life. . . . Now listen! For the first time since I began to preach I am entirely free from all engagements after October 1st. . . . I do not know what I may be led to cable you. . . . It is of supreme consequence to me only to do the will of God and that can be known only through believing prayer. . . . I must wait for clear signs of the Divine will before daring to take up a work so vast. The whole people have been chastened and the soil is mellow and ready for the sowing."

As a result of this correspondence and prayer Dr. Pierson cabled Mr. Spurgeon St. Paul's answer to the Macedonian vision (Acts xvi. 9, 10) and received a most cordial invitation from the officers of the Tabernacle to preach for at least three months. It was not an easy matter, with a *Review* to edit and an aged mother and dependent children to care for, to make arrangements for an indefinite absence from home, but God prepared the way in this also. On September 25th he wrote in his prayer diary: "Wife and I rose at 4 A. M. for special prayer to commit the whole matter of the European trip to God (1) my mother; (2) the children; (3) money needed; (4) house during absence; (5) a new humility and anointing for work."

These prayers were signally answered so that every step was made clear. Funds were provided from unexpected sources, and household arrangements were satisfactorily completed. What was of even greater importance, Dr. Pierson himself received new anointings of spiritual power to prepare him for the service to which he had been called.

On October 23d he arrived in London and on the following Monday Mr. Spurgeon had so far regained strength that he was able to leave for Mentone in the south of France. Before he left London, however, these two men met at Beulah Hill for a brief prayer and conference. Of this last meeting Dr. Pierson wrote: "Notwithstanding his illness, he knelt with me to ask God's blessing upon my labours. 'Oh, Lord,' he prayed, 'we do not tell Thee how to work or what to do, only work like Thyself.' The prayer was so beautifully sweet and childlike that it reminded me of Count Zinzendorf at five years of age tossing letters out of the window to his 'dear Jesus.' This man of fifty-seven approached his Lord with the frankness and freedom of a little child."

The prayer of faith was abundantly answered, not in the restoration of the beloved pastor's health but in the blessing of God that accompanied the ministry of his substitute in the Metropolitan pulpit. People at the Tabernacle were in the mood to hear the man who had come to preach and their own beloved Spurgeon further prepared them by his own "strong crying and tears" and by his weekly letters of hopeful encouragement. Some of these pastoral epistles are worth quoting not only because they reveal the man but because they show the way in which he upheld his American brother in the difficult work before him. Here are a few extracts from Pastor Spurgeon's letters to his people:

"I am relieved of great anxiety by the Lord's plainly directing me to secure Dr. Pierson to fill the pulpit during my absence. He is a man after my own heart and a great winner of souls. He will not aim at anything but the glory of God. He begs that the whole Church will grant him the aid of their united prayers and efforts. . . . Let nothing flag. . . .

The Opening Day

"No one suggested Dr. Pierson to me; it came from my heart and I think I was led of the Lord. I have had the closest fellowship of heart with this beloved brother as a champion of the faith. . . .

"He has come among you in humble but unwavering faith that the Lord is about to make bare His arm in our midst. I hope he has come to reap where others have sown and also to gather in some who have been withering by the wayside and were not in the field at all. I expect a great revival. I pray for it and I look for it. . . . My beloved brother brings you the divine proffer of a great blessing. Are we ready to receive it? Are we prepared to use a flood-tide? Oh! that every member may say 'I *am*'!"

From the first service these prayers and expectations of pastor and people were abundantly answered. Dr. Pierson came not with confidence in the flesh but with "weakness and much trembling." The Saturday night before his first service in the Tabernacle the responsibility weighed so heavily on him that he could not sleep. The sea voyage, which was always a trial, had upset his nervous and digestive system, so that he had violent agitation of the heart, with intermittent beating followed by accelerated action. He wrote: "I was alarmed for my life and rose with my wife at 3 A. M. to call on God for strength." This prayer was answered and in spite of continued weakness he went forward in faith with the strenuous services of the Sabbath.

The opening day at the Tabernacle on Sunday morning, October 25, 1891, augured well for the future. He preached to a crowded congregation from Acts x. 29, "Therefore, came I without gainsaying, as soon as I was sent for; I ask, therefore, for what intent ye have sent for me?"

The five thousand worshippers were hushed and attentive though they must have felt the striking contrast between the personalities of their pastor and that of his substitute. One who was present thus describes his impression:

"They are unlike physically and mentally, but one as to spiritual things. Dr. Pierson is a typical American, tall, thin and ascetic-looking. He is like a Puritan risen from his grave. He has a noble brow, an aquiline nose, a closely-clipped beard and mustache, a face that is almost too intellectual if it were not for the intense sympathy with his fellow creatures which beams forth from his expressive eyes. He has the bearing of a student but his speech was logic on fire. Both in matter and manners he was profoundly powerful. His action is graceful, suitable, forceful. Nothing seems studied yet there was unmistakable evidence that the doctor has a wide acquaintance with general literature and has diligently cultivated great natural talents.

"Mr. Spurgeon was, on the contrary, in many ways a typical Englishman. His burly form and genial gaze reminded one of a gentleman farmer out for a holiday. His tender, lustrous eyes seemed ever full of quiet fun.

"In style of oratory there is as wide a difference as between America and England. The sharp but loving home thrust of Spurgeon finds no place in Dr. Pierson's speech. There is in the latter not the abrupt stab but a clear-cut argument, a cogent reason, a clear definition leading to an appeal. Spurgeon appealed chiefly to the heart, Pierson to the mind and conscience. Mr. Spurgeon was an artist in word painting; Dr. Pierson does not picture in awful terms the penalties of a life of rebellion against divine law, but he takes up the evil

A Visitor's Viewpoint 233

thing, strips it of all the gay covering until it stands out naked and ghastly, a thing for loathing and disgust, from which his hearers long to shrink away ashamed. Spurgeon made you laugh; Dr. Pierson is not without humour of the kind that makes you chuckle and keep quiet.

"But Spurgeon and Pierson are more akin than the casual critic dreams. Just as the mantle of Carlisle fell upon John Ruskin, so surely the mantle of the Prophet of Newington seems to rest on the shoulders of the American divine. They are both inspired by the same profound faith in the Unseen, without which it is impossible to wield a living force for righteousness among the masses. Both men give one the impression of sincerity and of a loathing for hypocrisy or cant or conventional platitudes. Spurgeon once risked everything by standing for the unpopular truth; Dr. Pierson has shown the same rare independence of thought. Both men believe firmly in the divine decrees. In their teaching, sin is not represented as a necessary stage in the evolution of character, but as a crime against God which cannot be lightly passed over."

Here in the Tabernacle pulpit, Dr. Pierson immediately found himself at home. He was surrounded by an atmosphere of prayer; the church officers met for prayer before the sermon and sat with him on the platform; there was congregational singing in which all joined and when he referred to a passage of Scripture there was a rustle of leaves from thousands of Bibles. The people were in a spirit of prayer and their sympathetic coöperation and response was often revealed by the way in which they followed up preaching with personal appeals to the unconverted.

One result of this first sermon was revealed a year or two later in a letter written to Dr. Pierson by a stranger who was present on that day:

"Four years ago I was actively engaged in preaching and God was using me in the conversion of souls. Naturally of a nervous disposition, I found that by taking wine or brandy before speaking I was braced up and relieved of the exhaustion afterwards. . . . This sad habit grew upon me until I was helpless in speaking without alcoholic stimulant. . . . Then God laid me on my back with a severe hemorrhage, followed by delirium for a week. On my recovery I abstained for a few weeks, but was induced again to resort to stimulants and soon became cold and indifferent to spiritual things and mixed up in every form of evil. I can scarcely bring myself to write this but it may be a warning of God to others who are tampering with drink as I did. . . . Burdened with my sin but still away from the Lord, I went the first morning you preached in the Tabernacle. The Word was with mighty power and I cried to God for help. On November 1st, I heard you again and I cried to God a second time in my despair and He answered me. I yielded myself absolutely and unreservedly to Him and peace and joy flowed into my soul."

At the same time the Adversary was not asleep in the metropolis and sought from the first to turn aside the thrusts of the Sword of the Spirit by counter thrusts of unfriendly criticism. An irate reporter, who failed to obtain an interview, printed in British papers and cabled to America false reports of utterances with the evident intention of bringing discredit on the preacher, stating, without foundation, that he had attacked Mr. Spurgeon in his absence and had charged his congregation with doing things he had told them not to do.

But there were few critics in the audience, for Dr. Pierson was one of those preachers who, in the first few minutes of his discourse, compelled the conviction that he was thoroughly in earnest, was convinced of the truth he was preaching and was consumed with a passion for the salvation of men's souls. Men and women yielded to such sincerity and loving appeal whereas they would have been unmoved by the formal eloquence of an orator. They lost sight of the preacher in the divine message that he presented.

Much of the power evident in these Tabernacle services was due to the congregation. At the outset of his ministry there Dr. Pierson proposed a union of prayer for a great outpouring of the Holy Spirit and this suggestion met with a hearty response. He wrote home:

"The Metropolitan Tabernacle is emphatically a house of prayer. Here are numerous rooms in which prayer is almost ceaselessly going up to God. When one meeting is not in progress another is. There are prayer-meetings before preaching and others after preaching. No wonder that Mr. Spurgeon's ministry was so blessed. May not the whole Church of God learn something as to the power of simple gospel preaching backed by believing prayer."

In the south of France the tidings of blessing brought joy to the heart of Pastor Spurgeon and he wrote to his substitute:

"The Lord's name be praised that ever I knew you. He planned to set me aside and at the same time He made you ready to fill the vacancy. Every word about you makes me praise God for sending you. I feel that I can rest in you as one sent by my Faithful Lord to do faithfully His work. May you never have to regret anything in connection with your remarkable deed of brotherly love. . . .

"Moses may be weak but Aaron and Hur are strong in the Lord. I am mending as to the flesh but quite restored in spirit. Before long I hope to be on the watch-tower again and gratefully surveying the fort which you have held to the satisfaction of all the garrison. . . .

"I trust that Mrs. Pierson is not unhappy in the city of Gog, Magog and Fog. I cannot wonder but I do ponder over the great unselfish love that keeps you grinding in the fog that I may rest in the sun. God bless you and make it up to you.

"Yours ever heartily,
"C. H. SPURGEON."

This prayer too was answered and soon there were so many letters from those desiring counsel and requests for personal interviews with inquirers that it would have required five secretaries to answer them.

It may be well here to notice some of Dr. Pierson's ideals for preaching and his method of sermon preparation. These were revealed in his lectures to the students of the Pastor's College [1]—the institution so near and dear to Mr. Spurgeon's heart. The Bible was his sole text-book and to him was the supreme and unerring revelation of God and His will. He became saturated with its teachings and language so that on every subject and on every occasion the Scriptures furnished him the basis for faith and the rules for action.

In the preparation of a sermon he went to the Bible,

[1] These lectures were printed in a volume entitled "The Divine Art of Preaching." Later he also published a book called "The Making of a Sermon."

as inspired of God, and examined every word to discover its full meaning and every phrase to interpret its revelation. Thus the treasures of the Scriptures were inexhaustible, its arguments were unanswerable and its promises unbreakable. The results of his daily Scripture study were entered on the wide margins or the blank pages of his interleaved Bibles. As soon as one was filled he bought another, for he never rested satisfied with the discoveries of the past. There were always new mysteries to be revealed, new treasures to be dug up for the enrichment of life. "He who stops learning must stop preaching," was his adage. His insight into the meaning of texts was largely the result of his ability to compare Scripture with Scripture, and the Old and New Testaments were each searched for their contribution to the theme in hand. He said:

"The Holy Scriptures are inspired by the same Holy Spirit that dwells in the believer. All true insight into the Bible, therefore, hangs on the unveiling of the eyes to behold wondrous things in the Word. It follows, then, that the greatest help in the preparation of sermons is a prayerful, humble, devout study of the Bible. Every text in God's Word is a divine gem which is to be cut and polished upon the wheel of the Spirit. The true preacher prays and meditates on the Scriptures until he has a vision and he never preaches until he has the vision. To get one's sermons from the illuminating power of the Holy Spirit begets marvellous courage. Such a preacher is bound to speak the truth in love.

"I feel constrained to bear witness that no amount of study of commentaries or any other human product has been of help to me in any way comparable to the devotional, spiritual study of the Scriptures in the original tongue—carefully noting every word, phrase, case of a noun, mood and tense, number and person of a verb and the relation of clauses and phrases to each other. . . .

"The highest kind of homiletic analysis is not an *invention* but a *discovery*, not a product of ingenuity but a result of illumination. Take for example our Lord's intercessory prayer (John xvii.). A careful study shows that the four prepositions reveal our Lord's conception of the relation of the believer to the world.

    1. They are *in* the world.
    2. They are *not of* the world.
    3. They are chosen *out* of the world.
    4. They are sent *into* the world.

The same chapter reveals the progress of the believer:

"(1) Separation; (2) Sanctification; (3) Unity; (4) Glory. Nothing can be added, nothing can be subtracted from these; neither can the order be changed."

Some of Dr. Pierson's convictions as to preaching are also helpful:

1. Preach the truth of God, not human philosophy. Do not make the mistake of seeking your message from books and current events rather than from the Word of God. The only safe rule is to give your people nothing that you do not find in the Holy Scriptures.

2. Preach the fundamental truths. One may preach a great many things that are in the Bible and yet may leave out Christ and the only truth that can save men and that can teach them how to live.

3. Preach fundamental truth with a deep spiritual experience back of it. A man is powerless to teach sanctification unless he is living it.

4. Preach in the spirit of prayer and in dependence on the power of the Holy Spirit. If a man has doubt or is ignorant of the reality of the work of the Spirit, he has no right to preach.

"The Temptation Stairway"

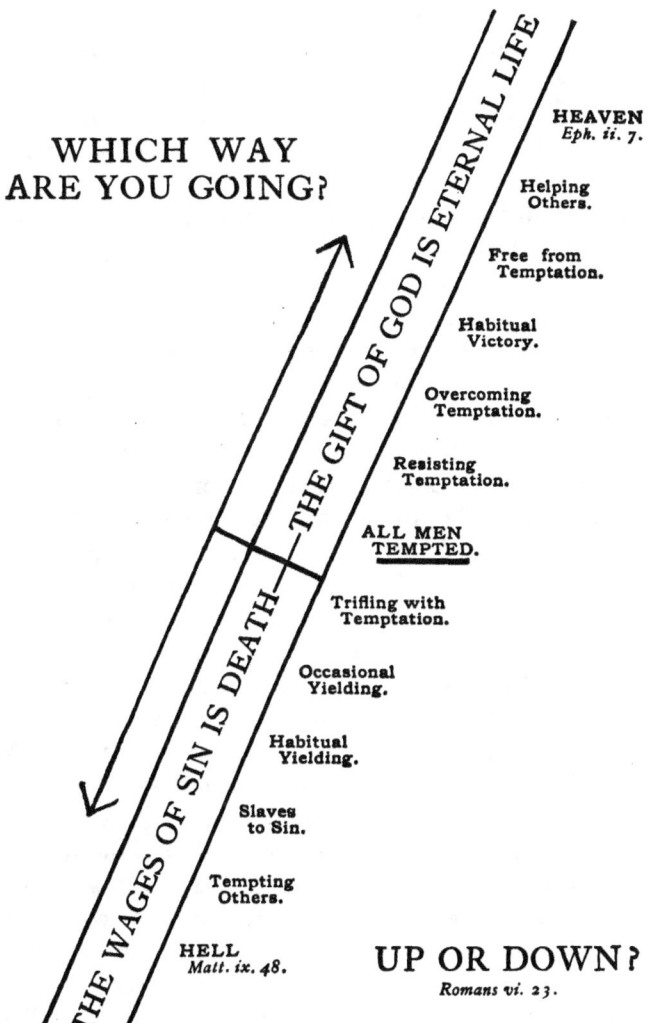

There were helps to memory that marked the outlines—alliteration, groups of threes or sevens—and there were sometimes graphic illustrations that could not fail to impress an audience. One such pictorial presentation is the "Temptation Stairway" used to illustrate the texts Ephesians vi. 12 and 1 Corinthians x. 13.

But while Dr. Pierson took his themes and his arguments from the Word of God he by no means neglected other sources of knowledge. He had an extensive and carefully selected library and an even more extensive acquaintance with all branches of literature. In his study at home were a hundred large boxes, indexed according to important subjects and letters of the alphabet—not a complicated system but one for ready reference. These boxes contained illustrative material, scientific, historical and biographical notes; poetry, essays and sermons. No pains were spared in making preparation thorough. After he had obtained his *message* from the Bible he searched personal experience, history, the lives of other men, science and philosophy for illustrations of the truth.

When he had satisfactorily gathered and arranged his material he made full and careful outlines, printing them by hand in almost copperplate style, so that they were easily legible for pulpit use. Some thirty bound volumes of these pen-printed outlines—containing a thousand sermons—reveal the result of his painstaking industry. He was accustomed to write out some sermons, not to be read or printed, but to insure clearness of thought and accuracy of expression.

The titles of some of the sermons most blessed in his ministry indicate the simplicity of the phrasing and the character of the subjects selected: "The Lessons of Pentecost," Acts x. 29; "First Things First," Matt. vi. 33; "The Heart of the Gospel," John iii. 16; "The Secret of the Untroubled Heart," John xiv. 1–27; "Awakening, Arming, Acting," Romans xiii. 11–14; "Micah's Question," Micah vii. 18–20; "The Word of God," James i.; "Redemption," Ephesians i. 6, 7; "Preservation and Presentation," Jude 24 and 25; "The Sum of the Gospel," Hebrews viii. 1.[1]

Concerning the results of his work in the Tabernacle Dr. Pierson wrote in his devotional diary on January 2, 1892:

"Another wonderful chapter in the dealings of the Lord. Three months of uninterrupted health and happiness. Everybody cordial and sympathetic and responsive. Fifty souls gathered in in December and many more inquiring. Immense after-meetings in the Tabernacle. Prayer-meetings of the profoundest interest.

"Am deeply impressed with the dealings of God. Never such fertility and freshness of gospel themes or such power in presentation. Mind full of subjects of vital importance touching the marrow of gospel truth. Spurgeon wants me to continue three months more. What God would have me do is the great question. Pray for greater simplicity and particularly for singleness of aim and humility of mind—not ever to *think* of myself highly. No grace is so difficult for me as humility. I want a lowly mind."

The three months for which Dr. Pierson had been

---

[1] Three volumes of sermons were printed from his Tabernacle ministry—"Heights of the Gospel," "Heart of the Gospel," and "Hopes of the Gospel."

asked to preach at the Tabernacle had scarcely expired when word came from Mentone that Spurgeon was sinking. Not only the great congregation but all London and the whole Christian Church mourned when he finally passed away on the last day of January, 1892. What Dr. Pierson was to the sorrowing members of his flock during the days that followed only those who passed through the trying ordeal can imagine. In spite of severe illness which weakened him painfully he was with them at the early morning prayer-meetings, and preached at the daily services of the week preceding the funeral. Altogether he delivered no less than thirty-three memorial addresses, each distinctly different. His words of comfort and cheer were like soothing ointment on painful wounds and an experience of grief that might have led many into doubt and despair was thus used to confirm faith and point the way to certain immortality.

Immediately after Mr. Spurgeon's death, Dr. Pierson sent his resignation to the officers of the church but they besought him to remain. Their hearts had been knit together by a common—or uncommon—suffering; he was the pastor's choice and the brother and co-pastor, James Spurgeon, president of the Pastor's College, was drawn to him by bonds of sympathy that daily increased in strength.

James Spurgeon wrote in a letter to Dr. Theodore L. Cuyler of Brooklyn, New York:

"My heart is enlarged with fuller gratitude to our heavenly Father for His care of us through the dear brother whom the American Church has lent for a while (would that it were a gift!) to the sister Church of England. I refer to Dr. Arthur T. Pierson, who

Results of London Ministry 243

has taken all our hearts by storm, and who holds us still captive under his gracious gospel spell. We can never tell what we owe him; and just now we feel as if we cannot spare him without risking a loss too heavy to be borne. The smitten flock here has been richly fed under his faithful preaching of the truth once for all delivered to the saints. Permit me, then, to express how much we owe to some of America's choicest sons in this time of irreparable loss and crushing anguish; and let me through you, my dear doctor, return our grateful acknowledgments for all this avalanche of love."

Above all God had set His seal on the work of the past three months. Hundreds had been brought into the church and literally thousands of letters testified to the spiritual fruit of his ministry. These letters were from all classes of men and women, from strangers and sojourners, from officers and parishioners. Each told its own story of help received to meet a peculiar need. One spoke of conversion during a sermon on "Christ at the Door" followed by conversation and prayer in the vestry; another was from a young man brought from skepticism and sin into Christian life and service; one came from a lukewarm Christian who had first been led to a sense of sin and then into full surrender and joyful fellowship. Others testified to new zeal in service for the master and new power in winning men to Him. But most of all they were from those who had been led to see new revelations of truth in the Bible, who had gained new confidence in its authority and a keener desire to search its mysteries.

Other letters told of whole Sunday-school classes converted; of husbands, brothers, sons who had been wandering in the darkness, now brought into the light.

These testimonies greatly humbled Dr. Pierson and led him to give heartfelt thanks to God. They also strengthened his confidence that he had been divinely sent to the Tabernacle for that critical period. But more than all else they confirmed his belief in the Bible as the very Word of God and in expository preaching as the most fruitful in spiritual results. He saw other men, of equal or greater ability, preaching without these results, on literature, science, or the topics of the day but with an uncertain faith in the Bible. Some of them drew large audiences and evoked public commendation and yet their ministry did not seem to bear fruit in men and women with transformed lives, with new love for God and a deepened desire to know and to do His will. These observations and his own experience were to him conclusive evidence of the divine inspiration of the Scriptures and of their power as the Sword of the Spirit.

It is little wonder that Dr. Pierson accepted, as God's call, the invitation of the officers and people to continue preaching until June. Beyond that date he could not promise as his family and especially his aged mother, then nearly ninety years old, required his presence in America.

Many of the congregation openly advocated the calling of Dr. Pierson to fill the vacant pastorate but this was obviously impossible as he was not a Baptist and he did not purpose becoming one. Dr. James Spurgeon had grown so attached to his American brother that he advised a co-pastorate with Dr. Pierson as preacher, even without any change of views. Immersion would not have been a stumbling-block, as he had for many years held the form of baptism to be an open

A Successor to Spurgeon 245

question and even as far back as his Detroit pastorate had caused a baptistry to be built in the church for those who might desire to be immersed. He would not have hesitated to be immersed if that would open the door to wider service but he refused to consider such a step at present lest it should seem to be taken in self-interest for the sake of securing the Tabernacle pulpit.

After a conference with some of the officers, who urged upon him a consideration of the pastorate, he entered in his note-book the reasons for and against such action. Twenty-eight arguments seemed to point towards his continuance at the Tabernacle, but when he looked at the other side he found forty-eight reasons against the proposition. As a result of his deliberation the following message was sent (February 25, 1892) to Rev. James A. Spurgeon:

"In my opinion it is not wise for me to encourage any expectation of a prolonged or indefinite stay among this dear people. . . . I foresee that the sooner this great church settles down to permanent work with a permanent pastor the better all around."

He received a unanimous request from the officers and people to return in October for another year of work in the church at the Tabernacle and he promised to do so if the way was still open to him and if the church was still without a pastor.

The work of the year culminated on Sunday, June 25th, with memorial services to Mr. Spurgeon and a farewell meeting to Dr. Pierson on the following evening. This meeting was in many respects remarkable: The Tabernacle was nearly filled with four thousand people and the mutual expressions of love were hearty and sincere. One of the members who was present wrote: "Had any one a year ago told the thousands who Sunday after Sunday throng the Tabernacle that in a brief twelvemonth they would lose their beloved and matchless pastor and that a minister, then a stranger to them, would so win their hearts and command their loyalty that they would regard him with scarcely less enthusiastic devotion than they felt towards Charles Haddon Spurgeon, the announcement would have been discredited and rejected. But the prediction would have been verified."

A son of Charles H. Spurgeon was called to occupy the pulpit for the summer months, while Dr. Pierson was in America. Ill-health had obliged this son, Thomas, to reside in Australia and there was little expectation that he would be available to fill his father's place permanently, even if that should be the desire of the people.

Dr. Pierson sailed for home in June, 1892, with the hearty "Godspeed" of a united congregation and from Liverpool sent back a message, like a last wave of the hand, as the ship bore him away to his own shores.

"*Dearly-beloved friends at the Metropolitan Tabernacle:*
"I cannot set sail without one more sweet word of prayerful and affectionate commendation of you all to the care of the Great Shepherd. My eight months' ministry among you has been one long experience of ceaseless mercy from our Father's hand, and of considerate courtesy and prayerful coöperation on your part. . . . Whether I come and see you or be absent, may I hear that you stand fast in one spirit as one man, striving together for the faith of the Gospel.

"I now speak for Thomas (The Twin), the dearly beloved son of your departed pastor. Pray for him.

You may all help, as I think you will, to make his ministry acceptable and profitable. Let his constant testimony be that in you he finds a praying people, and so shall the Word of the Lord have free course and be glorified. . . .

"When this letter is read to you I shall be on the sea, praying for you all. Let these words be true, 'And after eight days again His disciples were within, and Thomas with them; then came Jesus, the doors being shut, and stood in the midst, and said, Peace be unto you. . . . Then were the disciples glad when they saw the Lord.'

"Yours, with a loving farewell,
"ARTHUR T. PIERSON."

Thomas Spurgeon's ministry during the following summer proved a blessing to many of the people and there was a strong but not unanimous movement in favour of extending to him an invitation to the pastorate. This information was conveyed to Dr. Pierson anonymously at first and he immediately wrote to London:

"If the people of the Tabernacle desire to call Mr. Thomas Spurgeon and are hindered because they have invited me to supply the pulpit, I am more than ready to retire and leave them absolutely free. . . . If you should cable releasing me, it would be only a relief to my mind, so anxious am I not to go back to the Tabernacle without the clear leading of God."

Much correspondence followed on both sides and perplexities increased. False reports of newspaper interviews complicated the situation. Many letters came urging that he keep his promise to return and renew his ministry there. His engagement in Scotland as Duff lecturer required that he go to England in any event. His diary and letters to his friends at this period reveal how sore a trial it was to him "to even *seem* to crowd out a son of C. H. Spurgeon or to come into competition with him." He sought to relieve the complication by declaring again, " I am not a candidate and if the officers will release me I will be glad to retire even from a temporary supply." After much prayer and conference with friends he decided to leave the decision entirely in the hands of the officers of the Tabernacle and cabled them accordingly. They replied, "An enthusiastic welcome awaits you." Then he cabled back (Philemon 22): "But withal prepare me also a lodging, for I trust that through your prayers I shall be given unto you." He accordingly sailed on November 9, 1892, with the hope and prayer that as before his ministry had been blessed to a grieving people, so this time he might be of service in uniting a distracted congregation.

This second ministry was almost as markedly blessed as the first. There was not quite the same unanimity and the Baptist papers of London assumed a less friendly tone. Enemies even arose who manipulated correspondence and printed spurious interviews. His sensitive nature was hurt but he only wrote in his diary : " The newspaper controversy is very vexatious but when 'He giveth quietness who can make trouble,' I have given all my affairs into His hands." Nevertheless the strain of those months told on his health and on the health of his wife.

Gradually an unfortunate division arose between those who advocated a call to the American preacher and those who favoured the son of the former pastor. Dr. Pierson sought to eliminate himself from the contest by announcing repeatedly that he was not a candidate for the office, but his friends refused to accept his statement as final, until at last he wrote forbidding his name to be brought forward even as a temporary supply.

The congregation finally overwhelmingly voted to invite Thomas Spurgeon to return to the pulpit for twelve months' service " with a view to the pastorate," and Dr. Pierson brought his temporary ministry to a close in June, 1893. Again the hundreds of letters that poured in upon him left no room for doubt that God had acknowledged his message. Many testified that it required the second period of preaching to complete the work of the first.

A beautifully illumined memorial and oil painting of Charles H. Spurgeon were presented to him at a farewell reception, and a clock, with cathedral chimes to Mrs. Pierson. The congregation pledged to pray for their American friends whenever the clock struck ten.

One of his admirers sent the following parody on the familiar verses of " Father O'Flynn."

"Doctor A. P., you've the charmin'est way wid ye:
What a delight 'tis to sing and to pray wid ye!
Sunday! ava! We could spend all the day wid ye,
    You've such a way wid ye, Doctor A. P.

"Since you've been here many hearts you have won;
To thousands of folk untold good you have done.
Kindliest creature, and tenderest teacher,
    And pow'rfullest preacher in all Newington.

"Doctor A. P., how we grieve you are lavin' us;
Stalwart and true, you have ne'er been decavin' us,
Upwards and higher you've always been wavin' us,
    You're always for savin' us, Doctor A. P.

"Best blessin's go wid ye, frind, over the say !
  What'll we do when you're gone—and away !
You kindliest creature, you tenderest teacher,
  And pow'rfullest preacher in all Newington."

We cannot conclude this chapter better than by quoting a testimony from one of the deacons of the Tabernacle, Mr. William Olney, giving a portrait of Dr. Pierson during his London ministry :

" Dr. Pierson was of an extremely affectionate nature, and the Christian love he showed to one he showed to others so that much of the great influence which he exerted over the minds of men came from the love he showed in countenance and word and action. This tenderness of heart was linked with extreme austerity in Christian doctrine and practice so that the slightest departure from the Word of Divine Truth was visited with a fiery indignation which contrasted strangely to the usual tenderness of his disposition. At times also, the amiability of his character was hidden beneath an apparent cold exterior which came from detachment of mind when soul and thought were centred on the work of God or the study of some special subject.

" The ordinary, daily life of the dear man of God was so unworldly as to be well-nigh ascetic. His countenance reflected the purity of his soul, and, in connection with the table or secular amusements he would allow no gratification of personal taste to interfere with his work for God to which he made all else subordinate. He ate sparingly, his conversation was almost invariably concerning the Word and work of his Saviour. No one could be in his company for long without recognizing in him the image of his Lord.

An Officer's Testimony

'Even Christ pleased not Himself' was the motive power in almost all that Dr. Pierson did and said.

"His love for the Bible was extraordinary. Day after day he would seldom let the twelve hours pass without announcing that he had 'made a discovery,' in the fields of Holy Writ. These discoveries were of hidden meanings or of comparisons which sprang from his intense searching of the Sacred Book. Some of these gems of thought were never given to the public but others came out in his public sermons and lectures. His pulpit utterances gave him extraordinary popularity in London. Christian workers were drawn from many other places of worship to sit at his feet as he dispensed from Sabbath to Sabbath in the Tabernacle the result of his Spirit-taught discoveries in Divine Truth. A leader of one of the missions connected with the Tabernacle told me that they might as well close their Sunday morning service altogether when Dr. Pierson was preaching at the Tabernacle as the avidity to hear this servant of God brought most of the workers away from the mission for the earlier service on the Lord's Day. When Dr. Pierson left his ministry at the Tabernacle the attendances were as remarkable as at the close of Charles H. Spurgeon's life."

Another testimony worth quoting was from the officers: "The deacons of the Tabernacle feel that they have had two sermons—one from you or rather from God through you—and one in you."

XIV

IMMERSION AND ITS CONSEQUENCES—A BATTLE OF CONSCIENCE

IT would be difficult for any conscientious man, who was earnestly seeking to "fulfill all righteousness" as well as to preach it, to minister for two years to such a congregation as that which met in the Metropolitan Tabernacle, without being deeply influenced in his own life and character. When we consider that Dr. Pierson, in his London ministry, found himself face to face with a large body of people who listened eagerly to his messages and learned to love him deeply and yet differed from him radically in regard to one of the principal sacraments of the Christian Church, it is not to be wondered at that he was led to investigate again the teachings of Scripture and to review his reasons for belief and practice as to baptism.

The first time that he met Charles H. Spurgeon they talked in a friendly way on the subject of believer's baptism; then during his Tabernacle ministry many communications appeared in the press and hundreds of personal letters on the subject came to Dr. Pierson. In this way the matter was brought frequently before him and he was urged by Dr. James Spurgeon and others to join the Baptist ranks and to allow his name to be presented for election as pastor. He was not unwilling to submit to immersion, if his influence would thereby be increased, but few can realize the struggle that must take place before a man sixty years of age and one of Dr. Pierson's standing and strength of convictions would turn his back on the position he had held in the Presbyterian Church for over thirty years. Such a step, he knew, would separate him from many whom he dearly loved and honoured, would be misinterpreted by unfriendly critics and might even for a time hinder his ministry.

The form of baptism had never been, to his thought, an important question and it will be remembered that the subject had come up in connection with his Detroit and Philadelphia pastorates. In London his close friend, Benjamin Greenwood, argued long and ably for the Baptist position, but at as great length and as ably Dr. Pierson replied, meeting Scripture with Scripture. He was still occupying Spurgeon's pulpit when he wrote to one of the officers of the Tabernacle, on February 9, 1893, as follows:

"MY DEAR BROTHER AND FRIEND:

"So long as I am in the Tabernacle I cannot calmly and deliberately weigh these questions. Without being consciously a reflector of others' opinions, or in any undue measure influenced thereby, I have so high a regard for my Baptist brethren that I cannot help trying to see matters as they do; and not until I am alone with the Lord and His Word, away from all this *personal* contact, can I finally reach the clear conclusions I wish to attain.

"Thus far I cannot convince myself by any logic that the ground we have covered in argument is not a debatable territory, within which there is room for an honest and intelligent difference of opinion. The main objection to the Baptists in my mind is that, *as a body*, they do not concede this. My views on these topics, as held for years, are treated as examples of unscriptural ground held by a man who has such knowledge of Scripture as makes his position on these points the more surprising and inconsistent! . . . I might abandon infant baptism as of doubtful authority, and accept believer's baptism and immersion as on the whole most obviously conformed to the common impression of Scripture. But, as I now see it, I could not stand with the great bulk of Baptists in denying that there is any logical and Scriptural foundation for the Abrahamic Covenant and infant baptism, or that there are not as many texts that may lead an honest mind to find *affusion* a legitimate baptism, as others might lead to immersion. Should I be immersed, it would be only to conform to the more satisfactory mode of meeting the question of believer's baptism; and, however I might abandon infant baptism, I should never doubt that men equally Scriptural, honest, and quite as devoted as I, if not far more so, may, with as good grounds, draw other inferences. I hate bigotry, even when it goes by the name of 'positive conviction.' On some matters the Word of God admits of more than one interpretation. ' Let every man be fully persuaded in his own mind.' I believe that in God's eyes I am now a baptized believer, and I can never submit to immersion, if by so doing I am making a concession to those who would unchurch everybody who does not interpret the Scripture just as they do."

It was nearly three years later, long after he had finally left the Tabernacle and after Rev. Thomas Spurgeon had been installed as pastor and was engaged in a successful ministry, that Dr. Pierson finally decided to abandon publicly his former position and to submit to a re-baptism. We do not intend to give at length all the steps that led to this decision or the reasons that weighed with him but the event was so important in his own life that the transition calls for a brief explanation. In order to make his position

Letter to the Philadelphia Presbytery 255

clear to his brethren in the Philadelphia Presbytery he wrote them in 1894, two years before he was finally immersed, suggesting that a letter be given him to the Congregational body. We give extended extracts from this communication because it reveals the workings of his mind:

"In the year 1876, God gave me an experience of sudden illlumination, which brought into my soul a flood of light, and made the Word of God a new book. Much that I had been taught, and had assumed as true, then seemed at least of doubtful Scriptural authority; and every matter was submitted to the searching light of God's Word, according to His criterion: 'To the Law and to the Testimony; if they speak not according to this Word it is because there is no light in them.' Two things impressed me: first, that the Bible was to be the final arbiter in all matters of doctrine and duty; and, second, that it was the guide not of scholars only, but of the common disciples; and hence that would be a correct impression, ordinarily, which prayerful study would leave on the average mind of believers.

"By such criteria I sought to test whatever I had been wont to accept as true, and all the great vital doctrines seemed to become more clear under the most careful Bible study. The Being of God, the Atoning work of Christ, His divine character, the Personality and Deity of the Spirit, and His Regenerating and sanctifying work, the Inspiration of Scripture even to its words, the universal fact of sin, and need of the new birth, and the future state of Awards seem to me plainly taught in the Bible.

"The Presbyterian polity seemed likewise in accord with the synagogue with its bench of Presbyters.

... Thus far my Presbyterian training gave me no occasion for misgiving. But, on reading the Acts of the Apostles, I felt strongly that the obvious impression left on an unprejudiced reader would be that those who heard and believed the gospel message were baptized, and that such believer's baptism was so connected with confession of Christ, as to be itself the substance of such confession. ...

"Another impression left by the reading of the Acts was that infant baptism has, in that book, a very slender basis of authority. The common, unbiassed student would not infer that such was the primitive custom. In every case but one, where the baptism of households is referred to, their 'believing' is also recorded.

"These misgivings I silenced for years by quoting to myself the sanction of long custom, and by the logical argument which goes back to the Abrahamic Covenant.

"There is something sublime in such an ideal, the believing parent, in advance, setting to his seal that God is true, and claiming covenant promise in behalf of his child. Then, as the circumcised child, when about twelve years old, taking his part in his first passover, would *ratify* the parental act, so the baptized child taking part in the Lord's Supper on becoming of age would ratify his own baptism by confessing the faith anticipated by his parents and solemnly sealed by them in advance as his representatives.

"This seemed a true philosophy, and yet my doubts as to the Scriptural authority for this ordinance were not easily dismissed. The question arose, would any plain Scriptural command be neglected if I did not baptize my children? I was compelled to admit the absence of any such direct injunction, and that so far

Infant Baptism 257

as the explicit teaching of the Word goes, the practice found but little support or sanction. Almost if not quite all the arguments in its favour would be met if some form of infant consecration or dedication were substituted in its stead, whereby parents could in behalf of their children claim covenant blessings and set their seal upon the promises by a formal act, offering them to God, without applying to them a sacrament meant for intelligent believers as a seal and confession of personal and saving faith.

"I observed with increasing misgiving that in actual practice infant baptism is sometimes a snare. No doubt many holy men and women hold a high ideal of the ordinance, but practically it is too often administered in cases where parents are at best only nominal believers, and where no real pious training is assured to the child.

"In the Presbyterian standards, though they are more carefully worded than some others, I find no word concerning baptized children which emphasizes their need, as much as unbaptized children, of the regenerating influence of the Spirit. They are treated as within the pale of the church, under its inspection and government, to be taught all Christian duties, and 'when they come to years of discretion, if they be free from scandal, appear sober and steady, and to have sufficient knowledge to discern the Lord's body, they ought to be informed it is their duty and their privilege to come to the Lord's Supper.' . . .

"This language leaves a baptized child to infer that to be sober, steady and free from scandal, and to have knowledge to discern the body of Christ in the bread, are sufficient signs of a disciple and admit to the Lord's Table. Is not the fact that, judged by such criteria, many an utterly unregenerated person actually finds entrance to our communion? . . . If in our day of superficial and unsanctified morality, any truth needs emphasis, it is that 'except a man be born again—born from above—he cannot enter nor even see the kingdom of God.' A baptized infant needs, as much as any other, the new birth. . . .

"For a considerable part of two years, when I was at the Metropolitan Tabernacle in London, God blessed the simple Gospel to the awakening of hundreds of souls. I was sought by scores of inquirers who had been depending upon baptism in infancy to such a degree that they had no clear sense of their need of the new birth. They felt a false security in having been engrafted into Christ in infancy and could not see why any other fitness for the Lord's Table was needed. I did what most of my brethren would have done—sought to turn them from all such sacramental snares to the one basis of assurance, the acceptance of Christ by faith and the renewing of the Spirit.

"Another perplexity confronted me in meeting inquirers. Not a few, brought up as pædo-baptists, being converted under my preaching, conscientiously desired believer's baptism, on what they believed to be Scriptural grounds. . . . They asked my advice, and I found it difficult to give them honest counsel without departing from my Presbyterian position that infant baptism made other baptism needless.

"Yet a third class of converts consulted me as to the baptism of their children. Though brought up to believe this to be a duty, they could find no sufficient Biblical warrant for the practice. Of course they were not of the Tabernacle congregation but outsiders who had there found converting grace. I could not honestly say that I was myself satisfied of the Biblical basis of infant baptism, and could only counsel them to be fully persuaded in their own minds. This compulsory process of introspection forced from me the confession that whatever Scriptural ground might exist for parental covenant and infant dedication, I must resort to the tradition of the elders, and the antiquity of custom for the sanction of infant baptism. If a sacrament is a seal of faith, is it proper to apply to an infant child a seal of the faith which in the nature of the case exists only in the *parent ?*

"I have always found it best when in doubt, and I know not what to do, to do nothing until the way is made clear; or if compelled to choose, take the course least liable to error. Though my doubts have not yet settled into positive convictions, it has become clear that to give encouragement to infant baptism while such serious misgivings exist is compromising my conscience. . . .

"After more than sixteen years of prayerful study these are my maturest conclusions, and though I am conscious of no radical divergence from my former faith, it is due to perfect candour that I make them known. . . . Were there room in the church where I am for a position such as I have indicated, substituting infant consecration for infant baptism and leaving consecrated children to confess Christ in believer's baptism, the Presbyterian Church would, in my judgment, be worthy to stand as the true Catholic church of the world. It would present a type of apostolic brotherhood elastic enough to embrace all regenerate believers, yet rigid enough to exclude all vital error, magnifying the great essentials and yet allowing liberty upon things not essential. Perhaps the dream is not likely to be realized but it is what some of us yearn to see actual. . . . No denomination has a monopoly of truth, and I believe that within this body is conserved as large a part of vital Christian doctrine and practice as in any other one denomination. . . .

"Every motive of worldly policy counsels me to silence, but loyalty to God, to the truth and to my brethren demands utterance whatever consequences come to me personally. Moreover, I observe that as my spiritual life deepens, these misgivings come more to the surface and will not be silenced; and whatever is closely linked to one's own best spiritual states must for him be a way of duty. . . .

"Conscience and truth are revolutionists, and when truth as we see it demands testimony, then intrepidity, loyalty, intellectual honesty and moral candour must be our guides; and we must be even more anxious to be *true* than to be consistent. In accordance with this principle I now commit this matter to God and to my brethren. We are bidden to study to show ourselves approved unto God alone. However pleasant and precious to have the approbation of those we love, there is One whose 'Well done!' carries with it eternal blessing, and to His decision from which there is no appeal I am content to submit this Testimony."

At the time of writing this letter Dr. Pierson was not ready to take any radical step that would separate him from the Presbyterian Church. Gradually, however, he became convinced that, while he could see grounds for difference of opinion in the interpretation of the Bible teachings, he, himself, would not be perfectly at peace in his own conscience until he had been baptized as a believer. He did not even seek to lead his wife and children with him and one daughter just before her father's immersion, not knowing that he was intending to take the step, wrote to know if he would "greatly object" if she decided to be re-baptized.

In the two years following the Tabernacle ministry, Dr. Pierson was much in the companionship of his Baptist co-editor on the *Review*, Dr. A. J. Gordon. Together they made many tours and held conventions in the interests of missions and for the deepening of spiritual life. On more than one occasion he consulted with Dr. Gordon on the question of re-baptism and once asked him to immerse him. For several reasons, however, it was deemed inexpedient at the time and was postponed. In February, 1895, Dr. Gordon passed away after a brief illness and so the closest link to the American Baptist Church was severed. On the day of his friend's Home-going Dr. Pierson wrote:

"Gordon died to-day (February 2d) at midnight and the change it makes in my life is unutterable. Of all men on this side he was dearest to me, my counsellor in everything—no difference of opinion in anything important and perfect sympathy of heart and action."

In the summer of 1895, during the sessions of the Northfield Bible Conference, a deep spiritual experience greatly affected Dr. Pierson's life and thought. This is briefly recorded in this private journal under the date of August 17th:

"Praise God no blessing so rich ever came into my life. D. L. Moody consulted me about inviting Andrew

Murray and Webb-Peploe to Northfield and I advised him to cable them to come. They came and closed their ten days of joint labours day before yesterday. Never have I heard such teaching and been so blessed. . . . Two addresses moved me beyond anything I ever heard —Webb-Peploe and Andrew Murray spoke on 'Faith.' Never did I see so clearly my privilege of resting moment by moment on the Word of God. I entered that day into the consciousness of the rest of faith and Thursday night sealed my new consecration in the farewell meeting. Henceforth my motto is 'That God may be all in all.'"

Conventions followed in which he joined Andrew Murray, speaking at Toronto, Boston, Chicago and elsewhere. His deepened spiritual life led him to lay somewhat less emphasis on the *work* of foreign missions and more on the *spirit* of Christ in all life and service.

The British Student Volunteer Convention was called to meet in Liverpool for the first five days of January, 1896, and the committee in charge besought the help of their "foster-father." At the same time he was invited to hold a series of meetings in British colleges and universities and to visit some of the larger cities, with his friend, Rev. F. B. Meyer, to speak on the Deepening of Spiritual Life, on Prayer, and on Missions. He saw God's hand in the special preparation that had recently been given him for this work and dedicated himself anew to the proclamation of the spiritual truths of the Gospel.

The way for him to leave home was also clear, for his beloved mother, largely on whose account he had returned annually to America during his British minis-

The Ceremony in West Croydon 263

try, had recently passed away at the ripe age of ninety-three.

He sailed for England on December 22, 1895, and after speaking at the Liverpool Conference began his spiritual campaign in the British Isles. In the course of a few months he expected to visit Bristol and it was in his mind to ask his friend, George Müller, (who had passed through a similar change of views on baptism) to immerse him at that time. One night after speaking to students in Wales on immediate obedience to the heavenly vision, he became convinced that he, himself, was postponing obedience. He was engaged to preach for Dr. James A. Spurgeon in West Croydon Chapel, London, on the following Sunday, and so strong was his conviction that re-baptism was the way of obedience for him that he immediately wrote to him to perform the rite. This was arranged to take place in the presence of a few friends on Saturday evening, February 1, 1896. No more public ceremony was thought advisable lest there should be unnecessary stir created among the friends at the Tabernacle; no more private ceremony was desired lest there should seem to be a fear of criticism. After preaching at West Croydon Chapel on the following Sunday and attending an informal reception on Monday Dr. Pierson set out to continue his Bible lecture tour in Ireland.

At first it seemed that his worst fears were to be realized and that his re-baptism was to be only misunderstood and used to discredit his motives and to hinder his ministry. When the statement was made in American papers that he had been immersed in order to secure the London Tabernacle pulpit, his intimate friend, Dr. George D. Baker, replied, "If he told me so himself, I would not believe it." But even Baptist papers held his action up for criticism, as is seen in one editorial insinuation:

"Why was the interval between Dr. Pierson's conviction of the truth of Baptist views and his baptism so prolonged? Why did he not give his testimony for Baptist views in America, his own country, where he has for many years practiced and defended infant baptism? Why, if he determined to be baptized in this country, was he not baptized in public? Was it wise, was it considerate in view of circumstances in the recent history of the Metropolitan Tabernacle, to take steps which will inevitably be viewed by many as hostile to its interests?"

Thus for the first time in his nearly forty years of public life, as he remarked, he was accused of conduct and intentions which he considered worthy only of a fool or a consummate hypocrite. Although the Metropolitan Tabernacle had a settled pastor, whom Dr. Pierson earnestly urged his friends to support, it was claimed that he was plotting to secure the pulpit. Those who knew him denied the charges in vain; those who did not know him listened to newspaper criticisms. It seemed at first as though his whole campaign might have to be abandoned. Ireland, the home of the boycott, was especially inclined to boycott his meetings. In Dublin there was a noticeable falling off in attendance although there was no decrease in the manifestations of the Spirit's presence. In Cork, the arrangements for meetings were entirely cancelled.

To a sensitive nature like that of Dr. Pierson many of the unjust criticisms of those who should have been friends were like a searing with a red-hot iron. He

Under Fire of Criticism 265

was convinced that he had done right though he conceded that more worldly wisdom might perhaps have been exercised in the time and place of performance. He was taken ill with cold and bronchial inflammation that made it difficult for him to keep his engagements. For two years he had also been under unusual strain owing to the serious illness of his beloved wife. For thirty-five years she had shared his blessings and his hardships, but the continued separation from her family, the fire of criticism to which her husband was subjected at home and abroad, and the constant travel, together with financial worries, at last brought on nervous prostration. In the midst of all this trial and under these personal attacks Dr. Pierson felt convinced that it was Satan who was seeking to hinder God's work. He would not give in either to physical weakness nor to opposition. He committed his cause to God anew, summoned all his energies and pressed forward. The result was a series of meetings in Belfast which, for spiritual impression, were beyond anything he had ever seen. Rev. Charles Inwood, who was with him, wrote of this experience:

"I came to know Dr. Pierson personally in Belfast immediately after ———— had assailed him after his immersion. He came to us much bruised and sore of heart. His mission however was a magnificent success. The great Grosvenor Hall, accommodating over 3,000, was crowded every night and his address on Foreign Missions was by far the most eloquent and soul moving missionary address I ever heard. The response and affection shown him at that critical hour touched him profoundly. His heart, craving always for love, but especially then, was refreshed by his Irish brethren.

Many features in his character and work have left an indelible and sacred impression on me—his knowledge, his gifts, his warm and guileless love, his holy and blazing indignation where the honour of his Lord and His Word were at stake, his sympathetic and careful preparation for his public ministry and his love of prayer and childlike dependence on the Holy Spirit. Most of all I was impressed with his absolute abandonment of his whole personality to the ministry of the moment; every cubic inch of his being was in every message, in every sentence, in every word, every tone, every look as he spoke."

The committee in charge of the tour deemed it advisable for Dr. Pierson to publish some reply to the criticisms that had been passed, and although it was his rule to leave his personal reputation and vindication in the hands of God, he finally consented to make to these friends a statement that might prevent further misunderstanding. From this statement we quote:

"Without reflecting upon any one, let me most explicitly state that, in some way, there has arisen a singular and complete misapprehension, both of my words and spirit, which further silence on my part might seem to sanction. . . .

"My recent baptism at Croydon Chapel had reference simply and solely to *one thing:* my individual compliance with a duty never until very lately made entirely clear, as needful on my part in order 'to fulfill all righteousness.' . . .

"The address, which has been so criticized, was wholly informal and unstudied. Some sentences were, I frankly concede, open to misapprehension, and should have been more guarded. An unsuspecting man may often give occasion to others for ascribing to him a purpose and meaning which he does not for a moment intend. . . . I was inciting disciples to appreciate the power of united prayer to bring down ever-increasing blessing of the Holy Spirit.

"I have not the least intention or thought of again taking *any* pastoral charge. The impression grows upon me that God is calling me to a different and, in a sense, wider work that would rather be hindered by such limitations. I cannot but add my sincere regret for whatever controversy I may innocently or imprudently have occasioned.

"*Dublin, Ireland, Feb. 26, 1896.*"

The lesson that he himself learned from this experience is referred to in a letter to his friend Benjamin Greenwood:

"God has been teaching me one of the greatest lessons of my life—that I am beset with foes and that not only my temper but my tongue must be in His dear keeping. At West Croydon, I spoke as though in your parlour where I could not be misunderstood, but the very words I intended to say to strengthen the hands of my brother at the Tabernacle were misinterpreted. . . . I feel my own blundering more than my own worst foes could wish."

Meanwhile God continued to set His seal of approval on His servant's ministry in the British Isles. A pastor in Ireland wrote to the *Irish Baptist Magazine*, April 6, 1896:

"When it became known that Dr. Pierson had crossed the Rubicon and burned his boats by immersion [!] it was a matter of speculation how his change of front would affect his Irish audiences. . . . In Dublin the galleries were not required and the attendance of the clergy was sparse. But it would have done your heart good to have witnessed the delight in believers' eyes as they sat spellbound, drinking in the teachings as the Doctor made clear the philosophy of the plan of salvation—God's loving and beseeching men that by the Gospel of His grace man might be restored, in whom the image of God had been 'defaced but not effaced.' His address on the Inspiration of the Bible was simply exquisite and the faith of believers increased by leaps and bounds as they listened while he showed the rock foundation on which it rested."

But it was not in Great Britain alone that he was to suffer from misunderstanding and attack. The American papers took up the subject and while some, like *The Outlook*, said that "No one who knows Dr. Pierson will doubt that he has taken the step conscientiously or can intimate that it was because of any ulterior or selfish motive," other papers severely took to task the man whom they had formerly applauded. The Philadelphia Presbytery deemed it advisable to request his resignation on account of his position on infant baptism. He, himself, had no wish to leave the Presbyterian ranks but the Presbytery took the following action on April 6, 1896:

"Resolved that the Stated Clerk be instructed to acknowledge the receipt of Dr. Pierson's communication and inform him

"(1) That, holding his present views on baptism he could not continue an acceptable minister in the Presbyterian Church which teaches that baptism, in accordance with Scripture, is rightly administered by affusion or sprinkling and that infants of such as are members of the visible church are to be baptized.

"(2) That whatever Dr. Pierson may have meant to the contrary, this Presbytery is clearly of the opinion that a change of denomination is demanded by his immersion, by the views expressed in his letter and by the proprieties of the situation.

"(3) That we therefore advise Dr. Pierson promptly to seek admission into some denomination most in sympathy with his convictions on baptism. . . .

"We testify to our continued confidence in Dr. Pierson's piety, zeal and ability as a minister of the Gospel.

"W. M. RICE, *Stated Clerk*."

As a result of this action Dr. Pierson's name was dropped from the roll of the Presbytery and he never again joined any ecclesiastical body. His convictions were unchanged as to the general doctrines and system of government of the Presbyterian Church, and while he agreed with his Baptist brethren in many respects, he could not accept their position in excluding from church-membership and from the Lord's Table any regenerated believers in Christ who differed from them on the subject of the Scriptural teaching on baptism. In a reply to the Philadelphia Presbytery (dated May 20th) Dr. Pierson said:

"I can only say that to submit myself to baptism as a believer had come to be a condition of my peace and of unclouded fellowship with God. . . . My obedience [to this gradually growing conviction] was not immediate for I was ensnared by questions of expediency. . . . I foresaw that my baptism might mean not only denominational alienation but exclusion, loss of popular favour and possibly hindrance to service. I did not foresee to what extent it would entail misrepresentation, accusation and even persecution;

that it would be construed as a sign of vacillation and inconsistency and even weakness of mind and unworthiness of motive. It must, however, be my solace that whatever discord it might create in human relations it has brought conscious harmony with God, consistency with the gospel teaching and practice and liberty to preach a full gospel message. . . .

"No doubt some former friends will forsake me, but if so I can only affirm that my sole desire is to be loyal to Christ. It must be obvious that no man at my age is likely to take such a step until what was gain to him he counts loss for Christ. . . . Had I this action to take again I would only do it more promptly, for in the nature of the case my only motive could be a desire 'to fulfill all righteousness.'"

With less courtesy and consideration on both sides, this difference of opinion between Dr. Pierson and the Presbyterian Church might have caused bitterness and have brought discredit on the name and cause of Christ. For some years many Presbyterian pulpits seemed closed to the man who had served so long and so effectively in those ranks, but later there was scarcely any Christian pulpit where he was not welcomed.

It was some years before the misunderstanding of his motives was obliterated in the minds of some connected with the Metropolitan Tabernacle. It was therefore with much gratitude and depth of feeling that he was able to write to his family thirteen years later (July 7, 1909):

"My Beloved Children:

"On Sunday, July 4th, I had what was perhaps the most conspicuously blessed Sunday of my life. You will remember that after my first year at the Tabernacle misunderstanding sprang up for which I was not to blame. . . . For sixteen years I have been praying that this might be overcome and banished. I have tried to keep still, to say nothing, and do nothing but commit it to God. After all these years, the prayer has been most abundantly and wonderfully answered in a unanimous invitation from the pastor and officers of the Tabernacle to conduct the services there on Sunday, July 4th.

"The day was magnificent, the audience great and the enthusiasm overwhelming. . . . I preached in the morning on 'Love' from 1 John iv. 7–21, and in the evening from Hebrews x. 9 on the words 'He taketh away the first that he may establish the Second.' This key verse to the Epistles to the Hebrews relates to things that have been displaced, (1) The old covenant by the new, (2) The old Testament law by the New Testament Gospel.

"It was so plain that the Holy Spirit was moving mightily that I felt led to put the test to the congregation. When those who were willing to take salvation as offered in the Gospel were asked to rise, a few stood up at first, then more followed until in the vast audience not one person remained sitting. The emotion was intense. The officers afterwards approached me with reference to holding a series of services in the building. I want you to know how our prayers for all these years have been answered."

It was indeed a sign of the loving graciousness of God that on his last visit to Great Britain the last vestige of misunderstanding should be removed and the warmth of loving confidence restored between Dr. Pierson and all those to whom he had so faithfully ministered at the Metropolitan Tabernacle.

XV

LATER BRITISH MINISTRIES—SPIRITUAL REINFORCEMENT

IN the crucible of physical affliction many men have had their characters refined and their spiritual vision clarified. This was true of Dr. Pierson. The last fourteen years of his life were years of almost constant suffering. In January, 1897, when he was sixty years of age his head and ears began to trouble him so as to interfere considerably with his hearing and continuous mental work. Through association with George Müller and others the thought of God as his physician had taken great hold upon his mind and he determined to take this ailment to God in prayer without recourse to medical treatment. On five or six occasions his suffering was so severe that he started to consult a specialist but stopped and turned back before reaching the door. He had many warm friends among physicians and greatly honoured them and their profession so that he did not, on ordinary occasions, refuse the use of medicine, but at this time it seemed to him that God was testing his faith. In Boston, on January 25th, he consulted a physician who said that he evidently had inflammation of the inner ear and advised him at once to consult an aurist. Instead he determined to leave his case in the hands of God and exactly one month later all trouble disappeared. Upon a second examination the same physician found his ears in a perfectly normal condition. The trouble never returned.

This was Dr. Pierson's first marked experience of divine healing and he came more and more in his later years to depend on God to give him physical strength. Not that he condemned the use of medicine or surgery, nor did he believe it to be the duty of all Christians to depend on God alone to heal bodily diseases. His great emphasis was on man's duty to study the laws relating to physical and spiritual health and to submit body, mind and spirit entirely to God. His convictions on the subject he briefly formulated as follows:

1. Disease is one of the consequences of sin—of broken physical and spiritual laws.
2. Healing power is primarily in the hands of God.
3. God can heal and often does heal without the use of medical remedies.
4. God more often heals through the remedies that He has provided in nature and which He has enabled man to discover.
5. It is the Christians' duty to care for their bodies by the observance of God's physical, moral and spiritual laws.
6. In case of illness Christians should first of all put themselves in the hands of God to learn the lessons that He would teach them and then, either with or without the use of means as He directs, they should seek recovery that they may regain full power to serve.
7. If healing is granted, give praise to God and devote renewed strength more earnestly to the doing of His will. If healing is withheld still glorify Him in body and spirit, by life or by death. The way in which suffering and sickness are borne may be even stronger testimony than would come through the recovery of health.

In his later, as well as in his earlier years, he frequently sought and adopted the advice of godly physicians, but more and more his main dependence was on believing prayer. Often after hours of suffering he would rise in the night and alone, or with his beloved wife, would plead with God that physical infirmity might not interfere with service and that the Adversary might not gain the victory—as Moses pleaded, " lest the Egyptians hear of it and rejoice." Many answers to these prayers are recorded in his private diaries. Several times also Christian friends met at his bedside and anointed him for healing according to the Scriptures.

God was ever present to Dr. Pierson's mind and His omnipotence was so real a factor in his conceptions of life that it was most natural for him to expect divine interposition in man's behalf. In a powerful address at one of the Mildmay Bible conferences in London, he said: " I say to you with the solemnity of a dying man that *no man has ever yet laid hold on the Supernatural Power of God* as it is possible to lay hold on that power. God's great plan for human life is that the Holy Spirit, entering into man's spirit, shall transform man's convictions, his emotions, his sensibilities, his resolutions and even his body. . . . I do not say that all disease is a direct result of sin but I am bold to say that we know very little of what the Power of God means in transforming disposition and intellect and conduct, and we have still less conception of what blessing might come even to the bodies of saints, if with apostolic faith, apostolic *power* returned to the Church."

But the severest trials to faith were yet to come. On December 13th of the same year (1897) Dr. Pierson was seized with a sudden attack of acute inflammation of the

Physical Infirmities 275

bladder and for six months suffered almost constantly. Physicians could apparently give no relief and for the first time in his life he was confined to his home almost continuously for several weeks. Still he kept at work and frequently rose from his bed of illness to keep preaching engagements. Physicians told him frankly that his active service was at an end and that he must make up his mind to rest for the remainder of his days. But they knew neither their patient nor the plans of their patient's God. The next twelve years were without doubt the most active and spiritually fruitful of Dr. Pierson's whole career. As his body weakened his spirit seemed to grow stronger and more keen to discern spiritual things.

Sometimes for months together, during these closing years, he appeared to be in almost perfect health, but the results of sixty years of strenuous life were seen in the gradual breaking down of his physical system. His right wrist became stiff and swollen and so continued for ten years and yet during this period he wrote constantly. He seldom had recourse to the services of a secretary or stenographer but wrote carefully with his own hand his letters, articles for the press and the manuscripts of his books—all of which were published after he had entered his second half century of life.

Probably the most important and influential of these later volumes was the "Life of George Müller of Bristol," with whom, for twenty years, he had enjoyed a most romantic and helpful friendship. The death of Mr. Müller in Bristol, England, in March, 1898, brought a deep sense of loss to Christians everywhere, and was a great blow to Dr. Pierson, who had so recently been consigned by his physicians to the list of the inactive.

The "Prophet and Patriarch of Bristol," Dr. Pierson considered the most remarkable man he had ever met and the one who most deeply influenced his life. His first introduction to the facts of Mr. Müller's history was, as a young man, when he read a little book entitled "The Life of Trust" by Dr. Francis Wayland. This made an impression on him which was deepened a few years later, in 1866, on his way home from Europe, when he heard a Unitarian clergyman describe his visit to Mr. Müller and the interview which, he said, "was like talking with one of God's princes who had seen the Almighty face to face."

In 1878 and 1879 when Mr. Müller was in America, the personal friendship began which was fostered by correspondence and by visits in each other's homes in Detroit, Philadelphia and later in Bristol. In 1896 Dr. Pierson was asked to conduct a "mission" in Bristol and enjoyed daily interviews with the venerable patriarch then over ninety years of age. Here he heard again the wonderful story of the man's early life of sin, of his conversion at the age of twenty, of his desire to be a missionary, of his ministry in Bristol where his church sent out sixty of its members to become missionaries. Here he was admitted into the sanctuary of Mr. Müller's private prayer life and saw the simplicity and faith in which he lived and laboured. He visited the orphanages with their 2,000 boys and girls and heard the story of God's provision for every need, without any direct appeals for human aid. He listened also as Mr. Müller told of his long missionary tours and of the "Scriptural Knowledge Institute" which had established mission schools and had scattered two million copies of the Word of God. At sixty years of age Dr. Pierson was not too old to learn and, with humility and an eager thirst after knowledge, he listened as Mr. Müller gave detailed testimony to show God as a hearer and answerer of prayer. In one of these interviews he asked Mr. Müller if he had ever petitioned God for anything that had not been granted.

"Sixty-two years, three months, five days and two hours have passed," replied Mr. Müller with his characteristic exactness, "since I began to pray that two men might be converted. I have prayed daily for them ever since and as yet neither of them shows any signs of turning to God."

"Do you expect God to convert them?"

"Certainly," was the confident reply. "Do you think God would lay on His child such a burden for sixty-two years if He had no purpose for their conversion?"

Not long after Mr. Müller's death Dr. Pierson was again in Bristol, preaching in Bethesda Chapel—the meeting place of the Brethren. In the course of his sermon he told of this conversation and as he was going out at the close of the service a lady stopped him and said:

"One of those two men, to whom Mr. Müller referred, was my uncle. He was converted and died a few weeks ago. The other man was brought to Christ in Dublin."

While Dr. Pierson was prostrated with illness in his Brooklyn home, he heard of the death of Mr. Müller in Bristol and immediately he began to plan a biography. On hearing however that an official "Life" was contemplated, he wrote with characteristic generosity to Mr. James Wright, the son-in-law and successor of Müller, that he would gladly transfer his gathered material to any author whom the family might select.

As a result the request came back that Dr. Pierson himself should undertake to prepare the authorized biography.

The commission was accepted and carried out in spite of a partially disabled body and amid the pressure of many other duties. The author hoped, through the book, to perpetuate Mr. Müller's unique testimony to God's faithfulness.[1]

The purpose to distribute the biography freely to Christian workers was first broached in a meeting of the Brethren of Bethesda Chapel, Bristol, before the volume had come from the press. Prayer was offered for funds, for open channels of distribution and for blessing on all those who should read the life. No appeals were made but enough funds were supplied from the author's royalties and from gifts of friends to send out thousands of free copies to missionaries and ministers all over the world. Many more thousands of copies were sold and it was translated into French, Danish, Welsh, Japanese, Dutch, German, Swedish and other languages. The seed thus sown has yielded abundant harvest. Unnumbered letters from missionaries and converts, from missionary societies and Christians in the home churches, were a further testimony to God's faithfulness as a hearer and answerer of prayer.

At the first meeting between Dr. Pierson and James Wright, the son-in-law and successor to Mr. Müller, a curious incident occurred. As they met in his drawing-room and clasped hands two five-pound notes pressed against each other in the interlocked palms. Each had been prompted by the same impulse and said almost at

[1] The volume is entitled "The Life of George Müller, Patriarch and Prophet of Bristol."

Marked Answers to Prayer 279

the same moment—" It has been laid on my heart to ask your acceptance of a small gift in the name of the Lord." The strange coincidence amused and touched the hearts of both and as each insisted that the other retain his gift, both had the joy of giving and of receiving at the same time.

While preparing Mr. Müller's biography, Dr. Pierson spent much time in Bristol and preached frequently, as he did also in subsequent years, in Bethesda Chapel. When Mr. Wright died in 1905 he was requested to write the account of that life also. Mr. G. Fred Bergin, the present director of the orphanage work, became a close friend and has frequently testified to the blessings of those ministries among the Brethren and the Bristol orphans.

It was the privilege and joy of Dr. Pierson to receive in his own life many answers to prayer, similar to those so conspicuous in Mr. Müller's work. Many times he records the direct answers for the supply of temporal needs as well as for spiritual blessings. In January, 1896, he lost his only overcoat in New Port, England. The weather was raw and he had no funds available for a new coat. He made the matter a definite subject of prayer, and soon the coat was returned through a series of coincidences that plainly showed God's hand in the answer. That same week he was led in his early morning devotions to lay before God in special prayer the financial needs of his family. His bank account had been reduced to almost nothing and certain bills had come in unexpectedly from America that required payment. At breakfast he was handed a letter telling of money unexpectedly deposited to his account which left a balance of $90.00 beyond immediate needs.

In a letter home he wrote: "I have thought that perhaps God laid me aside from active service to show me that He could care for our temporal wants when ordinary sources of income are cut off, as well as when I am able to work."

Another signal answer to prayer came when, a few years later, he desired to erect a memorial chapel at Nowgong, where his daughter Louise had "fallen asleep" after a brief service in India. He wrote to his absent children (July 1, 1904):

"Ever since dear Louise departed we have felt inclined to rear some little memorial to her at Nowgong. Miss Fistler writes that a chapel is very much needed, and has sent suggested plans. This makes it seem plain that it is God's mind that this should be done, especially as there is no money wasted in the plan. I at once wrote that we, as a family, would undertake to build this little memorial. At family worship that morning we put the matter afresh before the Lord, and asked that He would give us some evidence *that day* of His approval or disapproval of our plans. I never had a more signal answer to prayer. Before night we had unexpected gifts sent to us, thank-offerings for the Mildmay Meetings, *amounting to almost the exact sum* needed for the building. This will enable us to present the chapel entirely furnished. How gracious of God to testify so lovingly and clearly to His approval of these plans."

God's bountiful supply never made Dr. Pierson a careless steward. Every new talent was received as a trust and he was ever studious to avoid waste of time or strength or money. Often did he joyfully forego a pleasure that he might give to some work which made a strong appeal. At one time he had arranged to

Hilarious Giving

spend a month with friends in Switzerland but appeals for help caused a change of program to a week in the Lake District, then further calls led him to take instead a day's walking excursion in the suburbs of London. Even intimate friends did not know of the many benefactions that flowed through his hand. He delighted to be the one to answer the prayers of others, and hundreds of God's servants have given thanks for timely help received through him. One day he was driving along a country road near his Northfield home, when he met a man trudging along carrying a valise to the railroad station three miles distant. It was out of his way but Dr. Pierson invited the man to ride and drove him to his destination. In course of conversation he learned that the traveller was a minister of a small parish. His son was lying very ill and his heart was heavy. In parting Dr. Pierson pressed a sum of money into the man's hand and in the outburst of thankfulness that followed he learned that he had again been God's messenger in a time of dire need.

Unostentatious giving was his delight, for he believed in keeping his left hand in ignorance of his right hand's generosity. But giving brought to him such hilarious enjoyment that his family and more intimate friends learned to recognize, by the peculiar elasticity in his movements and the particular sparkle in his eye, evidence of some new benefaction that had brought joy to his heart. Neither was his giving confined to times of plenty, for he learned to regard the impulse to give to a worthy cause as an impulse from his Lord, and he believed that the same God who made it possible for him to relieve another's extremity would make up any temporary deficiency caused by his gift. He that "lendeth to the Lord" will not long be kept a creditor of the Almighty.

Another scene of Dr. Pierson's British labours was the famous auditorium of Exeter Hall, London, where for seventy-five years many lecturers on social and religious subjects had swayed vast multitudes. Here Albert, the Prince Consort, appeared in 1840 on behalf of the abolition of the slave trade; here the first great temperance meetings were held and here John B. Gough delivered his wonderful orations in 1831; here Jenny Lind gave her famous concerts. In 1881 Exeter Hall became the headquarters of the Young Men's Christian Association and in this place twenty-two years later Dr. Pierson was introduced by Sir George Williams to deliver a series of lectures on the Bible—a series that proved to be a noteworthy contribution to Christian thought. The first meeting was held in the smaller hall for the benefit of two or three hundred young men and other Christian workers, but at the second meeting the audience of two thousand necessitated their adjourning to the larger auditorium and at the subsequent lectures the hall was crowded with three thousand listeners. Each week they came to hear this Bible teacher—one who did not merely extol the beauties of the Word, but who so exhibited its wonderful structure, its divine revelations and its superhuman power, that his hearers were compelled to acknowledge for themselves its unique, matchless beauty, heavenly wisdom and divine authority.[1]

These lectures, as well as similar series in 1904 and

---

[1] The three volumes of lectures are entitled "God's Living Oracles," "The Bible and Spiritual Criticism," and "The Bible and Spiritual Life."

1907, were delivered with the aid of large charts that presented the outlines and doctrinal teachings in origi-

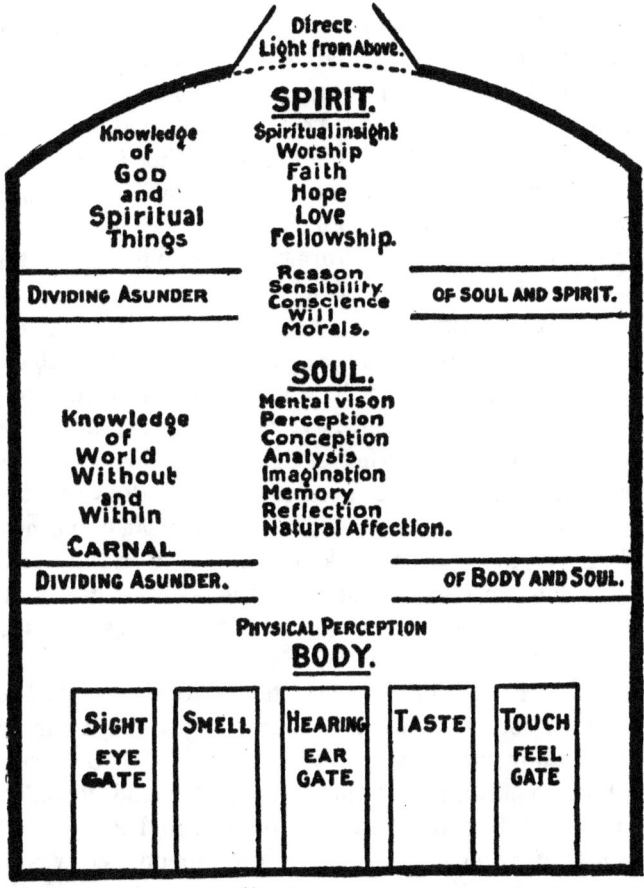

nal and graphic way so that they were doubly impressive. The accompanying diagram illustrates the way in which eye-gate was used as well as ear-gate.

The ready ability of the speaker to meet objections was shown on more than one occasion. His arguments were reasonable but he was unyielding in his contention for the authority of the Bible. One evening he remarked that no one claimed verbal inspiration for the English Bible—although that was remarkably accurate—but only for the text of the original writings.

"Then," exclaimed a gentleman rising in the front seat, "if we cannot read the original we might as well have no inspired Bible at all."

"Well," replied the lecturer quickly, "my daughter, who is a missionary in Japan, recently sent me a photograph of her child whom I have never seen. No doubt it is not a perfect likeness. Do you suppose that I said, as I looked upon it, that is not the original and therefore I might as well have no grandchild at all?"

The testimonies to the results of these lectures came from far and near. A Londoner said that as he came home in the train one evening a porter sat down next to him and after a little asked if he was "on the Lord's side." The porter added that the lecture in Exeter Hall on Wednesday had led him to confess Jesus as Lord and to own Him as His Saviour.

Dr. Pierson himself wrote home to his son that he had never seen God work so manifestly and constantly. "It humbles me," he said, "that I am only now learning how to stand out of the way and let God work."

It is not possible here to give in full Dr. Pierson's method of Bible study. His main dependence was on the Scriptures themselves.[1] He studied them in the original and with the help of a few select commentaries

[1] Some results of fifty years of Bible study are gathered in Dr. Pierson's "Knowing the Scriptures."

to discover, if possible, the mind of God. He gathered light from all sources and brought the many rays to a focus in his own mind that he might give out that light to others. Such volumes as "The Speaker's (or Bible) Commentary," Saphir's "Divine Unity of Scriptures," Bernard's "Central Teaching of Jesus Christ," Saphir's, Murray's and Moule's expositions of the "Epistle to the Hebrews," Graham on Ephesians and other studies occupied shelves within easy reach. On one occasion when speaking on a difficult passage in the Book of Revelation he said," No preacher can hope to understand this chapter unless he has read the book a thousand times; this I have done, and I know that I have not yet fathomed its full meaning."

Six rules for Bible study he gave to those who would enter into the deeper secrets of the Book.

"No book on philosophy or science or poetry or history needs these rules, but without them no one can penetrate into the real meaning of the Bible.

"1. *Search.* The wonders do not lie on the surface, like shells on the beach, but are hidden, like nuggets in veins, and must be dug up.

"2. *Meditate.* There is a process akin to rumination, which, as you dwell on the Scriptures, draws from them life power. Without such meditation, reading is like eating that which you do not digest.

"3. *Compare.* There is no error on earth which may not find apparent support from some isolated text, but no error in doctrine or practice can stand the test of the whole Scripture. We must compare Scripture with Scripture so that one passage may interpret another or may correct the false impression gained from another.

"4. *Pray.* 'Open/ Thou mine eyes that I may behold wondrous things out of Thy law.' The Spirit who inspired must be the Spirit to expound. **Prayer is the illuming secret to the intellectual eye.**

"5. *Believe*. In all other departments men believe what they know but in the divine revelation men come to know what they believe. Faith must accept God's Word in order to be confirmed in knowledge. As Isaiah said to Ahag: 'If you will not believe, surely ye shall not be established'—confirmed in knowledge.

"6. *Obey*. We can never learn the second lesson from God until we have practiced the first. 'If any man willeth to do His will he shall know of the teaching.' Doubt is usually the result of disobedience. When you see a command in the Bible, translate it into conduct and character. Obey what God teaches and He will lead you into larger knowledge.

"Thus by searching and meditating, by comparing and praying, by believing and obeying, we are enabled to see in this Book its Divine Author, we discover the remedy for man's depraved state and nature and we come to the deep knowledge of the mysteries of God."

The Bibles which he used for study were marked and annotated in a way that showed scrupulous neatness and diligent research. Prebendary Webb-Peploe says: "As I sat on the platform at the Northfield Conference with Dr. Pierson I could not fail to be struck with the extraordinary appearance of his broad margined Bible. Such a sight I had never seen as that book, interlined, marked with references, notes and other signs of deep and thoughtful study."

The joy he found in "discoveries" was only second to the joy of sharing these new found treasures with others. Whether his audience was made up of one interested listener, or was a group of old ladies, or was a vast crowd in Exeter Hall, at Mildmay, or at some

The Keswick Conventions

other convention, his enthusiasm was equally great if only his hearers were ready to see and believe the Word.

One of the most charming spots in the English Lake District is the town of Keswick on the shores of Derwentwater. Here for many years, in the last week of July, Christians have gathered to receive religious refreshment, and hither came Dr. Pierson in almost annual pilgrimages during the last thirteen years of his life to receive and to give reinforcement for spiritual life. He had become familiar with "Keswick Teaching," as it is commonly called, before he ever visited Keswick. In the year 1895 he had learned from experience the purpose and power of God to transform character and to give victory over every known sin. Then he was asked to attend a series of Keswick meetings in London in 1896 and the following year was invited to address the Keswick Convention.

Keswick teaching consists in definite progressive steps, from sin to sanctity. The basis of the movement is a conviction that the average Christian is too often without the experience of real spiritual power; that the average Christian life is worldly, and that it is the duty and privilege of every child of God to enter at once into "Newness of Life" and to walk in the power of the Risen Christ.

Six definite steps are presented at Keswick by the various speakers on six successive days: Monday—General preparation by a view of the sinfulness of sin; Tuesday—Dealing with sin; Wednesday—The keeping power of Christ; Thursday—Joy and rest in God; Friday—Power for service; Saturday—Missions. The steps are more fully described by Dr. Pierson as follows:

First: A searching of the heart through God's illumination, to reveal its secrets. This revelation to be followed by instant abandonment of every known sin and of every weight that hinders holy living (Ephesians iv. 22-24; Romans vi. 11-13; Hebrews xii. 1, 2).

Second: The death of self in every form.
1. Self-trust (Romans x. 1, 2).
2. Self-reliance (John xv. 4-6).
3. Self-will (James iv. 13, 15).
4. Self-seeking (Matthew xvi. 24, 25).
5. Self-pleasing (Galatians vi. 14).
6. Self-defense (1 Peter ii. 19-23; iii. 16).
7. Self-glorification (Galatians vi. 14).

Third: The absolute surrender of the will unto God in obedience. "No man can serve two masters."

Fourth: The believer filled with the Spirit—claimed by faith—apart from feeling (Romans iv. 21). This means that the Christian is
1. Sealed by the Spirit (Ephesians i. 13, 14).
2. Empowered by the Spirit (Acts i. 8).
3. Filled by the Spirit for teaching and service (Colossians iii. 16; 1 John ii. 2).

Fifth: Experience of the revelation of Jesus Christ as an indwelling presence (Matthew xxviii. 20; John xiv. 17, 23; Galatians i. 6; Hebrews xi. 17).

Sixth: Enjoyment of the privileges and victories of the higher and deeper Christian life.
1. The rest of faith (1 Romans v. 1, 2; Hebrews iii. 7-iv. 11).
2. Power over sin (1 Corinthians xv. 56, 57; Romans vi. 4; viii. 2).
3. Passion for souls (Romans ix. 1, 2).
4. Conscious fellowship with God (1 John i. 3).
5. Prevailing prayer (John xv. 7; James v. 16, 18; 1 John v. 14, 15).

No speaker is asked to take part in a Keswick convention unless he can testify to a conscious experience as a result of taking the steps indicated.

After-meetings are held each day but only for inquirers. At this session there are many sharp thrusts and many wounds, but the healing balm is applied by the same faithful hands and life comes out of death.

At the first visit of Dr. Pierson to Keswick he told of the way in which he had been led into the life of victory and blessing. It was no small humiliation to this man sixty years of age, who had, for forty years, been a leading teacher and preacher, to stand before that large assembly and unflinchingly confess his sins of impatience and pride and self-will that had marred his usefulness and then to describe how God had shown him his weaknesses and at the same time had revealed the divine source of strength. Rev. Evan H. Hopkins, in describing the scene, says:

"All hearts went out to him as he told how God had searched his heart during the visit of Rev. H. W. Webb-Peploe and Andrew Murray at Northfield two years before. He told of the new victories that had enriched his life and the new power that had marked his service. He expressed a desire to be more widely used in promoting in his own land the line of truth that had been so blessed to his own soul."

Dr. Pierson closed his testimony with an ascription of praise to God. The effect was electric and many others came forward to say that their way also had been cleared of obstacles and they had received new inspiration and strength for the conflict. In describing the place and the convention he wrote:

"Keswick is unique for its spiritual *atmosphere*. This

is, first of all, and all the time, an atmosphere of *prayer*. Prayer is the law of preparation, of continuance, of consummation; quiet waiting before the Lord, and patient waiting on the Lord, and for the Lord, is the habit. The singing is a feature, but not *the* feature, and the prayer gives even the praise a new quality. Thus the atmosphere is fragrant with the Holy Spirit's presence. If any speaker indulges in a rhetorical, ambitious flourish of words, or in some elaborately prepared speech, intended for effect, it is like a loud, discordant note in a generally subdued and quiet harmony. . . .

"And never have I seen such entire and engrossing pursuit of one thing, and such adaptation of all minor matters to the major purpose. There is no published program of subjects or of speakers, but a definite order is pursued; and if a Keswick speaker drops in the third day, he knows what is the point in the progressive unfolding of truth where he is to fit into the general impression, and promote it. But above all else was I impressed with the Holy Spirit's pervasive presence. To see 3,000 people quietly waiting before God in silent prayer, and expectant of blessing—singing, praying, praising, hearing, simply as those whose attitude is that of expectation—was a new experience. I yearn to see Keswick practically reproduced in America. With all the conventions now existing, there is not one that makes such a convention unnecessary."

After he had been introduced to the sacred fellowships of Keswick, Dr. Pierson frequently made trips across the Atlantic to testify and teach on the convention platform. His Bible readings drew large and attentive audiences. His clear and practical messages were always earnest and sometimes solemn but never sombre or purely emotional. One series of Bible studies which was most helpful was entitled "A Spiritual Clinique," in which he diagnosed spiritual diseases and prescribed the divine remedies. With a rare evidence of a knowledge of medicine this physician of souls pointed weak and ailing men and women to the Great Physician in whose hands no case is incurable. One hearer was so astonished by the profound knowledge of medical science shown in the address that he turned to a medical man who sat next to him and asked whether the speaker could be depended upon as a reliable guide in his excursion into the realms of medicine. The reply was—" Dr. Pierson has as complete a grasp of the subject as I myself possess."

At the convention in 1905 his addresses called forth from one Church of England rector the following extravagant comparison:

"There was great expectation, united prayer and unity as in the days of the apostles. On Friday evening 3,000 persons were gathered together in one tent. Upon these the Holy Spirit fell. The speaker was kept from completing his address by the sobs and cries of Christians who confessed their failures and sins."

That occasion was described by Dr. Pierson's own pen as follows:

" In the closing meeting of Friday night, there were the most manifest demonstrations and illustrations of God's working. Many Christians had focussed their prayers largely on this meeting and a company of about thirty met by agreement that afternoon for an hour or more of prayer. Definite requests were made that the Holy Spirit would sweep through the meeting in power, setting aside the appointed speakers, if He pleased;

breaking down souls in cries and tears, bursting through all needless restraints of fixed program, leading to boldness of testimony, keeping down all disorderly elements, leading to momentous decisions, inspiring new self-dedication, constraining all to remove hindrances to holiness and usefulness, and leading some to offer themselves for the mission fields of the world. Every specific request made that afternoon on the hillside was fulfilled to the letter.

"While Rev. E. W. Moore was giving an address on 1 Cor. iii. 2–15, on 'The Ordeal of Fire,' I, who was to follow him, felt God's refining fire going through me, revealing the wood, hay, and stubble of work and motive. So humbling and overwhelming was this conviction, that when called upon to lead in prayer and address the meeting, it was quite involuntary first of all to make a confession, and ask others, who likewise had felt conscious of God's direct dealing, to stand before God as those who then and there besought Him, to refine us now. In response to that invitation practically the whole tent full of people rose as one man, and, while prayer was being offered, many joined in an audible 'Amen.' Not one word of my proposed address was ever delivered, nor was the subject even indicated. There was no need of leadership. Another and greater One was in control, invisibly present and presiding.

"The prayer was scarcely concluded, when a spirit of penitent confession broke out in every quarter, and I stood there on my feet for about two hours and a half, witnessing the Holy Spirit's wondrous working. A soldier acknowledged desertion and theft, and left the tent to write out his confession, and some of us, later on, saw the letters that he had written. A commander in the navy declared his purpose to make his ship a floating bethel. No less than fifty clergymen, evangelists and leaders in Christian work, confessed to sins of avarice, ambition, appetite, lust of applause, neglect of the Word, of prayer, of souls; hundreds of other individuals confessed various sins of omission and commission, sometimes a half dozen or more on their feet at once.

"No improper word was spoken. All was subdued, but deep, intense, searching. The meeting might have gone on without decline of interest, had not motives of expediency and consideration for others prevailed. When we closed with old 'Coronation' at 10:30, there had been no disturbance. Penitence, confession, prayer, self-surrender, holy resolve, had led up to praise and adoration. Then the great throng quietly separated with the profound sense that God had visited His people."

On his return to America in 1897, Dr. Pierson conducted, with Charles Inwood of Belfast, F. B. Meyer of London, Dr. Cornelius Woelfkin of Brooklyn, and others, similar meetings for the deepening of spiritual life. The Keswick method of spiritual reinforcement was thus extended to Christians gathered at Northfield, Boston, Baltimore, Brooklyn, Syracuse, Chicago, Toronto, Rochester and elsewhere. After one of these meetings a fellow minister approached Dr. Pierson and expressed his regret that he had formerly thought the speaker cold and unfriendly in his manner.

"Brother Harris," replied Dr. Pierson, "do you know, I am an irascible old man; but *what would I be if it were not for the Grace of God!*" The secret of the misunderstanding in this case, however, was that Dr. Pierson had a rheumatic right hand and could not shake hands cordially.

His last visit to Keswick, in 1909, was an especially memorable time to him, but his friends were grieved to see the change that had come over him. While his spirit was as keen and enthusiastic as ever, it was obvious that his physical strength did not correspond with his mental alertness. All who heard him seemed intuitively to realize that he was delivering his valedictory addresses amid the beloved surroundings that knew him so well. This feeling seemed to be shared by Dr. Pierson himself.

"There was something infinitely pathetic," wrote a friend, " in the personal remarks which he made at the close of his first address on 'Foundation Truths in Holy Living'—something that seemed to indicate that the long fellowship was about to be broken, and that he must not part from his fellow Christians with the least shadow of misunderstanding between them. Speaking with manifest emotion, he said that before coming to the meeting that morning, that he might get right with God, he had made confession to God of a sin against Him which he would not mention to his audience, as it was quite sufficient that he had mentioned it with deep penitence to God. But it had occurred to him that he had been guilty of a sin to his brethren. 'In my zeal,' he said, 'to be true and genuine and sincere I have long neglected the cultivation of winning and attractive manners, and, no doubt, have been a stumbling-block to many souls; and I make that confession here this morning. We are told to speak the truth in love. Some of us may be so zealous for the truth that we forget the love, or so zealous for the love that we forget the truth; and I want to say that if anything in me has been repellent through undue frankness or brusqueness, I repent of it before God, and I acknowledge it with sorrow to you."

No one who listened to these words is likely ever to forget the effect which they produced, and when, a minute later, having made his own confession, he again asked any to stand up if the Lord had shown them something in their life that must be rectified, Godward or manward, and to take an instant, visible, decisive step in the recognition of this fact, a large number rose to their feet.

In the quiet of his own room that night he wrote home to his children a letter that reveals the man as few knew him:

"MY BELOVED SONS AND DAUGHTERS:
"Nothing has been made more plain to me since leaving home than that in cultivating morals and truth in the inward parts I have too much neglected to exhibit outwardly a winning manner. I have never meant to be abrupt or discourteous but have often impressed others as unsympathetic and taciturn or even cynical it may be. . . . I am sure that Truth is not to be at the cost of Love and that it is selfishness not to restrain the inner feelings from needless exposure in face and manner.

"I want to ask forgiveness for any offenses against love which I have committed in the home, and to remove all stumbling-blocks out of your way, my beloved children.

"God's infinite loveliness grows on me. To an extent hitherto unknown every detail has been committed to His hands and He has shown Himself marvellously faithful. I can only testify and exhort you more and more to commit to Him every matter however small in perfect trust. Let us be in a very uncommon sense wholly given up to Him. Time is short; eternity is long; and Christ is near. May God keep you on His shoulder for supporting strength, on His bosom for cherishing love, and cheer you Himself and hold you in His embrace.

"With tenderest love,
"FATHER."

Time would fail to tell of the many other British ministries of Dr. Pierson—in Wales and in Christ Church, London, in Harcourt Chapel and Westminster Chapel, and at many conventions and anniversaries of various denominations and societies. British Christians found in his sermons and addresses spiritual nourishment to their taste and he found in British Christians true friends and yokefellows. Many of these British friends were privileged to come into close fellowship with Dr. Pierson. To them he was not only a wellknown divine and an undaunted crusader but he was a genial companion whose fund of information and love of good stories made many hours pass delightfully. Many were the letters that he wrote in verse to acknowledge hospitality or gifts. Dr. J. B. Figgis of Brighton, whose pulpit he frequently supplied, gives an intimate view of his guests and with this we close the British reminiscences.

"I heard him sometimes in my own church, once in Bethesda, at Bristol, often on the platform, often in 'the Tent of Meeting,' but I never heard him that I did not come away with some great subject of divine truth made clearer to my mind and dearer to my heart. As to the Person of God, or Christ, or the Spirit, occasionally there was something left to be desired, but as to the divine power, the divine doctrine, and our human duty and God's grace to carry it into effect, nothing was ever wanting. There was a rich vein of Biblical exposition, Scripture compared with Scripture, and in between these were such striking illustrations as made the truth glow and shine.

"Our dear friend's coming to Keswick was wonderfully timed in the providence of God. Though by no means one of the founders, he was, in these latter years, one who much helped to make Keswick. This was natural, inasmuch as Keswick had largely helped to make him. No doubt his intellectual powers, his giant grasp of truth, his energy of expression, would have made him remarkable in any period of the Church's history; but the mellowing and soul-subduing power of sanctification, for which man has no credit, brought in traits of character of another and gentler order, and without these the other faculties must have been somewhat rigid, if not stern.

"His nature was exceedingly sensitive. Before a service one dared not speak to him unless he spoke to you, and after a service, nine times out of ten, one was awed into silence, and so was he. 'This one thing' he did, and everything was sacrificed to the one thing. I shall never forget how men of the strongest nature I ever knew were broken down under his appeals, and sat in the vestry after the service with the tears streaming down their cheeks.

"Not many knew him well in private. He and his wife twice spent two months under my roof. I was away resting most of the time; but it was good to hear of the sweetness of the family prayers with the servants of my household and with that devoted wife. Never was a husband so faithful and interested; hardly a letter was posted or a step taken, my housekeeper told me, that he and Mrs. Pierson did not go together. One often hears a husband jokingly taunted with leaving his packing to his wife. Dr. Pierson left neither his own nor his wife's but did both himself. He would turn to her during family prayers, and ask her thought on the passage read, and in other ways show that he had learned that great lesson of the New Testament to begin first to show piety at home.

"America sent us the greatest force of modern evangelism in D. L. Moody, one of the greatest preachers of modern times in Henry Ward Beecher, and one of the greatest expositors in Arthur T. Pierson, and we give God thanks that they came from the Great Republic beyond the seas as a token and pledge of the union of hearts which the statesmen of to-day are seeking so graciously to ratify."

A Believer's Bank-note Designed by Dr. Pierson.

XVI

LATER AMERICAN MINISTRIES—RECRUITING IN VARIOUS CAMPS

THE life of an unsettled preacher—unsettled, that is, geographically—is by no means an easy one. He is continually separated from his family and from his books and papers. He must travel in all sorts of weather and in all kinds of conveyances; must endure many discomforts in second or third rate hotels; must forego the conveniences of home and many of the joys of neighbourliness. He must be ready at all times in sickness and in health to respond to calls for service from those who perhaps have not the considerateness of friendly parishioners. Sometimes he is in danger of being "killed by kindness" from those who would be too lavish in their bounties or too eager to furnish entertainment without rest. But the itinerant teacher and evangelist endures all hardship submissively or joyfully, according to his nature, as a good soldier of Jesus Christ. There are at the same time many compensations in such a ministry— the joys of wide service; the eager coöperation of local committees whose enthusiasm might not survive a prolonged pastorate; the many new and priceless friendships formed; the opportunity to repeat the same tested messages to many different audiences; the blessed memories to be stored up for future testimony.

Such were the experiences of Dr. and Mrs. Pierson during the last two decades of his life on earth. Together they crossed the Atlantic twenty-six times, the American Continent six times and the Pacific Ocean twice. In all they travelled not less than one hundred and fifty thousand miles—a distance equal to six times round the world—on the King's Business. On principle they never carried accident insurance, holding that their "lives were in God's hands." In 1900 on a journey to England to attend a Keswick convention their steamer ran into a freight vessel, cutting her in half amidships. The *Campania's* injuries were slight and above the water line, but the other ship sank within sight of all, and only the captain and thirteen of the crew were saved. To the solemn sadness felt at the death of the unfortunate sailors was added a deep note of thankfulness when it was learned that the sunken vessel was loaded aft with gunpowder and dynamite, and that God in His gracious providence had prevented collision at a point which would have meant disaster to hundreds. Dr. Pierson talked personally to the rescued officer, led the meeting of the passengers for prayer and planned the practical help for the survivors. He wrote his children in America—"I hope you will hold a family service, and unitedly thank God for this deliverance. I feel doubly pledged thereby to the Lord. Let us more than ever be wholly His—and daily and hourly watch at His gates to know His will for the day."

Once on his way home from Rochester in 1905 and again on a journey from New York to Northfield, Massachusetts, the train on which Dr. Pierson rode was partially wrecked, but he suffered no injury. At another time when he was returning from a session of the Ecumenical Missionary Conference in Carnegie Hall, New York, he was crossing lower Broadway in company with his friends, Mr. George C. Stebbins and Mrs. Waring Stebbins. They were talking earnestly of the things of the Kingdom when a swiftly moving electric car struck them, throwing Mr. Stebbins to the ground, tossing Dr. Pierson to one side and rolling Mrs. Stebbins under the front of the car. Those who witnessed the accident expected to find one or more of the party killed and accounted it little short of a miracle that all escaped serious injury. A broken tooth was Dr. Pierson's only mark of the hazardous experience, but in his heart there was another stored up memory of the heavenly Father's care.

"In conferences and conventions oft," might have been written over the last twenty years of Dr. Pierson's ministry in America. He took no vacations but found recreation in a variety of employments. In summer, even when the thermometer registered from ninety to one hundred degrees, he kept his preaching engagements in Boston, New York and Philadelphia, sometimes against the strong advice of physicians. He could not be content with idleness and the best tonic to his system was an opportunity to witness for God. He might be more weary and weak after the effort, but he felt again that, in spite of pain, life was worth living. Summer and winter lectures in Bible schools occupied many months—in the Moody Bible Institute, Chicago, and in the Bible Teachers' Training School and the National Bible Institute, New York City.

The letters of testimony received after such addresses were varied by objections and criticisms, which at times could not but cause a smile at the writer's expense. One of these in which humour and pathos are mingled read as follows:

"DEAR SIR:

"Having heard you several times I want to say that your manner of dealing with religious matters is so touching that even an infidel like me may be attracted and even convinced that religion (though on the most incredible basis) can become a source of relief and peace for a wearied and perplexed soul. Last Sunday I was so touched that I had the intention to declare openly to-day that I will join the Church. But unfortunately yesterday heard the awful tirades of Rev. ——— and I became a backslider again!

"Respectfully yours,
"——— ———"

In no place was Dr. Pierson, during the last years, more at home or more helpful and appreciated than in the Bedford Presbyterian Church, Brooklyn, of which his family were members. Here he was friend and adviser to the pastors, Rev. Wm. J. Hutchins and Dr. S. Edward Young, and here he gave freely of his services and contributed generously to the building of chapel and church. His faith and enthusiasm were contagious and inspired the pastors and people with a confidence that they could, with God's help and their own united efforts, accomplish tasks that had seemed impossible.

He also rendered valuable service in the Fifth Avenue Presbyterian Church and in the First Baptist Church of New York City; in Boston and Worcester; in Philadelphia and Baltimore; in Detroit, Michigan; in Toronto, Ontario; and in Dallas, Texas. He addressed conventions in Atlanta, Georgia, and other Southern centres, and on the Pacific Coast in Los Angeles, San Francisco and other cities.

Some ministries to which Dr. Pierson was invited

The Parliament of Religions   303

were not much to his taste. In 1893 he was asked to speak at the Parliament of Religions at the Chicago Exposition, but though he held undoubtingly that Christianity has nothing to fear from comparison with the best of the ethnic faiths, he could not see the advantage in giving representatives of false religions an opportunity to exploit them before American audiences. He foresaw that where theories could not be tested by practical results, the one-sided views presented would be calculated to do more harm than good. While he honoured many of the men who were behind the movement he replied in no uncertain negative to their invitation to take part in a parliament which he believed " would give opportunity for the enemies of God to blaspheme."

At the same time he accepted an invitation to speak at the World's Congress of Missions, but not without some protest because of the broadness of the platform. He found it difficult to fellowship in such a cause with those who denied the deity of his Lord or who did not believe in the necessity for faith in His Atonement or who unduly exalted humanity to the place of practical deity. He was convinced that the message they carried to heathen lands was not the true Gospel. He expressed a dislike to attempting an address on a topic assigned by others, since, as he said, " I must feel a '*burden*' on a subject if my address is to be of any power."

On the opening night of the great Ecumenical Conference in Carnegie Music Hall, New York, in April, 1900, Dr. Pierson gave a stirring summary of " The Superintending Providence of God in Foreign Missions." It was a presentation of the evidence of divine guidance and government in the history of missions, a marvel of condensation, that mightily stirred the vast assembly.

At Northfield he was also ever a welcome teacher. The conferences have grown since the early days of 1884 and 1885 and to-day include gatherings of young men and young women; and summer schools of Sunday-school workers and missionary students. They begin in June and continue to October, conferences being followed by post conferences. Dr. Pierson sometimes jokingly remarked that the "Post-mortem Conferences" were usually given into his hands. He also frequently conducted the inspiring services of missionary day and delivered many notable addresses. In the summers of 1908 and 1909 he taught a nine o'clock morning Bible class in Old Testament history, and drew from one to two thousand listeners with Bibles and note-books every morning of the conference. There were no indications that at seventy-two years of age Dr. Pierson had lost any of his power as a Bible expositor.

The friendship with Mr. D. L. Moody which was begun during the Detroit pastorate and was strengthened with early Northfield conferences, continued during the succeeding years until Mr. Moody was suddenly summoned to lay down his work in December, 1899. One of the last letters written by this servant of God to his friend evidences the understanding that existed between them.

"MY DEAR PIERSON:

"I thank you from my heart for your fidelity to me. May God bless you for it. I am as anxious as you are to maintain the integrity of the Word of God, and for any suggestions you have made to me I thank God and you.

"Always your friend,
"D. L. MOODY."

At the funeral of this noble Christian evangelist Dr. Pierson was greatly impressed with the thought of the few short years of service that remained. He remarked to his friend John Wanamaker: "You and Moody and I were all born in the same year. This dear friend's Home-going is a call to us to make the best use of our time that is going so fast and to live for God more devoutly than ever."

As to Dr. Pierson's subsequent connection with Northfield we quote from William R. Moody, his father's successor in the educational and conference work centred at Northfield and Mount Hermon.

"When in 1899 the responsibilities resulting from the passing of the founder of the work at Northfield entailed duties and demands that were new to me, the friendship with Dr. Pierson became closer and to his wise counsel on many occasions, as well as to his sympathy and prayers, is to be attributed much of the continued blessing upon the conferences and schools.

"Of his ministry at the conferences, both as Bible teacher, spiritual guide and missionary zealot, thousands can testify. When in 1908 and 1909 he conducted the daily Bible class at the Auditorium, the attendance was from the first the largest of any day session. Nor was the interest abated in any degree, but continued throughout the two weeks. When he presented some deep spiritual truth his memory of Scripture and power in reasoning never failed.

"But that with which comparatively few are familiar was his influence upon the students in the Northfield schools. It might be expected that with maturity of thought and experience he would have failed to impress young people, but such was not the case. He possessed that which is the mark of greatest distinction in either a teacher or preacher—he could interest the young. To those of us who knew him, it has seemed that his lectures and informal chapel talks at the Northfield schools represented his best work. There was a freedom that was born of a mutual sympathy between speaker and audience which was less evident in some of the summer conferences. Especially was this true at Mount Hermon, where he was loved with a warmth unusual among boys for one so many years their senior."

It was among these young men in training for their life-work that Dr. Pierson spent some of his happiest hours. He recognized an unusual opportunity to inspire them for the service of the King of kings and delighted to speak to them on such topics as "Mental Habits," "Books and Reading," "Missionary Heroes," "The Formation of Character" and "The Power of the Word of God." Daily in the heat of summer or in the brisk cool days of autumn he drove over the river five miles and back to give a ten or fifteen minute address at their chapel services, and the students appreciated it.

He frequently reminded young men that a truly useful life begins to be serviceable near its source, and reinforced his statements from his wide knowledge. It was thrilling to hear him give a list of the accomplishments of the young men of history. "Virgil," he said, "stood at the head of the Latin poets, Luther led the hosts of the Reformation, and Newton occupied the front rank among discoverers, before they had reached the age of thirty. Before twenty-eight,

Herodotus had recited his nine books of history at the Olympic games, and Hannibal had brought Spain into subjection to the arms of Carthage. When twenty-five years old, Demosthenes was the golden-mouth of Greece, and Cicero the silver-tongue of Rome! Raphael at the same age was summoned by Julius II to adorn, with his immortal paintings, the panels of the Vatican, and Galileo nightly viewed the paths of the shining fields above in search of undiscovered stars! At the same age Shakespeare stood at the head of all dramatic writers! At twenty-two Alexander had overturned the Persian empire, and Napoleon and Washington were accomplished generals. Plato was, at twenty, the intimate friend and peer of Socrates, and called Aristotle, at seventeen, 'the mind of his school.' Pascal was a great mathematician at nineteen, and Bacon was no older when he laid the basis of his inductive philosophy. At twenty-five, Jonathan Edwards and George Whitefield were princes among preachers, and at thirty, Jesus Christ was sounding forth His Gospel which was to revolutionize the world."

The students loved Dr. Pierson as a father and one of the professors expresses the opinion that no man, since Mr. D. L. Moody went Home, had so great a hold on successive companies of Hermon men. "I shall never forget," he says, "the combined faith and grit with which he went on, doing better work than ever, under such handicaps as neuritis, rheumatism and broken ribs. I often wondered whether it was right but I always knew and felt that it was magnificent."

The principal, Prof. Henry F. Cutler, said of these Hermon ministries: "Dr. Pierson was an ideal scholar and an ideal friend. He was on such a familiar footing with our boys that they knew and loved him. They respected his scholarship. His diction was perfect and his appreciation of literature exact. He somehow left the impression that it was possible for each one of them to be such a man as he was, and that was the blessing to us. When he came on the platform at Mount Hermon the boys burst out in an applause which could hardly be restrained. When he left they always sang a song for him, 'The Lord bless thee and keep thee.' They truly reverenced Dr. Pierson, for he always gave them the Gospel. He was to us one of the Heroes of Faith."

At Northfield he was seen by his farmer neighbours and trades-people as a man without the barrier of conventionalities, and they all respected and many loved him. They knew that "his word was as good as his bond" and that his generosity was unbounded. Even those who were at first unfriendly or distant came to recognize in him a true brother and friend.

One characteristic incident was connected with his sale of a sandy hilltop within sight of his summer home. Dr. Pierson returned from a trip to find the barren hillside covered with sod and a pleasing little cottage built upon it. With the enthusiasm of a child he stood on his veranda and exclaimed, "Wife dear, isn't that a transformation? How we shall enjoy looking at that pretty hillside now. Let us go over and congratulate Brother ———— right away." They not only paid the visit but Dr. Pierson insisted upon paying back a part of the purchase money on the plea that the improvement had added value to his property.

It was in Northfield too that he was seen in relaxation on almost the only furloughs he ever took. Dr. Pierson's vocation was the preaching of the Gospel, but he had avocations many, and these were his mental and physical salvation. He could draw and paint with considerable skill, and his touch on piano or organ was that of no mean musician. He drew plans for more than one building, and with the help of his sons he constructed a small house on the hilltop for prayer and quiet study. Carpentering was a delight to him and a bench and outfit of tools were installed in every house he occupied. But for real abandon, one should have seen him on his Northfield farm, coatless, working in overalls, with an old straw hat on his head, shod with Gibeonitish shoes, and with saw, hammer, rake or paint pot in hand, busy with repairs, or gathering in the hay.

No form of summer recreation, however, held quite as much charm for him as did a family picnic. The days at Northfield were times of reunion for his widely scattered brood, which with children and children's children sometimes numbered twenty. To pack full pails and lunch-baskets into a wagon, with the mother and the less robust members of the family, and then to walk two or three miles, accompanied by sons and grandsons, to some lake or wooded hillside, and there to build a fire and eat on the ground,—this meant real pleasure for him. He could cook a beefsteak or broil a fish to a turn over hot coals, and this privilege he always assumed.

An amusing incident occurred a few years ago at one of these family picnics. A place rather nearer to the road than usual had been chosen, and Dr. Pierson was down on his knees blowing a dying flame into life—

under a swinging kettle of coffee. The sleeves of his negligee shirt were rolled up above his elbows, his old faded straw hat, which he was using as a fan, was fast becoming brimless, and his youngest grandson was standing near as an interested observer, when a team passed on the other side of the brook. The occupants of the carriage stopped, tied their horse, and then came nearer for a better view of the scene. Thinking that they might wish to picnic also, one member of the Pierson family invited them to remain, but they shook their heads and stood in ridiculous amazement gazing at Dr. Pierson, as they inquired: "Is that really Dr. Pierson—*the* Dr. Pierson whose books we have read? Dr. Pierson, the great preacher who occupied Spurgeon's pulpit—is that he there at the fire, cooking a meal?" They declined to come closer and after a time drove on—with the pleased consciousness of having discovered another side to the character and private life of a public man.

Such discoveries were not infrequently made by those who were welcomed into the bosom of Dr. Pierson's own family. On other occasions he often felt the weight of some responsibility or was aglow with the enthusiasm kindled by a great message, but in the hours of relaxation—when there was no need to be on his guard against misunderstanding or criticism—the man himself stood revealed, and to see him was to love him. He was ever forgetful of his own convenience in private affairs as in public ministries. Many times he would walk home, through city streets or along country roads, laden with bundles that public men and self-conscious youths usually scorn to carry. The same earnest simplicity of character that led him to make public confession of shortcomings led him to be somewhat indifferent in the matter of the clothes he wore, or the kind of conveyances in which he rode, or the lowly character of the service that he performed for others. He delighted to help in the work of the home, and cared not who saw him carry wood in summer or coal in winter. He was equally ready to care for the horse, to prepare a dinner or to nurse a sick one—if only by so doing he might relieve some one else of a burden, might obtain a change of employment for himself or might save money and thereby have more to give away.

It was the Dr. Pierson of the home, more than Dr. Pierson the public man, the preacher or the author, who moulded the lives of his children and set his impress on his children's children. When the first child was born in his Binghamton home, Dr. Pierson's father said to him: "My son, in that child is a greater responsibility than in your whole parish." As the years went by, the results of that parental counsel were increasingly manifest in his family. In these days even Christian parents often hesitate to exact strict obedience to unwelcome laws and many bring up their children more to self-indulgence than to self-denial. In consequence how many mourn the disgrace and disaster brought by wayward sons and daughters. The precept and example given by Dr. and Mrs. Pierson led every one of their seven children to confess Christ publicly before the age of fifteen, and when the time came to choose a vocation, each of them selected some form of Christian service; all who married chose life-partners who were in perfect accord with the Christian ideals upheld in the Pierson home. Of Dr. Pierson's children three volunteered for service in the foreign mission field, one entered home missionary work, and the others have given their spare time to city missions. All are active members of Christian churches and in their own homes seek to carry out the principles and practices instilled in them by their early training. These children testify to the incalculable blessing they received from the faithful adherence of their parents to lofty principles, from the prominence given to God as a real factor in daily life, from the insistence upon regular habits and the emphasis placed on faith, prayer, systematic giving and unselfish service. The regulations which were often irksome rules in childhood became bulwarks of character in maturity.

Another noticeable feature of Dr. Pierson's influence in his family is seen in the unity prevailing among the children. At times, though they were scattered in Europe, India, Japan, Central America, New York, Philadelphia and Arizona, yet they always kept up regular correspondence with their parents and with each other, for harmony and sympathy prevailed unbroken. This unity is no doubt due to the Christocentric atmosphere in which they were brought up, and especially to the simultaneous prayer circles which at the father's suggestion were established in each home.

XVII

THE JUBILEE YEAR—A VISIT TO THE FRONTIER

FEW men live to see their lives rounded out to any degree of completeness. When the end comes they seem to have accomplished so little and frequently feel that they are just beginning to learn how to live. This was in some degree the feeling with which Dr. Pierson viewed his own life when he came to look back over the seventy-four years, which included a half century of public ministry. But his friends formed a different estimate of his career and the closing year marked, in a unique way, the completion of a cycle of service, a fullness of testimony and an attainment of ideals that formed a fitting conclusion to his life. The divine plan stands out with wonderful clearness.

Anniversaries were ever red-letter days in the Pierson calendar, and this closing year was singularly rich in such celebrations. In May, 1910, came the commemoration of Dr. Pierson's fifty years as a minister of Jesus Christ and in July he and his wife passed the golden mile-stone in their wedding journey. These jubilee celebrations presented a threefold opportunity,—for bearing witness to the loving faithfulness of God; for tributes of affection and esteem from friends all over the world, and for reunions with family, with classmates and with sympathetic fellow workers. During this last year, he also found opportunity to gather together, in a jubilee volume, some of the results of his fifty years of Bible study.¹ Copies of this book he distributed freely to ministers, missionaries and other Christian workers all over the world. Finally, it was not until this last year of his pilgrimage that Dr. Pierson was able to pay his long desired visit to the distant mission fields and to come into personal contact with missionaries in the midst of their work.

The fiftieth anniversary of his ordination as a minister of the Gospel was appropriately celebrated in the old Thirteenth Street Presbyterian Church, New York City, the church with which he had first united as a boy of fifteen and in which on May 13, 1860, he had been ordained to preach. His jubilee sermon was a striking utterance and was based on three Old Testament texts:

"And he went on his journeys from the south even to Bethel, unto the place where his tent had been at the beginning; . . . unto the place of the altar, which he had made there at the first: and there Abram called on the name of the Lord" (Genesis xiii. 3–4).

"Let us arise, and go up to Bethel; and I will make there an altar unto God, who answered me in the day of my distress, and was with me in the way which I went" (Genesis xxxv. 3).

"And thou shalt remember all the way which the Lord thy God led thee these forty years in the wilderness, to humble thee, and to prove thee, to know what was in thine heart, whether thou wouldest keep His commandments, or no" (Deuteronomy viii. 2).

The speaker reviewed the way in which God had led him during his seventy-four years and emphasized

---

¹This volume was published under the title "Knowing the Scriptures."

An Anniversary Address

again with increased earnestness the lessons that had been impressed upon him by his own experience and observation. He urged especially the importance of a right start and a true foundation: a Christian home life, a family altar, Christian education under consecrated teachers, an early confession of Christ, Sabbath observance, a Christian marriage and a dominant purpose to serve God. Then, in his own graphic way, he went over the marvellous events, inventions and changes that had taken place during the preceding half century; the progress in science and exploration, in religious and political reforms, and in missionary achievements.

But the facts that impressed the speaker, even more forcibly than the scientific wonders of the century, were the gracious dealings of God with himself. The days of his pilgrimage had been approximately marked off into decades, each closing with some crisis or new experience: the first ten years ended with his departure from home; the second were spent at school and college, from which he was graduated at the age of twenty; during the third decade he was learning his first lessons in preaching and at its close he had gained a broader vision of the world and of his ministry through missionary studies and through his first visit to Europe; from 1867 to 1877 he had passed through his second period as a pastor and at the close of this decade came the burning of the Detroit church and his new experience in evangelistic work; the next ten years marked the climax of his pastoral work and ended with his visit to the World Missionary Conference in London, the publication of his "Crisis of Missions" and the acceptance of the editorship of *The Missionary Review of the World;* from 1887 to 1897 he was engaged in his missionary crusades among the churches of Great Britain and America and in the last year he paid his first visit to Keswick; the final full decade, 1897 to 1907, was devoted to Bible lectures and addresses on the deepening of spiritual life. Thus in seventy years, step by step, he had been led through stages of preparation for the pastorate, for an evangelistic ministry, for missionary work, and finally for teaching, in ever widening circles, the deep spiritual truths concerning life and service.

In fifty years of his ministry Dr. Pierson delivered over 13,000 sermons and addresses and wrote over fifty books, in addition to unnumbered tracts, poems, songs, booklets and articles for religious periodicals.

But to discover the facts on which his own mind dwelt with greatest satisfaction in the retrospect of his life, we must turn to the pages of his private diary. There we read his review of the loving care with which God had surrounded him and some of the lessons that he had learned.

"From my infancy," he wrote, "even in all my sins and wanderings, my unbelief and disobedience, my life has been marked by ceaseless gracious interpositions of God. When I first left home and entered boarding-school, He sought me and turned my youthful steps into the way of life. Then during my college and seminary years He supplied all my needs and three times when I have felt led to resign my pastorate, without knowing from whence the support for my family was to come, He bountifully cared for us so that we lacked no good thing. . . . He has taught me with infinite patience to be 'anxious for nothing.'

"In times of spiritual trouble He has fortified me

A Stirring Testimony

with His promises and has never left me nor forsaken me. Blessed be His holy Name forever and ever; how could I have ever doubted Him. . . . How graciously He has led me into a clearer knowledge of Himself and of His power to subdue evil temper and sordid ambition and other known sins;[1] and how, in spite of my weakness and shortcomings, He has used my feeble efforts to serve Him."

At a meeting which was held in his honour in the auditorium at the Northfield Conference, August 13, 1910, he delivered a remarkable address in which he told of God's leading and he repeated the rules and promises that had been tested in his own experience. In response to the tributes from William R. Moody, Dr. S. Edward Young and Rev. J. Stuart Holden he merely said:

"A man can receive nothing except it be given him from above," and he quoted the words of St. Paul, "It is not expedient for me to glory . . . but I will come to visions and revelations of the Lord" (2 Cor. xii. 1). He then mentioned four Scripture texts which had greatly influenced his life.

1. "Psalm i. 1, 2—'Blessed is the man that walketh not in the counsel of the ungodly, nor standeth in the way of sinners, nor sitteth in the seat of the scornful; but his delight is in the law of the Lord and in His law doth he meditate day and night.' This is the sole secret of prosperity and peace: Meditate in the Word of God and take delight in it. In more than fifty years of study I have only begun to understand it.

---

[1] The volumes that reveal Dr. Pierson's belief as to the Scriptural teaching on holy living are entitled: "Shall We Continue in Sin"; "Godly Self-Control": "His Holiness" and "A Spiritual Clinique."

2. "Proverbs iii. 6—'In all thy ways acknowledge Him and He shall direct thy paths.' Since the time when my father first gave me that text when I was a boy leaving home, it has been a principle in my life—never to make a plan without first seeking God's guidance and never to achieve a success without giving Him the praise.

3. "Matthew vi. 33—'Seek ye first the kingdom of God and His righteousness and all these things shall be added unto you.' This promise has been wonderfully fulfilled in my experience. Whenever I have taken a step on faith, and have sought to devote myself primarily to the advancement of God's interests, He has seen to it that I and my family have lacked nothing. I have made it a practice never to put a price on my services, and yet, even during the last twenty years, when I have received no stated salary, there has never been any lack. On the contrary I have been able to give away more money than ever before.

4. "John vii. 7—'If any man will do His will, he shall know of the doctrine, whether it be of God or whether I speak of myself.' There is no need of skepticism or unbelief or doubt. Any man who is willing to do God's will can *know* and the only way to *know* is to will to do. After more than fifty years of closest study, observation and experience, I can testify that *it pays to be a follower of God.*"

As he reached this climax, there was a note of assurance and of triumph in the voice that sent a thrill of conviction through his hearers. None who were present that morning will forget the power of his testimony to the faithfulness of God, or the earnestness with which he pleaded with each one in the audience to hold nothing in reserve but to make a full surrender to the gracious, covenant-keeping God.

The golden anniversary of Dr. and Mrs. Pierson's

marriage was celebrated at their summer home in Northfield, on July 12th, and was a joyous reunion. The happy bride and groom of fifty summers were surrounded by children and grandchildren and never was there a more united family circle than that which met on the hillside, and with poems, gifts and loving words paid their tributes of devotion. To many of their earth-wide circle of friends, Dr. Pierson sent a message of love with the following verses which he wrote for the occasion:

> " With fifty years of wedded Love and Life
> Our Father God has crowned us—Husband, Wife.
> Five daughters and two sons our Home have blest;
> One only—dear Louise—yet called to Rest.
> For all these golden years and sunlit ways
> We ask our friends to join our hymn of praise;
> No gifts we crave so much as priceless Love,
> And prayers in our behalf to God above:
> That if, a while, His Grace prolongs our stay,
> His Pillar may direct our pilgrim way;
> Then bid us welcome to His Home on high
> Where Love is throned and Joy can never die.
> Blessed indeed, from Sin and Death made free,
> In Heaven to keep The Golden Jubilee!"

The reunions of this closing year were many and they were singularly complete. Friends and loved ones with whom Dr. Pierson had not met for years were brought together to celebrate his anniversaries. There were not only family gatherings but there were luncheons with classmates, dinners with honoured yokefellows in the world's work, and visits with boyhood chums. Each occasion was a time of rejoicing and was seized upon by Dr. Pierson as an opportunity to testify again to the goodness of God.

These anniversaries and reunions also presented a

fitting occasion for friends far and near to express to Dr. Pierson their love and debt of gratitude for his faithful ministries—tributes that are too often only "post-mortem praises." Letters, telegrams, and gifts poured in upon him from every land under the sun and filled his heart with thanksgiving, while at the same time they humbled him, as he confessed to his own failures and gave God the glory for success.

Another spontaneous tribute was paid to Dr. Pierson one Sunday afternoon in the summer of this closing year when he had consented to address a meeting at the West Twenty-third Street Branch of the Young Men's Christian Association, New York. The auditorium was crowded with men when the secretary introduced the speaker by saying: "It may not be known to many of you that Dr. Pierson was one of the original one hundred young men who formed the first Young Men's Christian Association in New York City, and he is now the oldest living founder in America."

Instantly the entire audience sprang to their feet and for some minutes their applause, which shook the building, could not be restrained. "At last," said one who was present, "the grand old gentleman, blushing like a schoolboy at the unexpected tribute, arose and tried to speak but could not and, after a courtly bow, sat down until he could control himself to begin his address."

Another highly appreciated message came several months later from the General Assembly of the Presbyterian Church, in session at Atlantic City, the church in which he had laboured for thirty-five years, and from which he had been unwillingly separated for a decade and a half. The telegram of greeting read:

Message from the General Assembly

"The General Assembly of the Presbyterian Church in the United States of America, at the close of a session devoted to Foreign Missions, sends you affectionate greetings, and expresses its gratitude to God for the service you have been enabled to render by voice and pen towards the world-wide extension of the Redeemer's Kingdom. We beseech the Great Head of the Church that He will grant you the richest comforts of His grace, and if it be His will, will give you restoration of strength for further labours in the Gospel. We salute you in the spirit of Romans viii. 28-31."

This resolution was followed in the Assembly by a prayer offered by Robert E. Speer, in which he said:

"Our Father, we come to Thee in prayer and love for one who many years ago, seeing the carelessness and indifference of the Church, saw also a great vision and raised a prophetic voice for the extension of Thy kingdom. . . . We thank Thee for his godly life and world-wide sympathies. Give him, we pray Thee, at this eventide of life, the peace which Thou alone canst give. Spare his life, if it please Thee, to serve Thee yet in Thy Vineyard. If this be not Thy will, we pray that his mantle may fall on some others who shall yet come after him. . . . May there be a long line raised up, with a yet larger vision, who will give their simple trust and loyal service to his Lord and ours."

In the midst of congratulations and rejoicings attendant on his anniversaries, Dr. Pierson remembered the things that were behind not as attainments but as causes for thanksgiving and he looked forward, with unspeakable longing, to further years of service. "If I could only begin life over again with my present knowledge of God how different it could be made," he would often say. "What wood, hay and stubble would be left out of the building, and how much more of gold, silver and precious stones might be put into the structure: I pray God that I may be spared to finish the work He has given me to do."

This prayer was partially answered in the opportunity that came at last to visit the foreign mission field. It was a fitting close for his earthly pilgrimage. After preaching all summer in New York and Philadelphia, speaking frequently to his beloved Mount Hermon students and delivering the post-conference addresses at Northfield on "Spiritual Disease and Spiritual Health," Dr. Pierson prepared to fulfill his lifelong ambition to visit the Far East that he might see for himself the work of Christian missions. For the first time in his life this tour had been made possible, in the providence of God, by the generous gifts of friends. Enfeebled health alone stood in the way, but this had never yet been permitted to be a barrier to service. Moreover the journey could now be taken in company with friends who were on their way to China, and other considerations seemed to outweigh the question of health. Even the physicians hoped that a change of scene and new experiences might diminish rather than increase bodily discomforts. The money that had been put into his hands—as a jubilee offering—also opened a coveted door of opportunity to help meet the needs that he might see on the field. After much thought and prayer he decided to make the journey and on the nineteenth of October, with his wife and daughter and their friends, Mr. and Mrs. Ralph Walker, of Leicester, England, Dr. Pierson sailed from Vancouver for Japan.

The journey across the Pacific was unusually rough so that when the party reached Yokohama it was

Wonderful Days in Japan

found that Dr. Pierson was unable to follow the full program made out for him by his missionary daughter, Mrs. Curtis. He was not ready, however, to give up doing the work for which he had come. Mere sightseeing had little attraction for him and whenever he was asked to visit some celebrated place he refused unless it was closely associated with the problem of reaching non-Christian peoples or had to do with the work of the missionaries. "I am here for one purpose," he would say, "and have no time or strength for anything else."

All that he saw interested him intensely and in spite of the fatigue that resulted from travel and speaking he would not give up. One morning after delivering an address at the Methodist school in Aoyama he rode several miles to visit the Great Asakusa Temple. Here he saw, for the first time in his life, people actually engaged in the worship of idols. He longed for the "gift of tongues" that he might speak to them in their own language of the true God and only Saviour. When he returned to the mission he was prostrated, but he only said: "It has been a wonderful day." The vision of coming victory awakened by the sight of the Christian school in contrast to the idol temple made him unmindful of the suffering he endured. In Kyoto he also visited the Honywanji Temple of which he had often read and about which he had written. It seemed a strange anomaly to him that the party of Christians were obliged to remove their shoes on entering this idol shrine, as though they were treading on holy ground.

As he came into touch with the missionaries he was moved by the evidences of their consecration and noble self-denial and longed to be able to help them in their great work. After visiting some of the schools and hospitals and churches he wrote home:

"Contact with these missionaries has given me a clearer conception of the work than forty years of study at home. We find here enterprises of the triumphantly successful sort, where one additional worker, or a gift of five hundred dollars, would double or treble the efficiency and the results. If some generous givers from home could only get a glimpse of the work and its needs they could not withhold the money. We feel constantly moved to strip ourselves of all that can be spared and to study the closest economy in order that we may invest all we have in enterprises that will pay thirty, sixty, or a hundred fold."

Wherever he went he made it his first business to inquire as to the greatest needs of the work and it was one of the crowning joys of his life to be able to use funds intrusted to him to relieve and cheer the burdened workers. Daily, in his weakness he prayed for the coming of the kingdom of God in these lands and in his hours of pain would sometimes exclaim: "This journey is worth all that it has cost me. How gracious of God to permit me to see this work about which I have read and spoken for fifty years and to give some help where it is so much needed."

At Kyoto he visited the Doshisha University and the hospital and church of Dr. Saiki, a Japanese Christian who had been connected with his church in Philadelphia. The physicians had ordered Dr. Pierson to give up speaking and sightseeing, but when he learned that the new Young Men's Christian Association building had been completed and that he was in-

A Visit to Korea

vited to speak at a dinner in honour of the event, he felt that he must rise up and go in order to represent his friend the donor, John Wanamaker.

Whenever possible he rejoiced in the opportunity of speaking to the missionaries and native Christians. Once when urged to spare himself he replied: "I might decline this service in any other cause, but here is one way in which I can have a share in the sufferings of Christ." Such thoughts sustained him even when he was racked with pain or harassed by doubt as to God's will and his own duty.

After a month in Japan he journeyed to Korea and remained in Seoul for six weeks. Here he spoke through an interpreter in one of the churches and arranged for a series of daily Bible readings with the missionaries. But the strain was too great. The physicians forbade any more public speaking and sent him to the Severance Hospital. Dr. Pierson found it difficult to submit and declared emphatically: "I have come ten thousand miles to do this work and now you tell me I must not. I would rather die than sit down here and give up the idea of delivering the message God has given me." The physicians were perplexed, for they realized that the results of enforced idleness might be even more serious than the strain of public speaking. They finally limited him to two addresses a week and new power seemed to be given him as he spoke to the missionaries on the "Names of Christ." Into these farewell messages he put all the ardour of his soul as he explained the character and mission of the Living Word, the Eternal Son of God, the Merciful Saviour of Man.

One Sunday afternoon, when he was in such pain that he reluctantly gave up meeting the missionary community, his son-in-law, Rev. Frederick S. Curtis, asked if he had any message to send. With much effort at first he began to dictate a few words, but as he went on vitality seemed to return and the Word of God became a "fire in his bones." This farewell address on "Heavenly Visions" (Acts xxvi. 19) greatly stirred the hearts of those who heard it.[1]

When the physicians finally told him that it would be impossible to carry out his program of visiting China and India, the thought of abandoning the tour caused him intense suffering. He fought day and night against what he considered must be unbelief in himself that prevented victory over every obstacle. "What am I thinking of to lie here and calmly die?" he exclaimed. "I am playing the part of a fool." With admiration the physician afterwards remarked: "What an old war-horse! What an unconquerable spirit!"

Dr. Pierson finally consented to turn his face homeward, but he was sustained by the thought that he might there regain strength to complete his missionary tour by travelling eastward. He also hoped that in America he might be able to tell of some of the wonders he had seen. He had come to know many missionaries and some Japanese and Korean Christians and as he saw and heard of the apostolic character of the Korean church, their faith, their self-sacrificing spirit and their hunger for Bible study, he determined to enlist the coöperation of friends at home in the effort to establish Bible schools in that land.[2]

---

[1] See *Missionary Review of the World*, September, 1911.

[2] This he was not able to do personally, but friends have undertaken to establish in Seoul an interdenominational Bible school to be known as the "Arthur T. Pierson Memorial Bible School."

Homeward Bound

After three months on the mission field, the travellers turned their faces homeward. Many times there were physical crises which a man of less energy and less faith could not have survived. A few days before the party sailed from Kobe the physicians declared that the patient might not even live to reach Hawaii; but he rallied and landed in San Francisco in better condition than when he had left Japan.

Though prevented from continuing his journey and unable longer to fill public engagements, he was not ready to give up the fight. The closing weeks of his life were to the end made up of days of service, and of thought for others. His last birthday was celebrated in Los Angeles, where he was cared for in the home of Rev. Thomas C. Horton, formerly an associate pastor in Bethany Church. A birthday party of members of the family had been planned to brighten his sick-room, and after he had spent three hours in the morning dictating Bible study notes to a stenographer he busied himself during the afternoon in writing bright, loving and humorous verses for each member of the household.

Even on his sick bed, when the physicians gave no hope of his recovery, his sense of humour did not forsake him. He joked with his attendants and frequently called on his son-in-law for amusing readings and recitations. One morning, after a night of alarming weakness and pain, he said to his daughter, who was helping him make his toilet: "Helen, an effusive woman in my congregation used to tell me that when I was preaching she could see a heavenly light on my face. Be careful not to wash it off."

A few weeks before he was called Home, the heavenly Father gave His servant strength to make the journey eastward from Los Angeles to his Brooklyn home where he could again gather *all* of his children and grandchildren around him. As they met for prayer and conference, he rejoiced in the reunion and in the ministries of loved ones. Soon he was to join also his only absent daughter and his parents in the Father's House.

In the providence of God Dr. Pierson's mental and spiritual faculties were unclouded to the last and his sick bed was a place of continued ministry. When he could no longer speak to groups he talked with individuals and led them into more intimate fellowship with his Master. The doctors and specialists who were called in for brief consultations and the attendants who ministered to his physical needs were ministered to by him in spiritual things and testified to the blessing received from even a brief contact with him. All were impressed by his unwavering faith, his zeal for service and his love for the things of Christ. To the end he was able to prepare editorials for the *Missionary Review of the World* and to write devotional Bible studies for the *Record of Christian Work*. Only a day or two before his final departure he was correcting the printer's proofs that were published two months later.

Dr. Pierson neither feared nor courted the thought of death. It was to him the gate of entrance to the presence of the King, but it meant also the abandonment of work which he dearly loved and which he had no desire to relinquish. His earnest wish was to regain strength and when scarcely able to stand, he would insist upon walking that his muscles might not lose their power. Nevertheless he was ready to go if the Master called. One day, in Los Angeles, when he had experienced a sinking spell from which he feared he might not rally he asked Mr. Curtis to read to him from Revelation xiv. 13: "And I heard a voice from heaven saying, Write, Blessed are the dead which die in the Lord from henceforth; yea, saith the Spirit, that they may rest from their labours; for their works shall follow with them."

He then commented concerning his own exodus on these words from which he had preached the funeral service of Charles H. Spurgeon:

"*Blessed are the dead*—this is the only time after Christ's resurrection that the term 'death' is applied to believers. But the further expression, *that die in the Lord,* gives a wonderful modification of the thought. They are said to 'rest from their labours' and that 'their works shall follow with them,'—as the Greek indicates: to go as a companion. 'Labours' are here contrasted with 'works.' Labours mean toil, 'works' mean blessed activity. Rest is given from all vexatious toils but all joyous activities go with them. I believe that if I 'die in the Lord' I shall leave behind me all vexatious trials, but that all gracious activities will go with me. I expect to go to more active service. I have a desire to depart and be with Christ but I also have a desire to abide in the flesh because of the needs I see for work in God's kingdom. . . .

"I think I may soon be going to my Father's House and if I am taken I wish to be laid away where I fall. I desire no encomiums, only the simple reading of God's Word and prayer. Should anything be said, let it be only this, that to the last I gave a faithful testimony to the love and power and faithfulness of God. Let there be no mourning, nothing but rejoicing that I have been called to higher service."

During the last days of his illness, when fever, pain and weakness prostrated the body, and when he could not even converse, verses of Scripture and prayer were almost continually on his lips. The words most frequently repeated expressed the longing of his soul, "That we might be partakers of His holiness" (Hebrew xii. 10). In the circumstances of his Home-going, the mercy of God was manifested, for there were no painful words of parting and no hurried commissions. Twenty-four hours before the final call came he sank into a semi-stupor from which he did not rally, and on June 3, 1911, at a little before 8 A. M. he fell asleep in Christ. The abiding expression on his face, after the spirit had taken flight, was one of peace and joy.

The morning after Dr. Pierson's decease, his little six-year-old grandson and namesake, who had not yet heard of his loss, crept into his mother's bed and said: "Mother, I had such a beautiful dream last night. I dreamed that I saw steps going up into heaven. It was all gold up there. Oh, it was very beautiful, mother."

"Did you see any one you knew?" his mother asked.

"Yes, I saw the Lord Jesus."

"Did you see any one else you knew?"

"No, I don't think so, mother."

"But some one did go up yesterday into heaven to be with the Lord Jesus. Some one whom you love and who loves you very much."

"Who was it, mother—was it—was it grandpa?"

All day the little fellow was happy in telling friends that his grandfather had gone to heaven on the golden

Entrance Into Life

steps of his dream. So the vision seemed to those who were left behind. The sting of death was taken away in the certainty of life in Christ and all felt the peace that came to the heart of the little child in the thought that the beloved one had entered heaven by the " new and living way," after a life brought to completion according to the plan of God.

The funeral services were held in the Bedford Presbyterian Church, Brooklyn, New York, in the presence of a hushed and crowded assembly. These services were conducted by intimate friends [1] and were an appropriate testimony to the triumphal ending of Dr. Pierson's earthly life and labours and in harmony with his wish. The opportunity was taken not to extol the servant but to praise his Master. Dr. S. Edward Young, the pastor of the church, presided, Dr. John F. Carson read appropriate passages of Scripture and Dr. Wilson Phraner, then in his ninetieth year, offered prayer. The congregation joined in the hymns " Jesus, Lover of My Soul " and " When I Survey the Wondrous Cross," and Mrs. W. R. Moody sang " Moment by Moment " and " Out of my Bondage, Sorrow and Night, Jesus, I Come." A missionary message was given by Robert E. Speer and a brief address on the " Word of God," by Dr. J. H. Jowett who had recently arrived from England to become pastor of the Fifth Avenue

---

[1] The honourary pall-bearers were also intimate friends and sympathizers—Rev. Cleland B. McAfee, D. D., Pastor of the Lafayette Avenue Presbyterian Church, Brooklyn; Rev. Henry W. Frost, of Philadelphia, Home Director of the China Inland Mission; Rev. Charles R. Erdman, D. D., of Princeton Theological Seminary; Rev. John McDowell, of Newark; Mr. Ralph L. Cutter and Mr. Frank H. Marston, of Brooklyn, Mr. William R. Moody, of East Northfield, Massachusetts, and Mr. Alwyn Ball, Jr., of Rutherford, New Jersey.

Presbyterian Church, New York. In his address Dr. Jowett commented on the parable of the wedding garment and said: " To the eyes of the heavenly spirits that look on this scene this service may be not a funeral but a wedding and the appropriate dress may be not a robe of mourning but a garment of praise; if so I am sure that our departed friend would rejoice." This was the key-note of the day—the note of triumph was dominant.

Henry W. Frost, Director of the China Inland Mission, one of the pall-bearers, voiced the feeling of the assembled friends when he wrote of the services: " The funeral was unlike any other I have ever attended. Praise seemed to be uppermost in thought and expression. How could it have been otherwise when the course had been so well run and the fight had been so nobly fought? Jesus Christ was magnified in life and in death."

All that was mortal was laid to rest quietly in Greenwood Cemetery and above the spot, where the body awaits the resurrection day, stands a permanent message in stone. It is a simple granite shaft on which rests a globe showing the countries of the world and in front is an open Bible on which are carved the Scripture verses which voice the Great Commission and the basis for hope of Eternal Life:

> *" Go ye into all the world and preach the Gospel to every creature "* *(Mark xvi. 15).*
>
> *" God hath given to us Eternal Life and this life is in His Son "* *(1 John v. 11).*

So passed one of God's earthly warriors. Clad in the whole armour of God, he had wrestled for over seventy years, not against flesh and blood, but against principalities and powers and against spiritual wickedness in high places. Having fought a good fight, he finished his course, he kept the faith. Henceforth there is laid up for him a crown of righteousness, which the Lord, the righteous judge, shall give to him in that day;—and not to him only but unto all them also that love His appearing.[1]

[1] Ephesians vi. 10–12 and 2 Timothy iv. 7–8.

THE END

Arthur T. Pierson.

ARTHUR PIERSON, at seventeen
From a daguerreotype taken during his college days

HAMILTON COLLEGE, AT CLINTON, NEW YORK, IN 1854

UNION SEMINARY, NEW YORK, IN 1857

The original building on University Place. Arthur Pierson's room was in the basement—the window to the right of the entrance.

ARTHUR T. PIERSON
[In his first pastorate at Binghamton]

SARAH FRANCES BENEDICT
[At the time of her marriage to Mr. Pierson]

FIRST CONGREGATIONAL CHURCH, BINGHAMTON, N. Y.
First Pastoral Charge of Arthur T. Pierson

THE PRESBYTERIAN CHURCH AT WATERFORD
[Mr. Pierson's Second Pastoral Charge]

ARTHUR T. PIERSON IN DETROIT
[From a photograph taken at about the age of forty—in 1878]

SECOND PRESBYTERIAN CHURCH AND PARSONAGE, INDIANAPOLIS

THE FORT ST. PRESBYTERIAN CHURCH, DETROIT

BETHANY CHURCH AND SUNDAY SCHOOL, PHILADELPHIA

INTERIOR OF THE FAMOUS BETHANY SUNDAY SCHOOL

SPURGEON'S METROPOLITAN TABERNACLE, LONDON

INTERIOR OF METROPOLITAN TABERNACLE, LONDON

A speaker's view of the Audience Room from the Pulpit [on a level with the first gallery.]

DR. and MRS. PIERSON AT BIBLE STUDY

From a photograph taken in England in 1896

The Gospel according to St. Mark

CHAPTER I.

1 THE beginning of the gospel of Jesus Christ, the Son of God;

2 As it is written in the prophets, Behold, I send my messenger before thy face, which shall prepare thy way before thee.

3 The voice of one crying in the wilderness, Prepare ye the way of the Lord, make his paths straight.

4 John did baptize in the wilderness, and preach the baptism of repentance for the remission of sins.

5 And there went out unto him all the land of Judæa, and they of Jerusalem, and were all baptized of him in the river of Jordan, confessing their sins.

6 And John was clothed with camel's hair, and with a girdle of a skin about his loins; and he did eat locusts and wild honey;

7 And preached, saying, There cometh one mightier than I after me, the latchet of whose shoes I am not worthy to stoop down and unloose.

8 I indeed have baptized you with water: but he shall baptize you with the Holy Ghost.

9 And it came to pass in those days, that Jesus came from Nazareth of Galilee, and was baptized of John in Jordan.

10 And straightway coming up out of the water, he saw the heavens opened, and the Spirit, like a dove, descending upon him:

11 And there came a voice from heaven, saying, Thou art my beloved Son, in whom I am well pleased.

12 And immediately the Spirit driveth him into the wilderness.

13 And he was there in the wilderness forty days, tempted of Satan; and was with the wild beasts; and the angels ministered unto him.

14 Now after that John was put in prison, Jesus came into Galilee, preaching the gospel of the kingdom of God,

15 And saying, The time is fulfilled, and the kingdom of God is at hand: repent ye, and believe the gospel.

16 Now as he walked by the sea of Galilee, he saw Simon, and Andrew his brother, casting a net into the sea: for they were fishers.

17 And Jesus said unto them, Come ye after me, and I will make you to become fishers of men.

18 And straightway they forsook their nets, and followed him.

19 And when he had gone a little farther thence, he saw James the son of Zebedee, and John his brother, who also were in the ship mending their nets.

20 And straightway he called them; and they left their father Zebedee in the ship with the hired servants, and went after him.

21 And they went into Capernaum; and straightway on the sabbath day he entered into the synagogue, and taught.

22 And they were astonished at his doctrine: for he taught them as one that had authority, and not as the scribes.

23 And there was in their synagogue a man with an unclean spirit; and he cried out,

24 Saying, Let us alone; what have we to do with thee, thou Jesus of Nazareth? art thou come to destroy us? I know thee who thou art, the Holy One of God.

25 And Jesus rebuked him, saying, Hold thy peace, and come out of him.

26 And when the unclean spirit had torn him, and cried with a loud voice, he came out of him.

27 And they were all amazed, insomuch that they questioned among themselves, saying, What thing is this? what new doctrine is this? for with authority commandeth he even the unclean spirits, and they do obey him.

28 And immediately his fame spread abroad throughout all the region round about Galilee.

29 And forthwith, when they were come out of the synagogue, they entered into the house of Simon and Andrew, with James and John.

30 But Simon's wife's mother lay sick of a fever; and anon they tell him of her.

31 And he came and took her by the hand, and lifted her up; and immediately the fever left her, and she ministered unto them.

32 And at even, when the sun did set, they brought unto him all that were diseased, and them that were possessed with devils.

33 And all the city was gathered together at the door.

34 And he healed many that were sick of divers diseases, and cast out many devils; and suffered not the devils to speak, because they knew him.

35 And in the morning, rising up a great while before day, he went out, and departed into a solitary place, and there prayed.

36 And Simon, and they that were with him, followed after him.

37 And when they had found him, they said unto him, All men seek for thee.

38 And he said unto them, Let us go into the next towns, that I may preach there also: for therefore came I forth.

39 And he preached in their synagogues throughout all Galilee, and cast out devils.

40 And there came a leper to him, beseeching him, and kneeling down to him, and saying unto him, If thou wilt, thou canst make me clean.

41 And Jesus, moved with compassion, put forth his hand, and touched him, and saith unto him, I will; be thou clean.

42 And as soon as he had spoken, immediately the leprosy departed from him, and he was cleansed.

43 And he straitly charged him, and forthwith sent him away;

44 And saith unto him, See thou say

A PAGE FROM ONE OF DR. PIERSON'S BIBLES

KESWICK and DERWENTWATER FROM THE TOP OF SKIDDAW

DR. PIERSON SPEAKING IN THE TENT AT KESWICK, ENGLAND

THE NORTHFIELD HOME FROM THE STUDY ON THE HILL
[An early morning view showing the mist rolling up the valley of the Connecticut River]

OFF DUTY AT NORTHFIELD
Dr. Pierson with his grandson, Arthur Farrand Pierson

THE BROOKLYN HOME OF ARTHUR T. PIERSON

His residence from 1895 to 1911. It was here that he passed away.

A MESSAGE IN STONE
Model of the Monument in Greenwood Cemetery, Brooklyn, New York

www.ingramcontent.com/pod-product-compliance
Lightning Source LLC
Chambersburg PA
CBHW051627230426
43669CB00013B/2208